IMAGES
of America

PIMA COUNTY

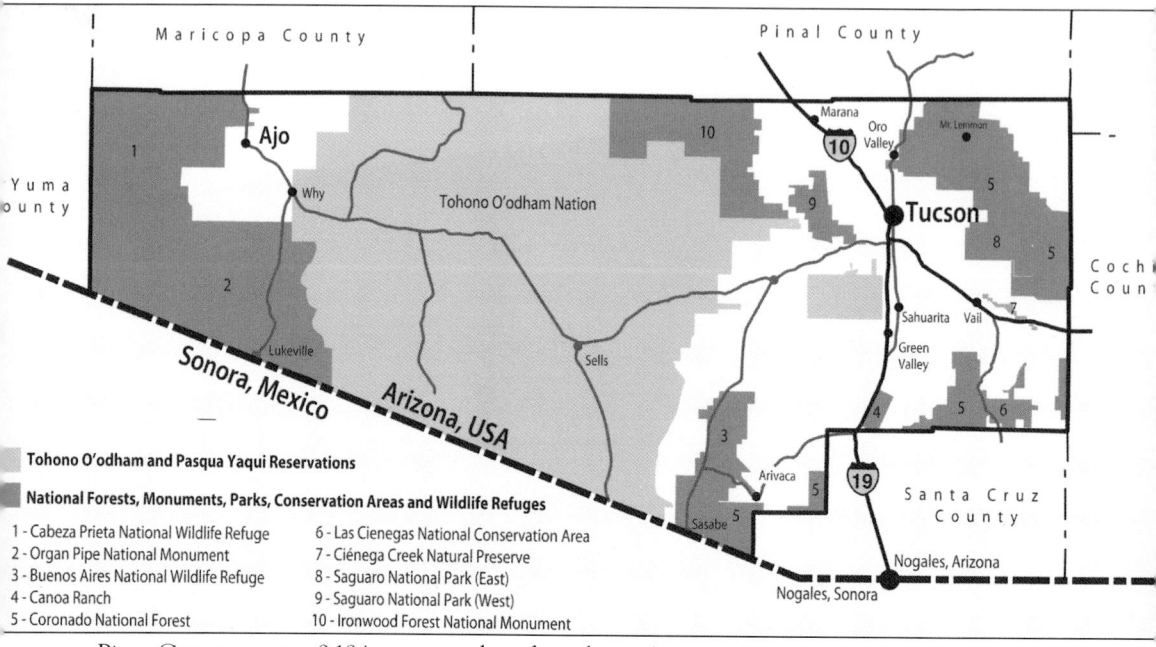

Pima County covers 9,184 square miles of southern Arizona. Ranging in elevation from 1,200 feet to 9,185 feet, the county has a diverse range of ecological and geological zones. The Tohono O'odham and Pascua Yaqui reservations together account for ownership of 42.1 percent of county land. Large areas of the county are also protected by a network of local, regional, and national lands, shown here in darker gray. (Courtesy of University of Oklahoma.)

ON THE COVER: Early members of the Sahuaro Ski Club prepare for an outing to the Santa Catalina Mountains for a ski trip. Composed primarily of individuals stationed at Davis-Monthan Air Force Base, the group was formed in the mid-1940s. The organization held fundraisers to build a ski area in the mountains near Tucson. (Courtesy of Arizona Historical Society, MS1255f452_M.)

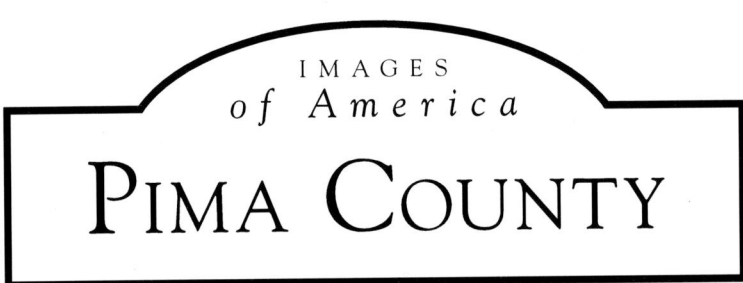

IMAGES of America
PIMA COUNTY

Pima County and the Arizona Historical Society

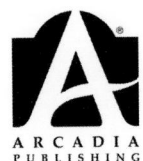

ARCADIA
PUBLISHING

Copyright © 2012 by Pima County and the Arizona Historical Society
ISBN 978-0-7385-9531-3

Published by Arcadia Publishing
Charleston, South Carolina

Printed in the United States of America

Library of Congress Control Number: 2012945562

For all general information, please contact Arcadia Publishing:
Telephone 843-853-2070
Fax 843-853-0044
E-mail sales@arcadiapublishing.com
For customer service and orders:
Toll-Free 1-888-313-2665

Visit us on the Internet at www.arcadiapublishing.com

In recognition of Arizona's centennial year, this book is dedicated to the people and places of Pima County that created and shaped our state's history.

Contents

Acknowledgments	6
Introduction	7
1. The Heritage of a Borderland	9
2. A Mosaic of Peoples and Cultures	19
3. Places to Live, Work, and Play	43
4. Attractions and Tourism	87
5. Building a Tradition of Conservation and Sense of Place	113
Index	126
Bibliography	127

Acknowledgments

This publication celebrates Pima County's centennial year and reflects a joint effort by the Pima County Board of Supervisors and the Board of Directors of the Arizona Historical Society.

Special thanks go the Pima County Board of Supervisors: Ann Day, District 1; Ramón Valadez, chairman, District 2; Sharon Bronson, District 3; Ray Carroll, District 4; Richard Elías, District 5; and Pima County administrator C.H. Huckelberry for their grasp of history, commitment to community, and encouragement and support to prepare this book to honor the people and places that have shaped Pima County through its history.

Special thanks also go to Arizona Historical Society executive director Dr. Anne Woosley, Bill Ponder, and Kyle McKoy for their support, collaboration, and partnership in this centennial tribute to the history of Pima County. This book, prepared by Jill McCleary of the Arizona Historical Society and Linda Mayro and Simon Herbert of Pima County, is the product of the work of many and would not have been possible without the support and assistance from the superb staff and volunteers at the Arizona Historical Society, including Kate Reeve, Alexandria Caster, Christina Seliga, Dave Tackenberg, Valerie Kittell, Chrystal Carpenter, Alexa Tulk, Dianne Nilsen, Meghan Morris, and Paul LaFrance. Thanks also go to Bill Singleton of the Pima County Communications Department for his expertise in preparation of some of the historical maps and to Neva Connolly and Roger Anyon of the Pima County Office of Sustainability and Conservation for the editing skills and word crafting.

The images, maps, and illustrations found in this book are primarily from the rich archives of the Arizona Historical Society in Tucson. As Arizona hits its 100th year as a state in 2012, the authors are indebted to all the families and organizations that have donated their photographs, manuscripts, and artifacts to the Arizona Historical Society. Without their donations, Pima County's deep and diverse history could not have been told.

All images appear courtesy of the Arizona Historical Society (AHS) and the University of Arizona (UA) except where noted.

Introduction

Pima County has long been a desert frontier shaped by its environment and the histories of Native American, Spanish Colonial, Mexican, and American Territorial peoples whose living traditions and cultures are intrinsic to the region's vitality. How the environment and cultures have changed and adapted over time are at the very root of Pima County's long story.

Tucson is Pima County's oldest city, its name derived from the expression *stjukshon*, a Northern Piman term meaning "at the base of black mountain." The village of Tucson was first noted in the journals of Spanish explorer-missionary Fr. Francisco Eusebio Kino in the 1690s as he journeyed north along the Santa Cruz River, which sustained the native O'odham people, their ancestors, and generations of other peoples to come. Tucson would eventually become the principal city of Pima County, and it remains a unique crossroads of commerce, cultures, and change.

Archaeologists have shown that some 10,000 years before the first Spanish explorers entered southern Arizona in what is today Pima County, the first prehistoric peoples hunted large game such as mammoth and bison, which became extinct at the end of the last ice age. People continued a hunting-and-gathering way of life for several thousand years, but momentous changes occurred around 2000 BCE, when cultivation of maize first began. Agriculture transformed Native Americans' economies and allowed settled village life to be established along rivers and streams. The ensuing Hohokam culture dominated southern Arizona for nearly 1,000 years, sustained through intensive agricultural food production supplemented by wild plant and animal resources. Through the exchange of surplus foods, cotton, pottery, shell, turquoise, and other materials, they developed extensive trading networks and complex political alliances. By the time the Spanish arrived in the 16th century, the Hohokam had vanished, succeeded by the O'odham or Pima peoples, who today view the Hohokam as their ancestors.

The Spanish *entrada* into Pima County in the 1690s brought with it enormous change. Sent to New Spain as a missionary, cartographer, and explorer, Jesuit priest Fr. Eusebio Francisco Kino brought European architecture, crops, livestock, language, economics, art, and religion to the region and established more than 20 missions for the native O'odham throughout what is today northern Mexico and southern Arizona. This region, which extended from Sonora, Mexico, to the Gila River in Arizona, was known as Pimería Alta (homeland of the Upper Pima). Around the same time the Spanish arrived, the nomadic Apache were migrating southward, eventually moving into the area north and east of Pimería Alta. Raiding of both native Piman villages and Spanish settlements for grain and livestock became a well-established practice by the 1700s, and Tucson, the northernmost of the mission communities, was essentially unprotected. In 1775, the military fort of El Presidio San Agustín del Tucson was established across the river from the mission, in what is today downtown Tucson, serving to protect the growing Tucson community. Spanish land grants at La Canoa and other areas were attempts to expand Spanish settlements and agricultural production to generate wealth for Spain. However, this was not to be.

Following a period of relative peace and prosperity, colonial New Spain fought for its independence, which it won in 1821, bringing more change. The Mexican Republic did not continue the missionary policies and the support of Spain, and with the flag of Mexico now flying over its walls, the Tucson presidio struggled on much as before. Apache raiding once again increased in intensity, and Tucson's population of 400 people of diverse ethnic backgrounds sought common protection within its walls. Outside contact was limited to occasional supply pack trains from other Sonoran towns and the few American frontiersmen and traders who ventured to this remote outpost.

By 1846, Mexico and the United States were embroiled in a war that resulted in the annexation of Texas by the United States and the loss of nearly two thirds of Mexico's former territory. When the war ended in 1848, Mexico ceded a vast territory to the United States comprised of what is today California, Nevada, Utah, New Mexico, and Arizona north of the Gila River. As before, Tucson remained a frontier town, and Pima County was still part of Mexico.

The discovery of gold in California in 1849 shattered Tucson's isolation, as gold-seekers and adventurers sought their way westward and the United States sought a southerly route for a transcontinental railroad to California. Unfortunately, the selected route was still part of Mexico, so the US government sent James Gadsden to Mexico City to negotiate a land sale with the Mexican government. While Mexico needed money after the war with the United States, Mexico would consider selling only enough land to give the United States its southerly route. After considerable debate, the Gadsden Purchase was completed in 1854 for a sum of $10 million. Tucson and the Gadsden Purchase area were made part of Dona Ana County in the Territory of New Mexico.

During the American Civil War, the Gadsden Purchase and New Mexico Territory became a political football, with the Confederates claiming the southern half as a separate Arizona Territory. Union troops were sent to Tucson in 1862, and in 1863, President Lincoln separated Arizona Territory from New Mexico Territory. Four counties were established in 1864, Pima, Yuma, Yavapai, and Mohave, named after Native American tribes. With the end of the Civil War, southern Arizona and Pima County were open for settlement and commerce. By 1871, the population of Tucson had grown to 3,000 people. It was now the mercantile center of Pima County as well as the capital of Arizona Territory. New adobe buildings spread out from the original confines of the presidio walls. The Village of Tucson was incorporated in 1871, establishing property ownership and local government, and the San Xavier Indian Reservation was established for the Tohono O'odham community in 1874.

Stage lines and freighters brought adventurers, miners, homesteaders, ranchers, farmers, and families to the new Pima County in Arizona Territory. Although its reputation as a lawless Wild West territory is justified, Pima County was rapidly moving toward better times. By the 1870s, schools had been started, civil law had been established, a jail and courthouse were built in Tucson, stage and mail lines to various settlements competed for business, ranches and farms were expanding, and mining in towns like Ajo, Quijotoa, Arivaca, Gunsight, and Silverbell was growing.

In 1880, the railroad finally reached Tucson, connecting Pima County with the East and West Coasts. This brought an era of even more rapid growth, new people, and change. The University of Arizona was established in 1885 in Tucson. Arizona became the 48th state in 1912, and to protect Tohono O'odham lands to the west of Tucson from encroachment by new settlers, a second extensive reservation was established in 1917.

Arizona's growth industries were based on cattle, copper, cotton, citrus, and especially climate (the "Five Cs"), and because of its dry and warm climate, Pima County would find its future in health-seekers, tourists, and new residents attracted to rugged mountains and the Sonoran Desert. By 1950, economic growth would be tied to expansive population growth fueled by real estate development.

To preserve the sense of place that defines Pima County, a strong conservation ethic has grown up that strives to balance growth with preservation of the natural and cultural environment. Pima County provides an authentic piece of Arizona where one can still seek and find a diverse land, heritage, and living traditions that have been shaped by generations of diverse peoples who came before and who live here today.

One

THE HERITAGE OF A BORDERLAND

Pima County, with its long and complex cultural history, has an equally rich and varied natural setting of deserts, mountains, and valleys, where the intersection of many cultures and diverse environments has created a series of changing borders on what might better be called the desert frontier of the American landscape.

Through much of its history, Pima County was a cultural borderland where, beginning many centuries ago, successions of peoples have come into the region and shaped the environment, from nomadic hunters and gatherers to Hohokam farmers who settled in large villages to early Piman peoples first encountered by Spanish explorers and missionaries. In the 17th century, Pima County became the northern frontier of New Spain, with Tucson as the "post farthest out." Mexican independence from Spain in 1821 brought changes, but it was not long after that Americans began their westward move to the California goldfields in 1849, prompting the Gadsden Purchase in 1854 and the establishment of today's border with Mexico. This brought the railroad in 1880 along with American settlement, commerce, government, and culture.

This borderland of peoples, cultural traditions, and land uses define Pima County's sense of place. This is very much a working and living landscape—home to Native Americans who view and use the land in traditional ways, home to descendants of Spanish settlers whose religious faith shaped the land and defined its cities, home to descendants of Mexican families who settled here bringing a rich vitality to the community, and home to descendants of American pioneers whose courage brought them westward seeking new opportunities.

Today, Pima County remains a borderland, sharing a 125-mile-long border with Mexico; sharing the borders of two Indian nations, the Tohono O'odham Nation and the Pascua Yaqui tribe; and sharing in the cultures and traditions of all those successions of people who met and lived in this desert frontier.

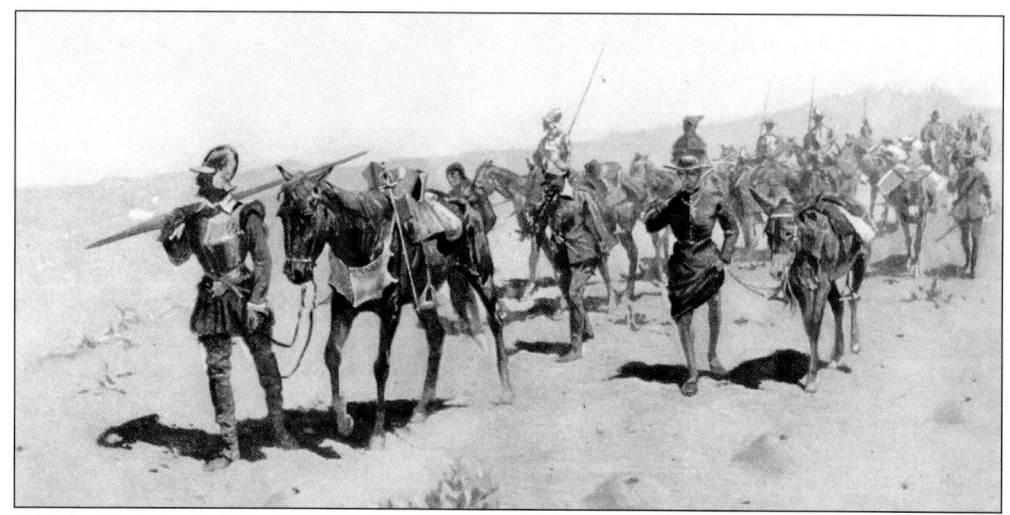

The American Southwest has attracted explorers and those with a pioneering spirit for centuries. As part of New Spain, conquistadors searching for riches crossed present-day Arizona. Above, a Frederic Remington drawing depicts Francisco Vásquez de Coronado's massive expedition through the Americas in search of the Seven Cities of Cíbola. Coronado used well-established Native American trade routes to cross Arizona. (AHS 16312.)

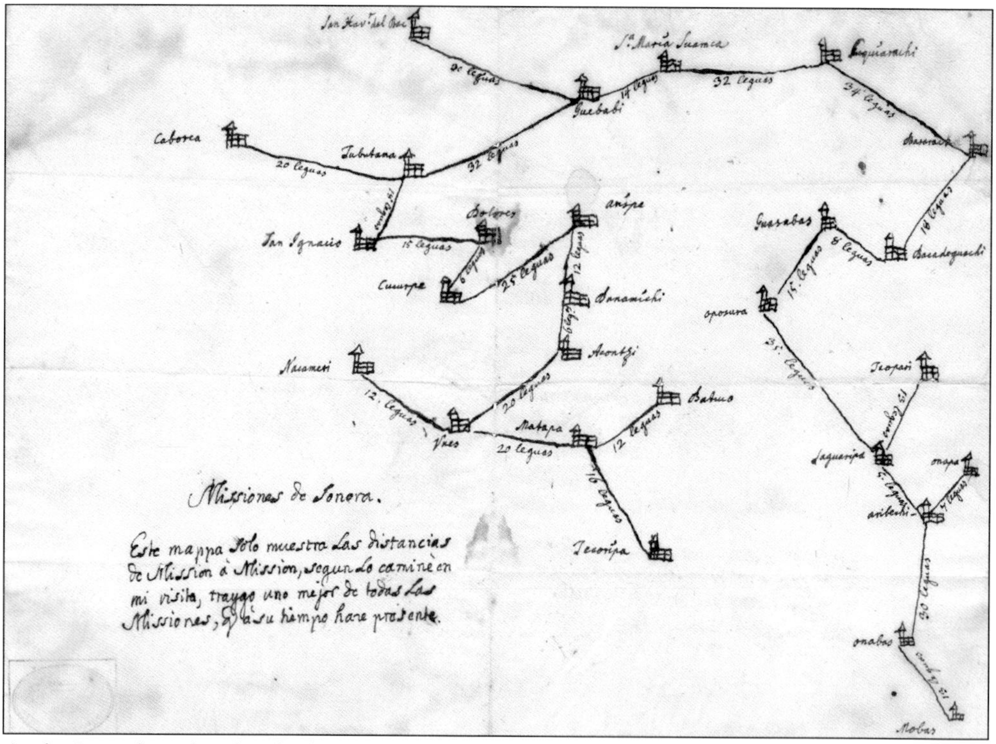

As the Spanish explored and colonized New Spain, they brought the Christian faith and established a mission system. The missions were intentionally placed with the goal of converting Native American tribes to Christianity. Additionally, the missions provided a stable food supply and protection against enemies. This hand-drawn 1744 map shows the extent of the mission system. San Xavier, in present-day Pima County, is shown at the highest point on the map. (AHS G4771 E4 1744 B3.)

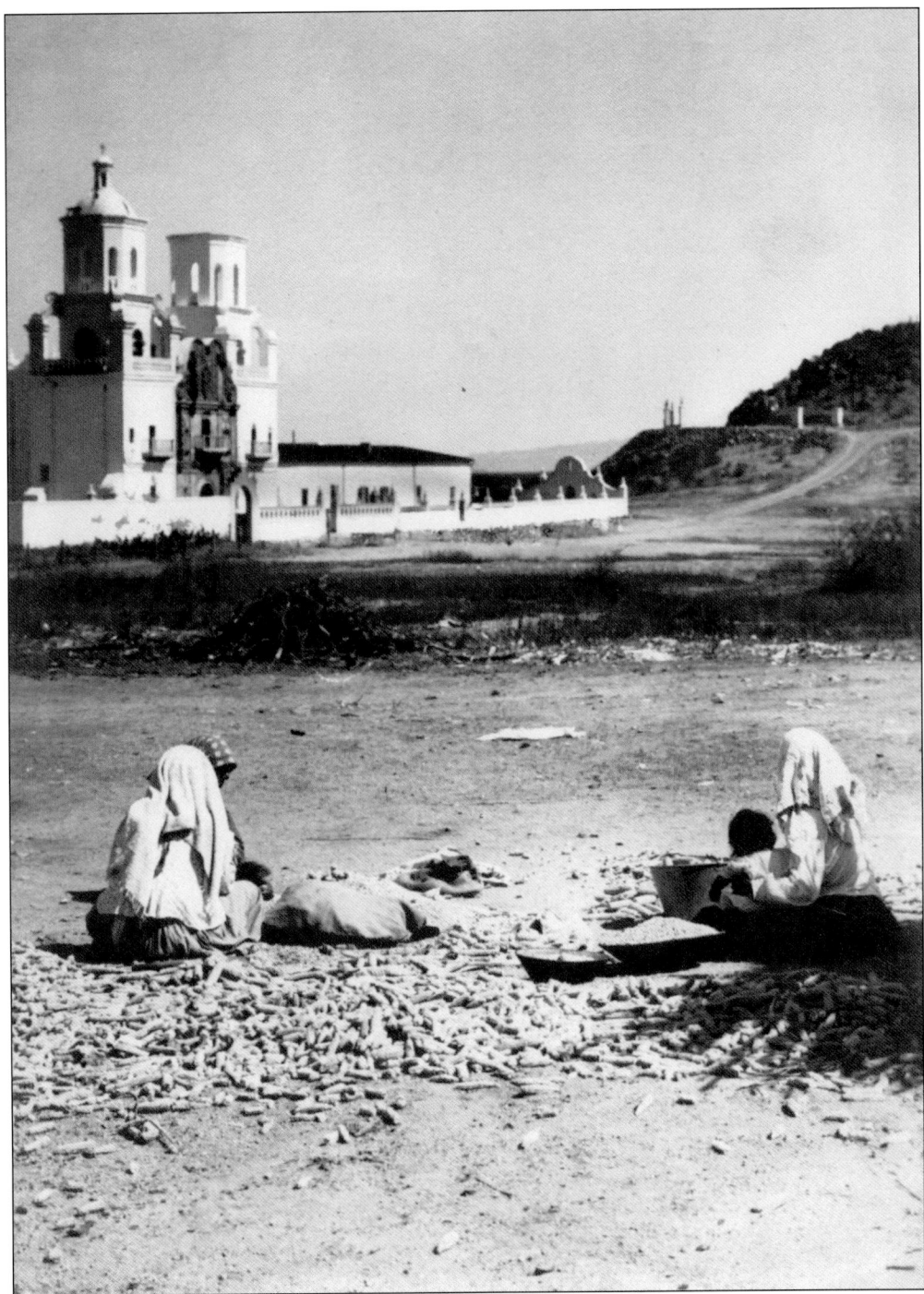
The Tohono O'odham Nation is a federally recognized independent sovereign Indian tribe located in southwestern Arizona. Tohono O'odham, which translated means "desert people," have lived in the area of Pima County from time immemorial. As a result, they have a rich history in Arizona and a culture that continues to thrive today. Pictured here are Tohono O'odham women processing corn in front of Mission San Xavier del Bac in southern Pima County. (AHS 91793.)

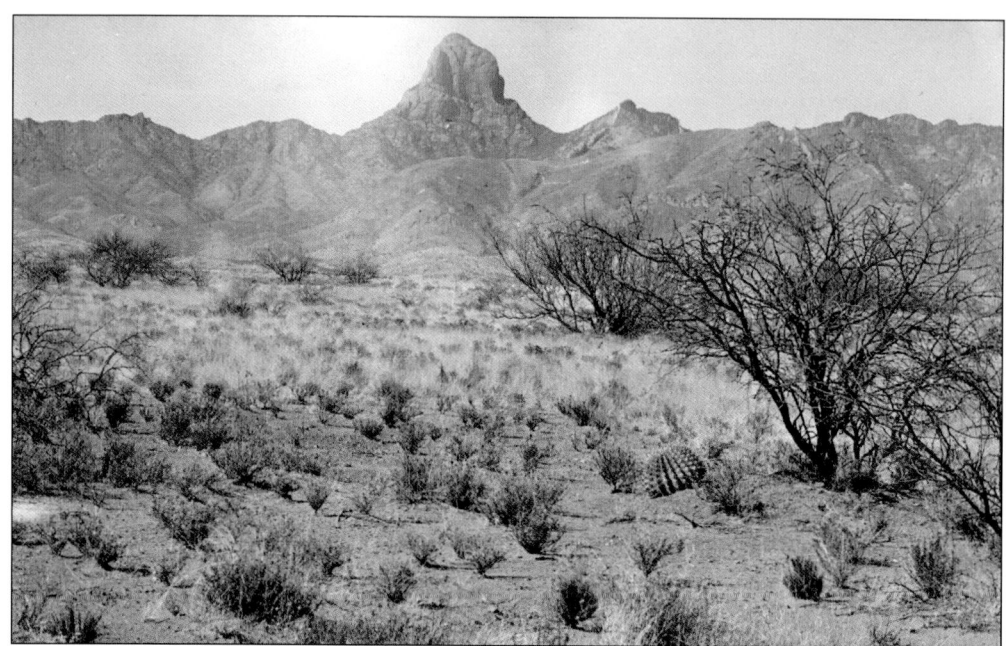

The 7,730-foot Baboquivari Peak provides a striking view in the Sonoran Desert. It is the most sacred place to the Tohono O'odham people and is home to the creator, I'itoi. The peak and approximately 2,000 acres surrounding it were designated as a wilderness area in 1990 and are a popular destination for hikers, climbers, and tourists. (UA Photograph Files.)

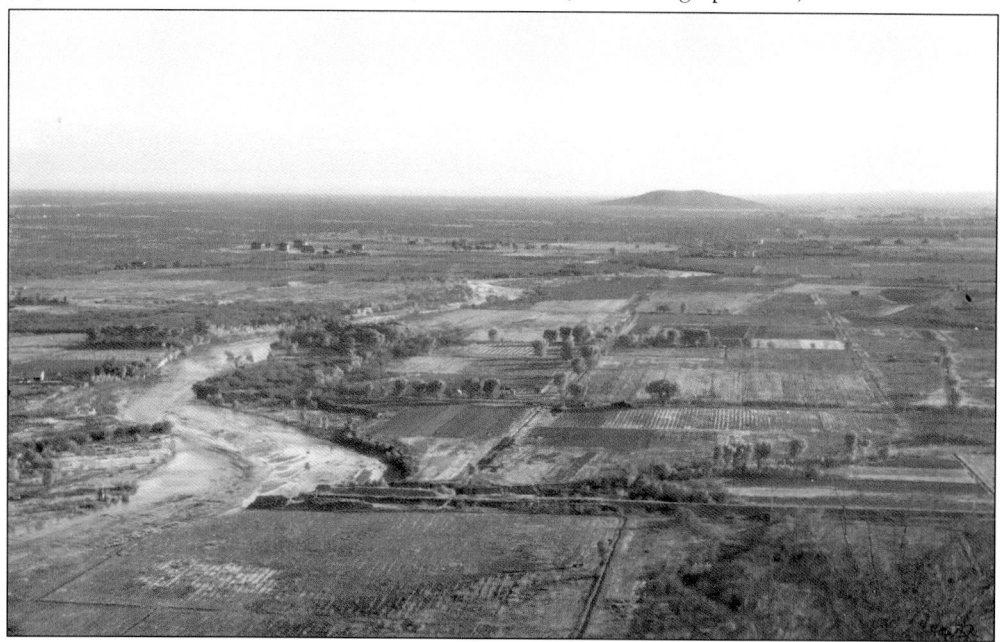

Agriculture played a large role in the development of Pima County. It is believed that Native Americans transitioned to farming and foraging activities in the area as early as 1500 BCE. As American settlers came to the area, they continued agriculture practices near the major river valleys. This view from Sentinel Peak in Tucson shows the extent of the farming still occurring around the Santa Cruz River in 1927. (AHS PC180f262_524.)

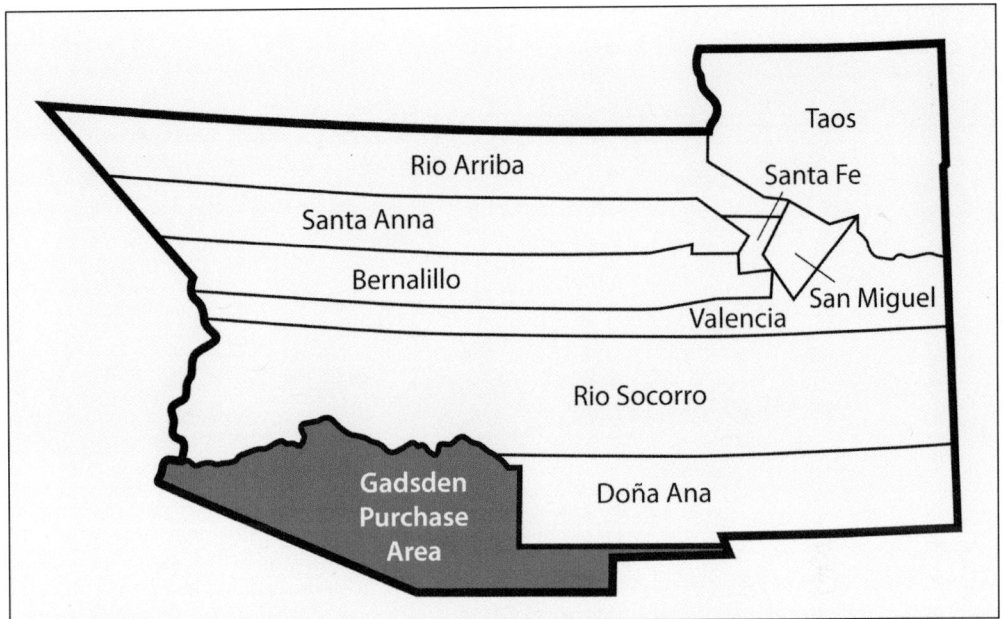

Seeking a southern route to California for a transcontinental railroad, the United States purchased 29,640 square miles of northern Mexico in 1854 through the Gadsden Purchase. This brought the small village of Tucson and the area that would become known as Pima County into the US territories. (Courtesy of University of Oklahoma.)

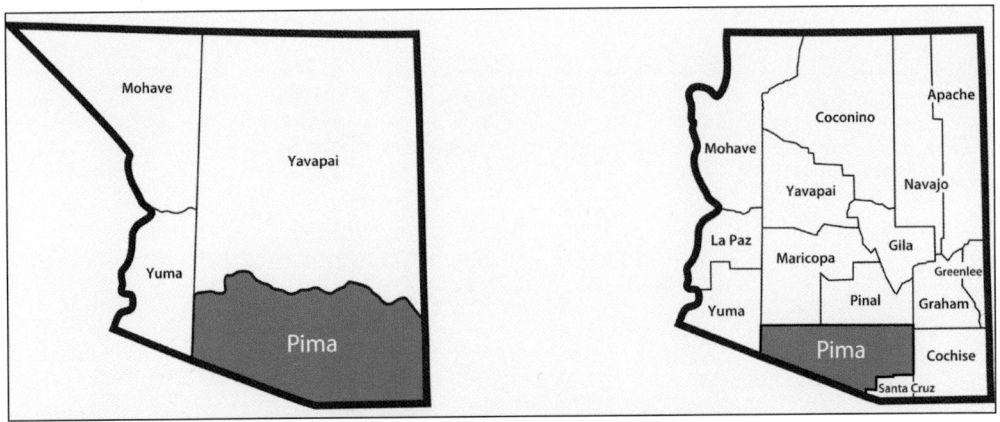

In 1864, the first territorial legislature for Arizona divided the state into four counties and named them after Native American tribes, Pima, Yavapai, Yuma, and Mohave, shown at left. Pima County covered approximately 26,000 square miles and spanned the southeastern portion of the state. By 1909, Arizona Territory's counties had been further refined from four large counties to 14, shown at right. Despite this reduction, Pima County still ranks as the 22nd largest county in the United States, making it larger than New Hampshire or Massachusetts. (Courtesy of University of Oklahoma.)

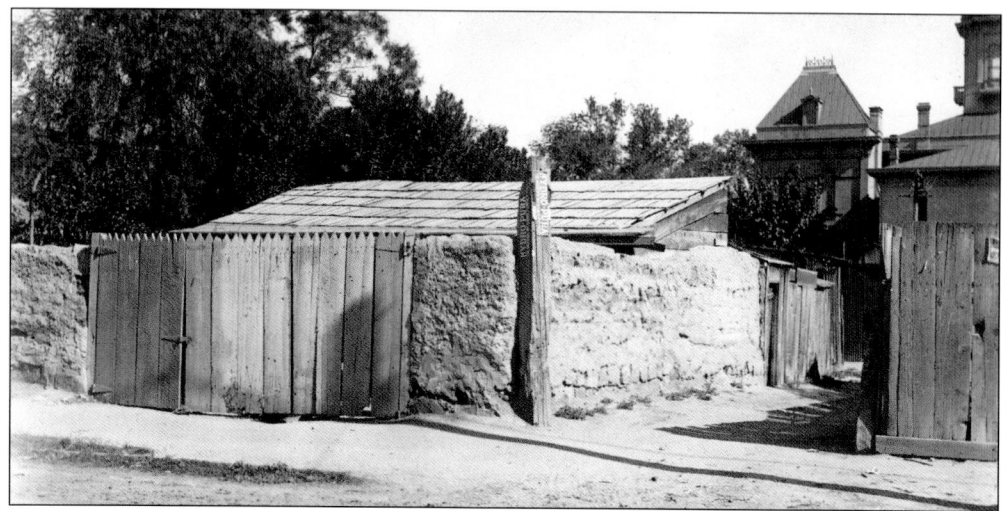

On August 20, 1775, Hugo O'Conor, an Irishman serving in the Spanish military, and Franciscan priest Francisco Garcés established the location for a new presidio near the site of a Tohono O'odham village. Built for protection from Apache Indian raids, the presidio became the foundation for present-day Tucson and expanded the Spanish system farther north from Tubac. The importance of the walls as a defensive structure started to decline in the second half of the 19th century, and the walls were no longer maintained. Above, the remains of a small portion of the presidio wall were put to use as the city of Tucson grew around it. Below, archaeological investigations have sought out the location of the original walls. This image was taken during archaeological excavations in the 1950s. (Above, AHS 5209; below, UA Photograph Files.)

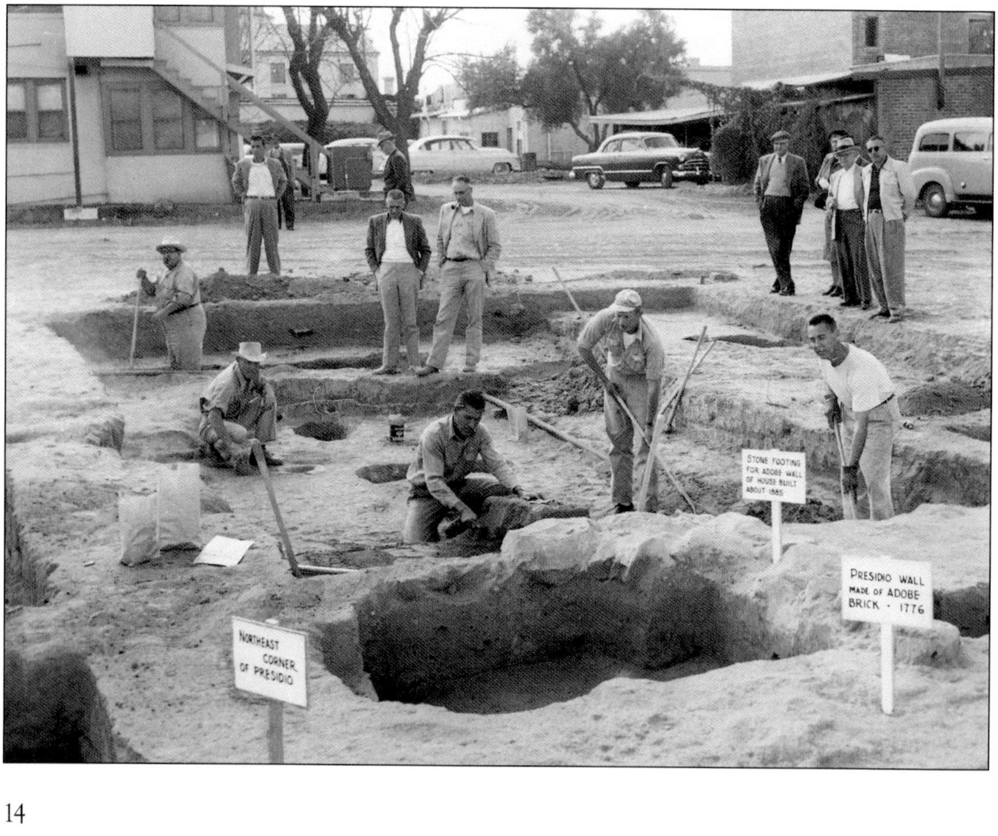

Photographer Willis Haynes began taking photographs across the small town of Tucson in the 1880s. He captured common street scenes such as this one, showing a Tohono O'odham woman walking along a typical dirt road next to simple adobe buildings. The name "Wah Long" shows on a sign in the background. (AHS PC60 18885.)

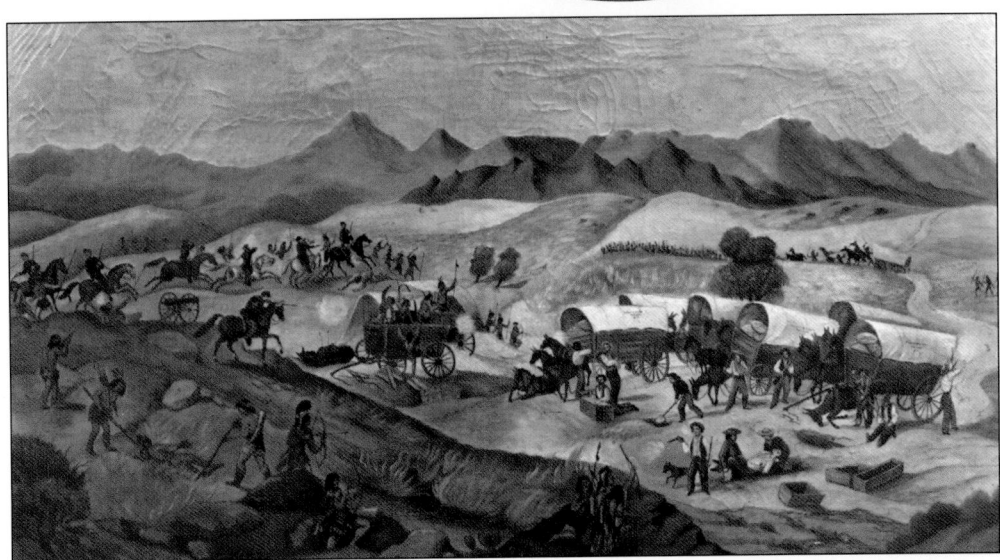

The threat of Apache attacks was a concern for pioneers who came to Pima County. Stories of murder and mayhem fueled continuous demands for protection from the federal government. In response, a system of frontier forts was constructed throughout the Arizona Territory starting in the early 1860s. This painting by Edward Zinn depicts an Apache raid on a supply train between Fort Lowell and Fort Grant. (AHS 49346.)

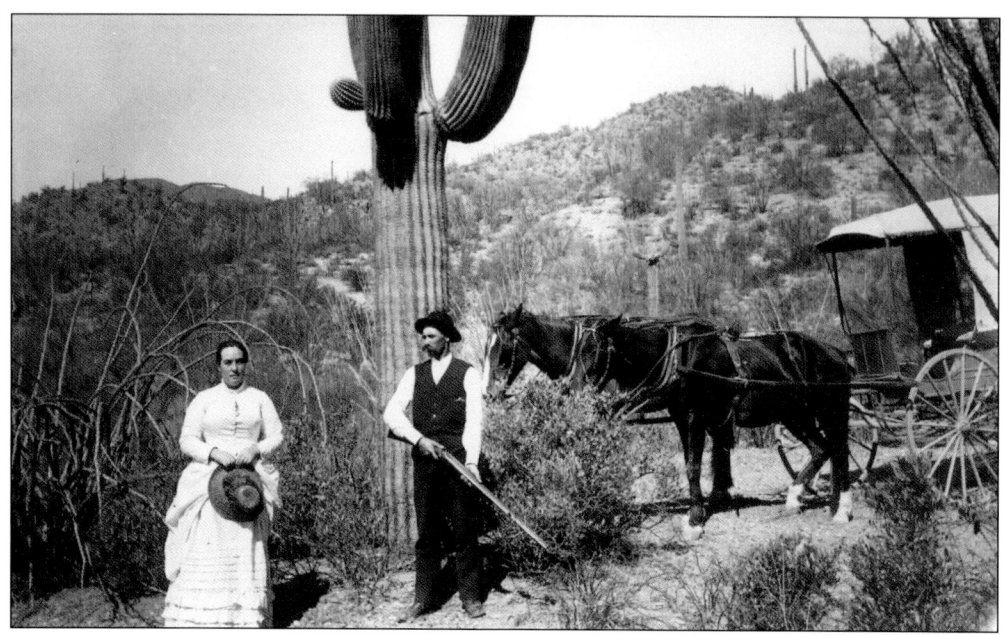

American prospectors and trappers began to explore Pima County as early as the 1820s, but permanent movement of Americans into the county was slow. After the Gadsden Purchase of 1854, it took two years for American troops to show up in Tucson and formally take possession of the land for the United States. As Tucson became a rough frontier town, visitors from the East Coast often decried what they thought to be the primitive living conditions and low morals of the people. However, with the passage of the Homestead Act of 1862, intrepid pioneers found their way to Pima County seeking a life in the West. (Above, AHS B91447a; below, AHS B91121b.)

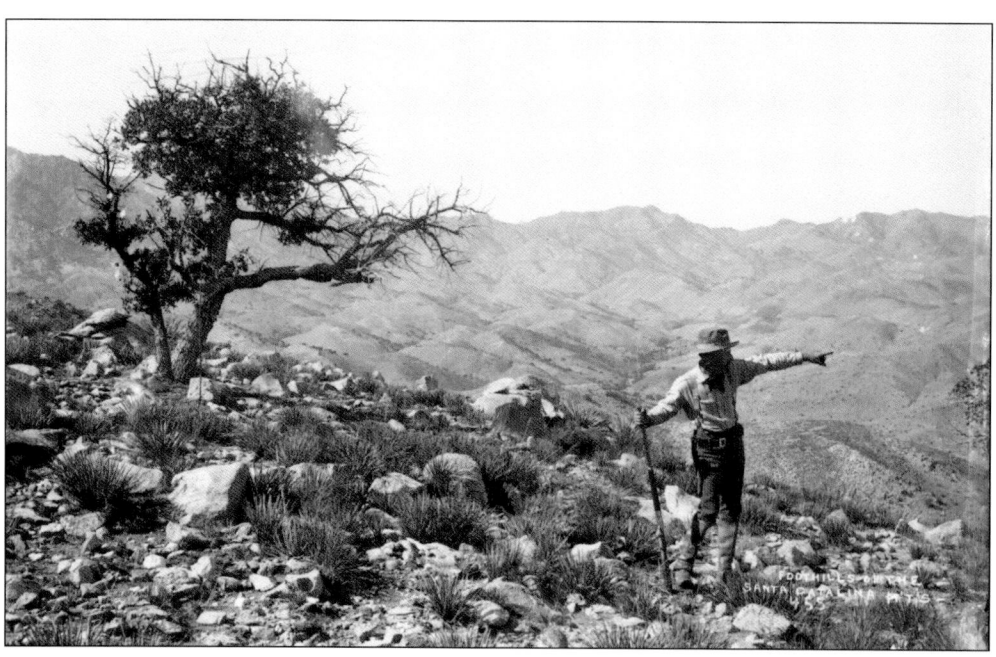

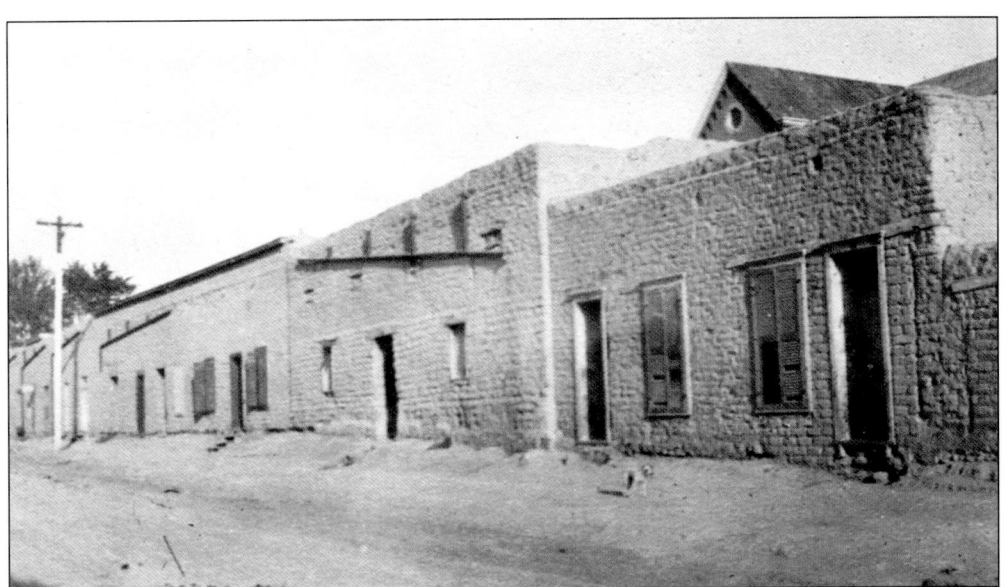

This unassuming collection of adobe buildings was located on Ochoa Street, near the present-day St. Augustine Cathedral, then in the heart of Tucson's business district. Rented between 1866 and 1868, the building shown at center served as the first administration offices and courtroom for Pima County. The single-story adobe building on the right reportedly housed the Arizona Territorial Capitol when Tucson was the capital between 1867 and 1877. (AHS 47863.)

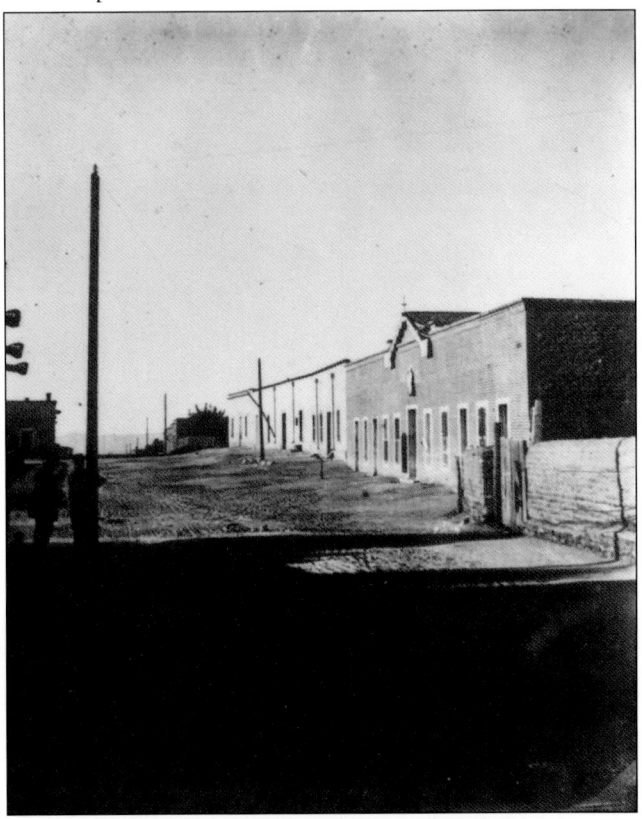

By 1868, the difficulties that came with trying to govern Pima County from a series of rented rooms persuaded the county board of supervisors to spend $200 to buy land for a permanent courthouse. Charles U. Meyers was contracted to build the courthouse at a cost of $10,150. This photograph shows a view of the courthouse's west facade, with the gable roof over the main entrance. (AHS B111291.)

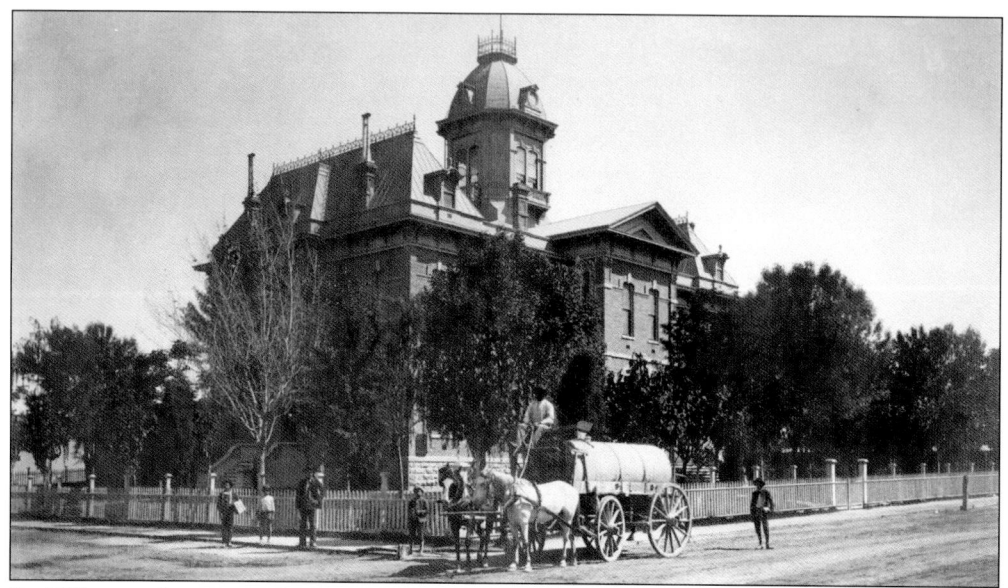

By 1881, growth in Pima County's population and a commitment to improving county services led to the need for a larger courthouse. This resulted in the first architect-designed courthouse in Pima County, designed by A.W. Pattiani. The Victorian design for the courthouse consisted of a symmetrical two-story building that was strikingly different from the simple adobe buildings that surrounded it. (AHS 2904.)

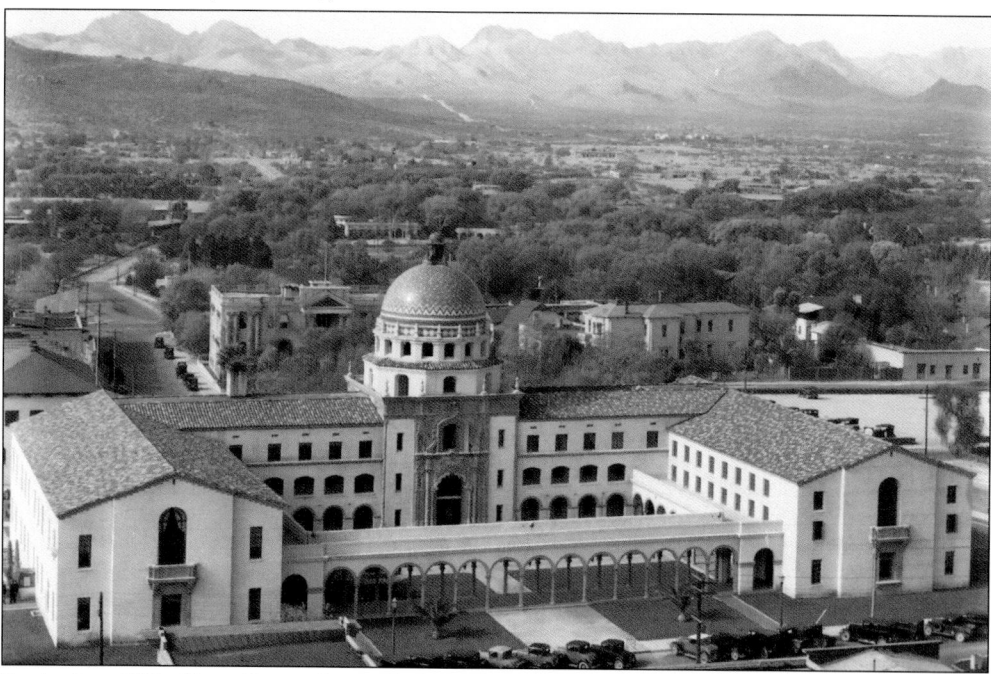

By the late 1920s, Pima County's courthouse was in decay. Architect Roy Place designed the new structure in a Spanish Colonial Revival style that included brightly colored mosaic tiles on the roof of the central dome. While the building continues to house county government and judicial functions, it is referred to as the "old" Pima County Courthouse, since the superior court moved to a new location in 1974. (AHS B25912.)

Two

A Mosaic of Peoples and Cultures

While there has been a long tradition of settlement in Pima County, the oldest and deepest traditions are those of the indigenous peoples, who have lived in the region for at least 10,000 years. These many generations of peoples are considered ancestral groups by the Tohono O'odham (Desert People), the Hia Ce-d O'odham (Sand Dune People), the Akimel O'odham (River People), and the Pascua Yaqui tribe, who all live in southern Arizona today.

Even as Spanish explorers and missionaries in the 17th century pushed their way northward into Pimería Alta from the south, Apache people were migrating southward and moved into the foothills of mountain ranges to the east of Tucson, from which they hunted, gathered foods, and easily raided O'odham villages, Spanish missions, and ranches along the San Pedro and Santa Cruz Rivers. Ongoing strife largely prevented much settlement of the region until 1886, when the great Chiricahua Apache leader Geronimo surrendered to the US military, effectively ending 200 years of conflict.

As borders moved and sovereign rule changed from Spain to Mexico, and then to the United States, all citizens in the region became citizens of the next sovereignty. What had been a small and predominantly O'odham, Hispanic, and Mexican community became American in 1854, when it was poised to change forever. The coming of the Southern Pacific Railroad in 1880 brought many new immigrants and settlers, like Chinese, Anglos, African Americans, Mormons, and Jewish settlers, among others. The Pascua Yaqui, an indigenous people from northern Mexico, also moved here in the late 1800s to begin a new community.

By 1900, Pima County's population had grown to nearly 15,000, and its Hispanic and Anglo populations were about equal. By 1950, there had been an explosion of growth to nearly 150,000. Today, Pima County continues to be both a crossroads and a destination for numerous peoples, and, as before, a virtual mosaic of cultural traditions, all woven into the rich cultural fabric that defines Pima County.

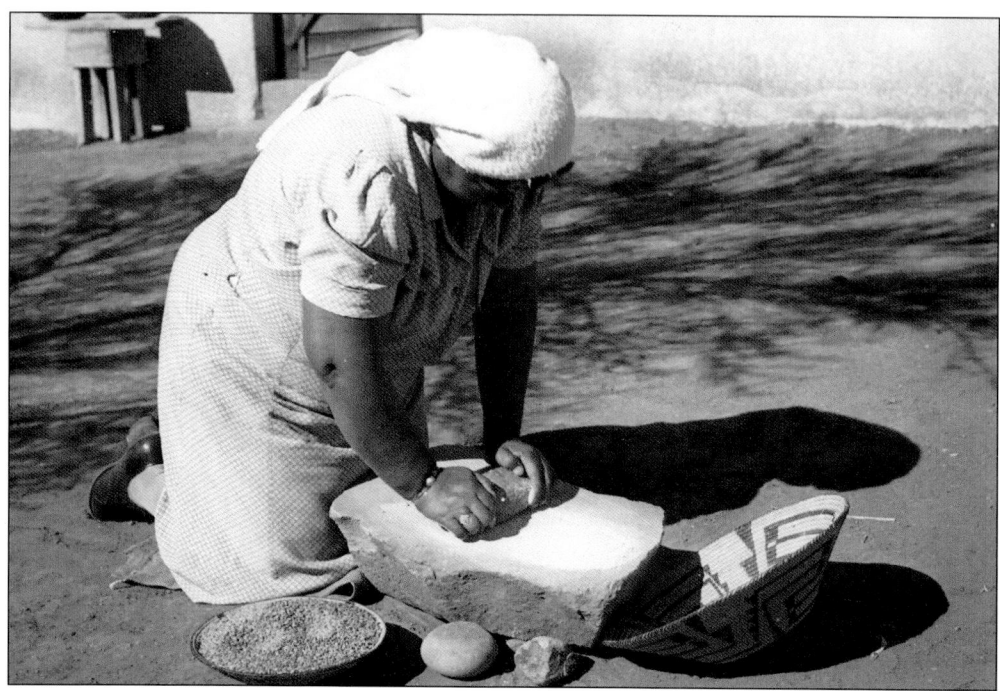

The Tohono O'odham Nation is one of the largest tribes in the Southwest, with nearly 28,000 enrolled members living both on and off the reservation. In 1937, the Tohono O'odham (then commonly called the Papago) adopted a constitution and became a sovereign nation. Above, a Tohono O'odham woman grinds grain using stones. A traditional basket collects the grain at the end of the rock. Below, a young Tohono O'odham child sleeps soundly in a cradle made of fabric hanging by rope. (Above, AHS 52166; below, AHS BN86800.)

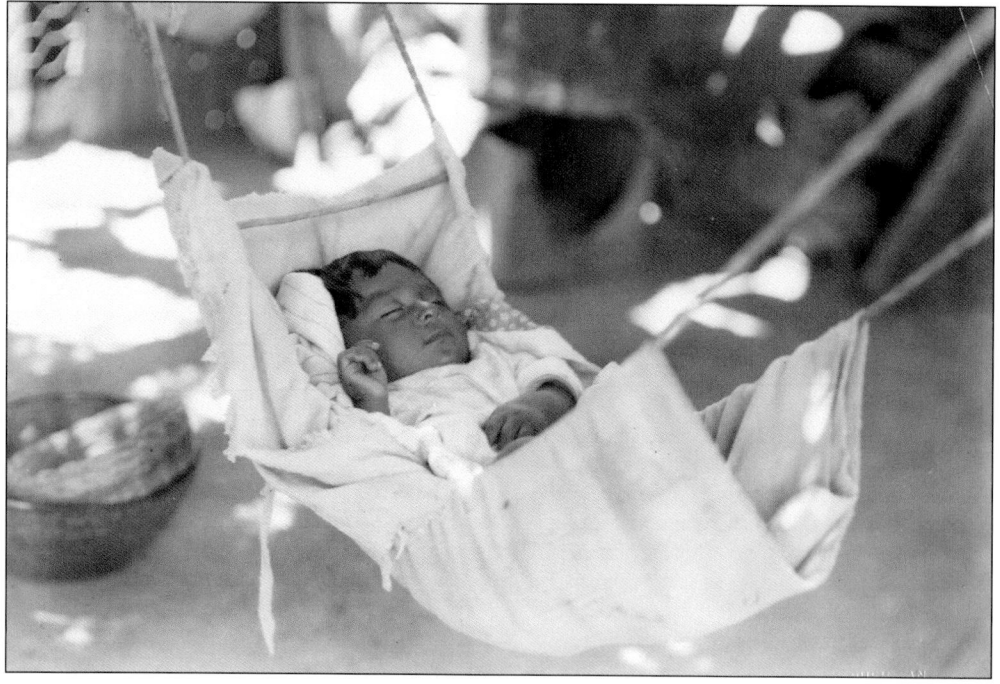

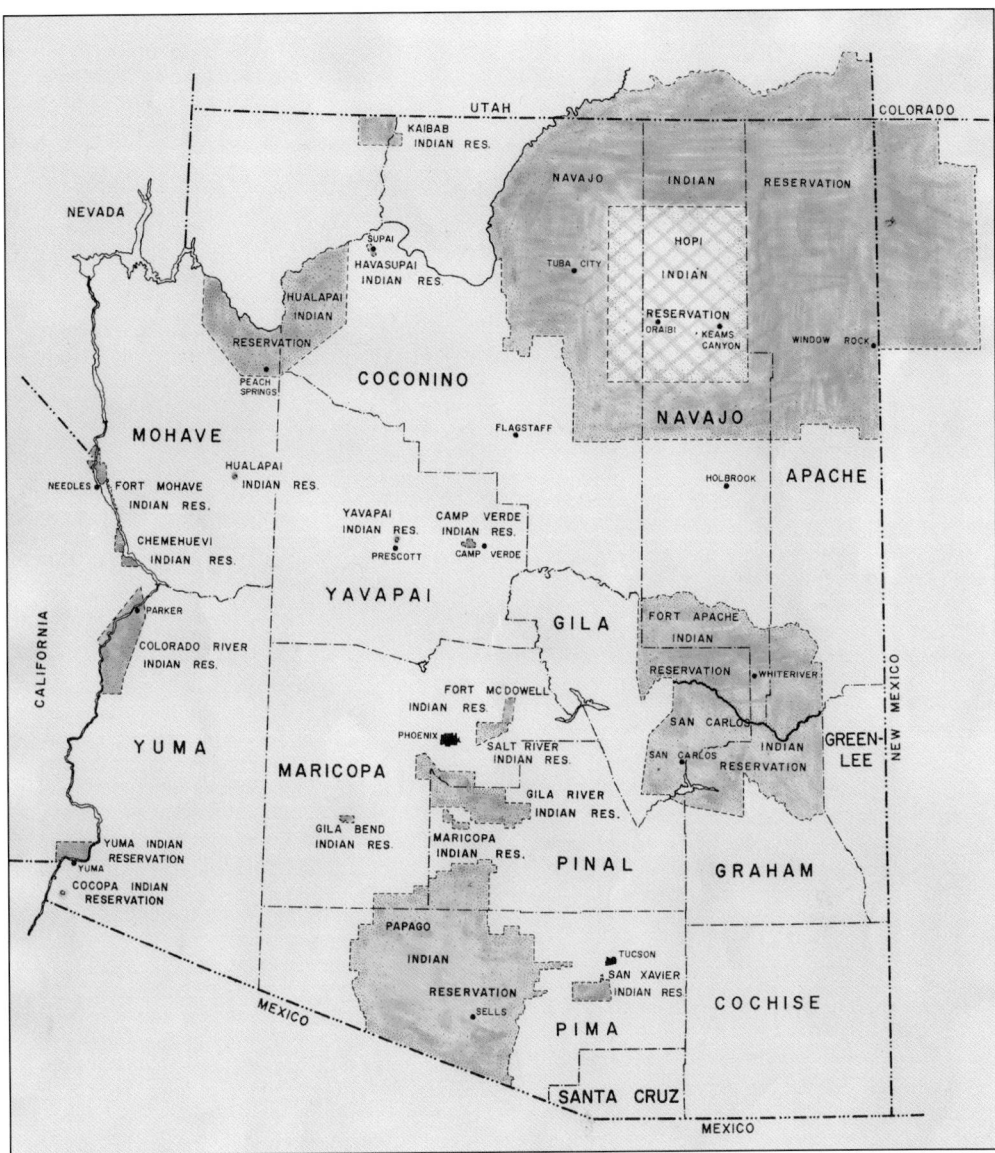

This 1960s map of Arizona shows the extent of Native American reservations across the state. With over 20 federally recognized tribes and over 250,000 Native Americans, Arizona has a rich diversity of cultures throughout its counties. In Pima County, the San Xavier, Pascua Yaqui, and Tohono O'odham (referred to as "Papago" on this map) reservations together account for ownership of 42.1 percent of county land. The capital of the Tohono O'odham Nation, Sells, was once called Indian Oasis. The name was changed in 1918 in honor of Indian commissioner Cato Sells. (AHS G4331 G6 196u M3.)

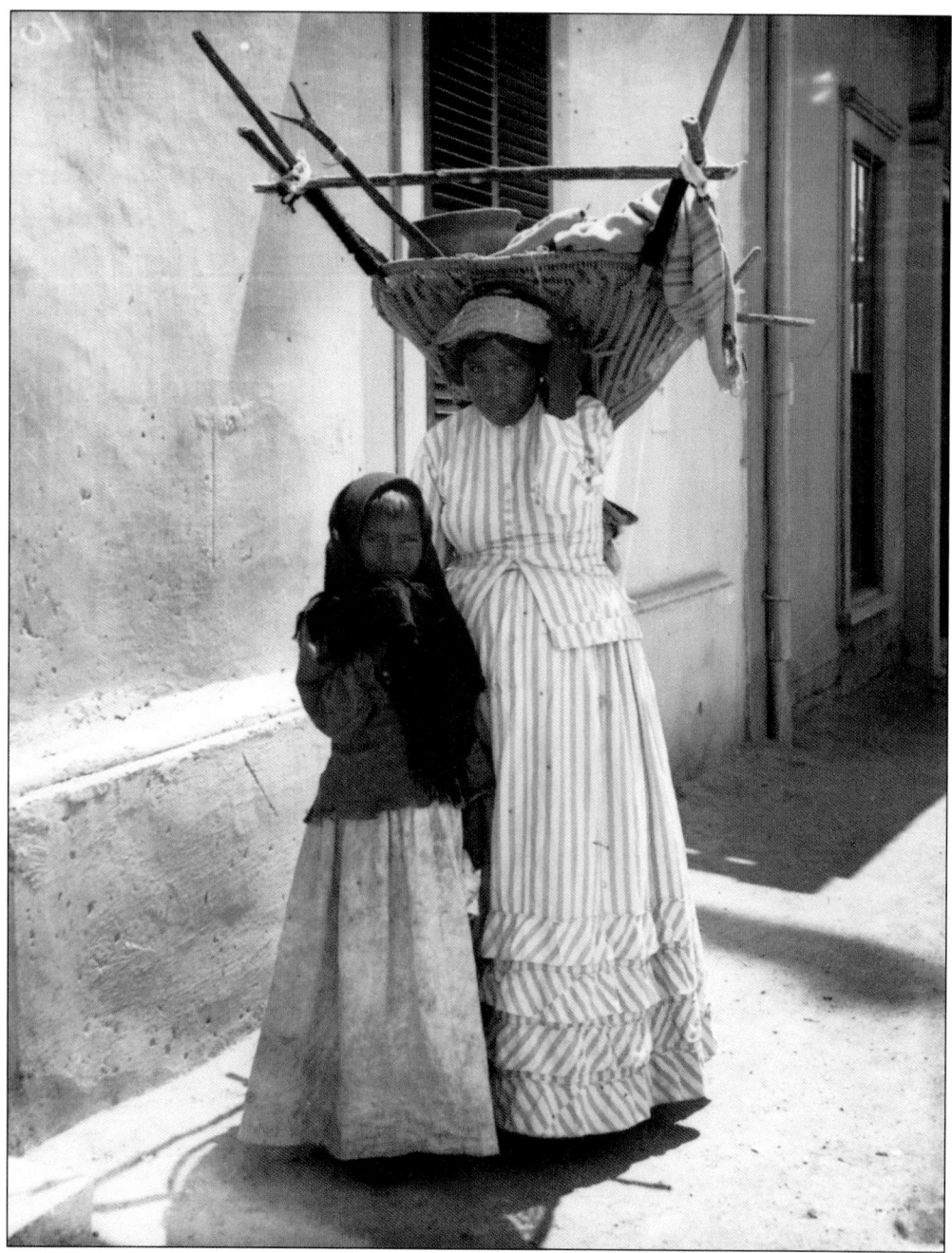

Although the photographer did not leave the name of the Tohono O'odham woman in this photograph, she represents a common sight in historic Pima County, which is of Tohono O'odham women carrying cone-shaped burden baskets, called *kiahas*. Often walking the distance from San Xavier to Tucson to sell their goods, Tohono O'odham women used *kiahas* to transport pottery, wood, hay, and a variety of other items. The basket rested on the back and stayed in place with a band that crossed the woman's forehead. (AHS B91770.)

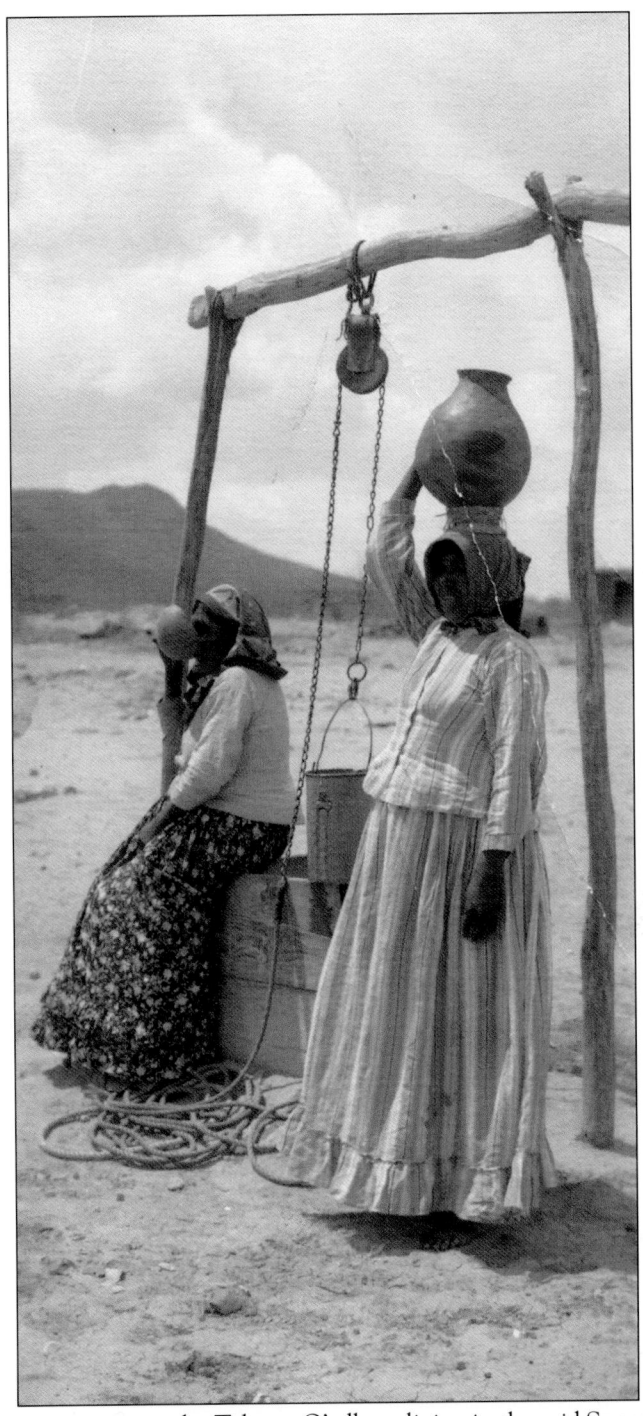

Water was a precious resource to the Tohono O'odham living in the arid Sonoran Desert. Often having to walk a great distance, girls and women would frequently travel to a well or other water source in the morning and bring water back to their families. Many of the pots and jars created by Tohono O'odham women were not only used to transport water but also to store materials or sell to tourists as souvenirs. (AHS 91794.)

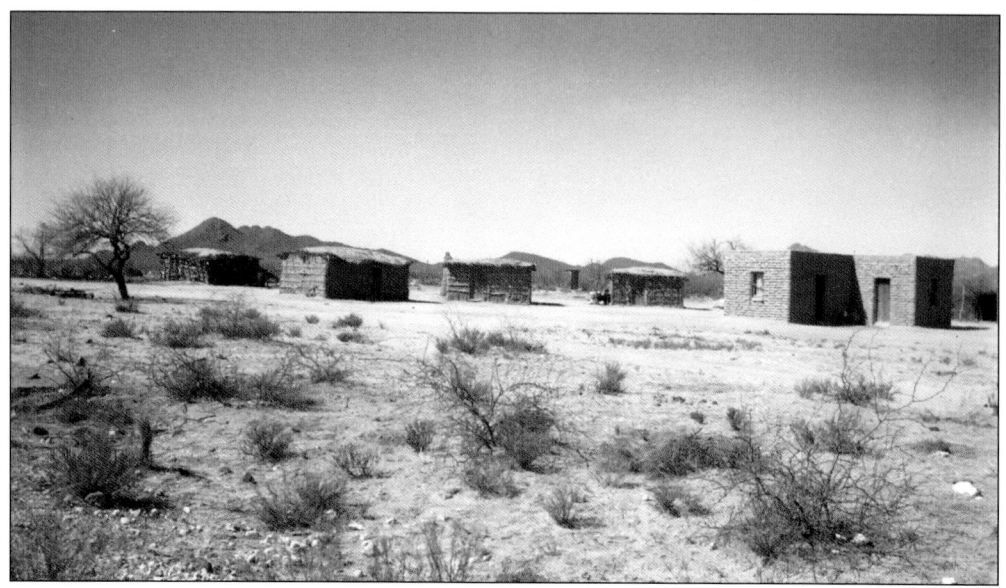

The lands of the Tohono O'odham are located within the Sonoran Desert and occupy portions of Pinal, Maricopa, and Pima Counties. With a land base of 2.8 million acres, it is the second largest tribal land base in the United States. The Tohono O'odham that reside on reservation land live on one of four separate areas. The largest is called the "main" reservation of 2.7 million acres and includes the community of Sells, which functions as the nation's capital. San Xavier, located just south of the city of Tucson, is the second largest land base and contains 71,095 acres. The image above shows dwellings on the Tohono O'odham reservation. In April 1927, photographer Norman Wallace took the snapshot below of rancher Ceverius Juan on the Tohono O'odham reservation in Covered Wells. (Above, AHS 101562; below, AHS PC180f.365_0316.)

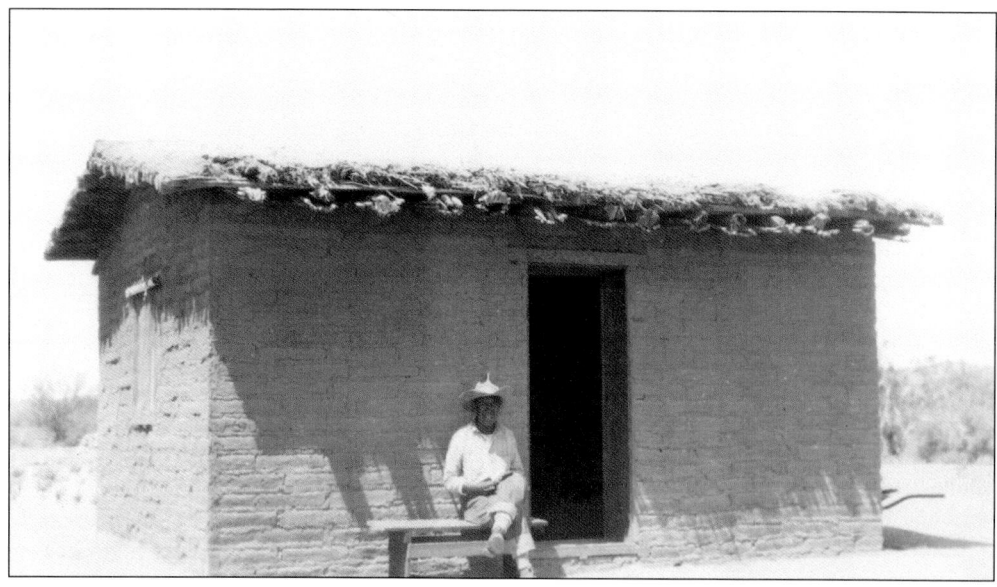

Like many indigenous peoples around the world, the Tohono O'odham have rich and complex oral traditions. The O'odham language continues to be spoken by most tribal members. It is one of many within the large Uto-Aztecan family of languages found throughout much of the western United States, Mexico, and Central America. Various dialects of O'odham language are spoken, and each dialect is concentrated in a different part of the reservation. At right, a Tohono O'odham woman and her children pose for the camera in San Miguel, Arizona, around 1905. The image below shows a typical dwelling and family near the Mission San Xavier del Bac around 1902. (Right, AHS PC63f.3_92190-16; below, AHS 52616.)

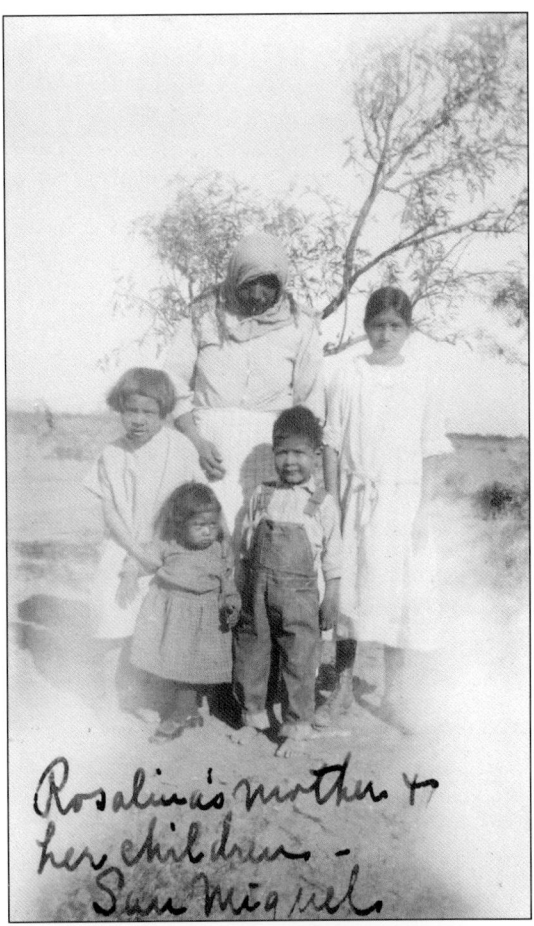

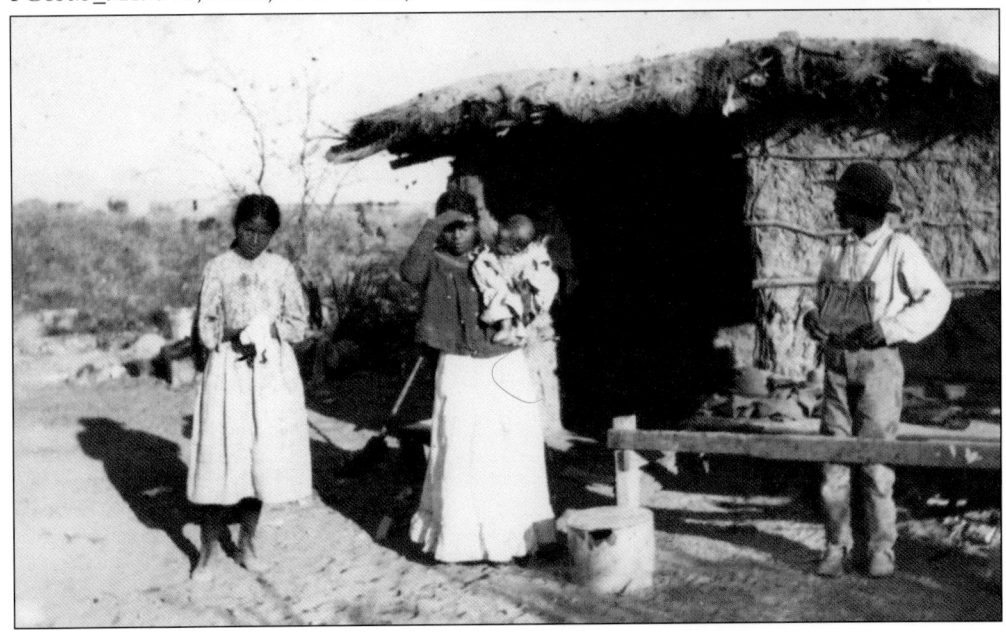

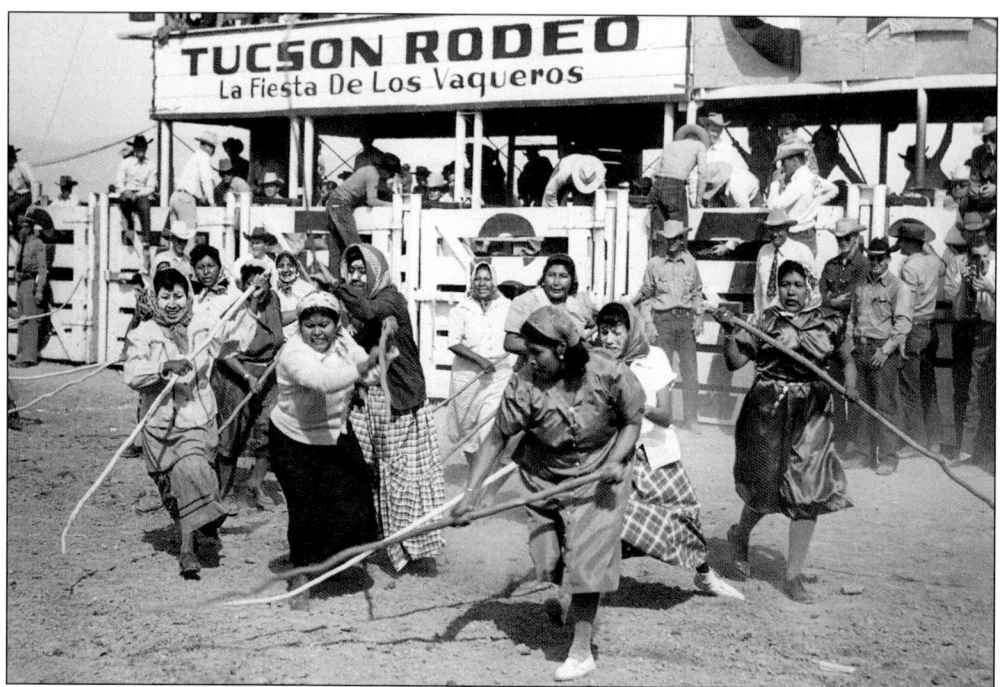

The game of *toka* (double ball) is a competition played by Tohono O'odham women involving playing sticks and two linked balls. Similar to lacrosse or field hockey, the women use bent sticks to push the puck to the goal. Here, a group of women competes at the Tucson Rodeo, also known as La Fiesta de los Vaqueros. (AHS MS1255f410b.)

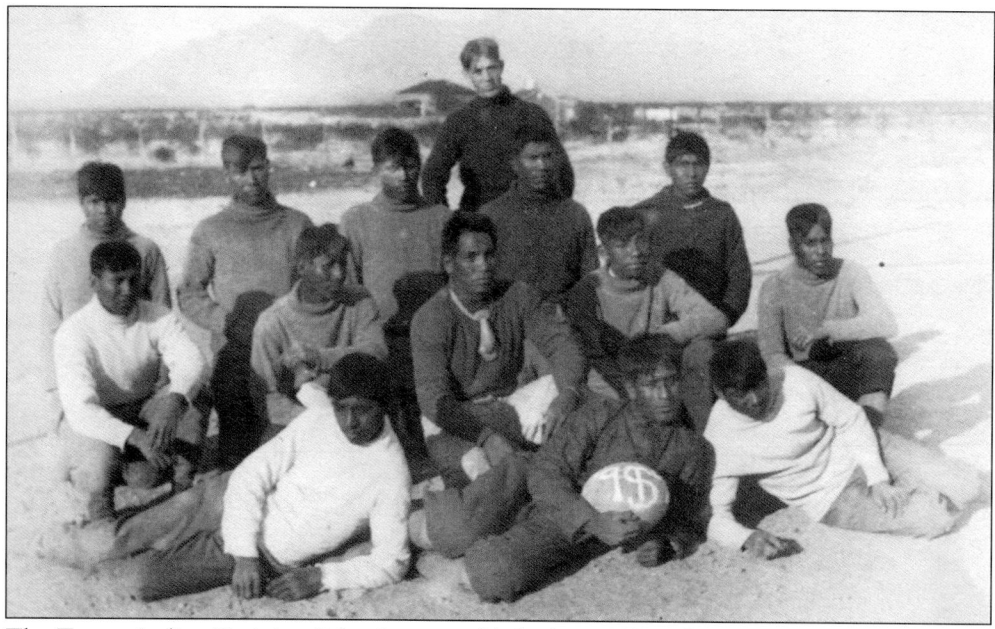

The Tucson Indian Training School was established in 1887 and ran organized sports for the students throughout its 72-year history. In this photograph, the school's football team stopped practice to pose for the camera on January 6, 1900. Photographer George Sinsabaugh captured images of the students during a visit to Tucson. (AHS PC120bu.)

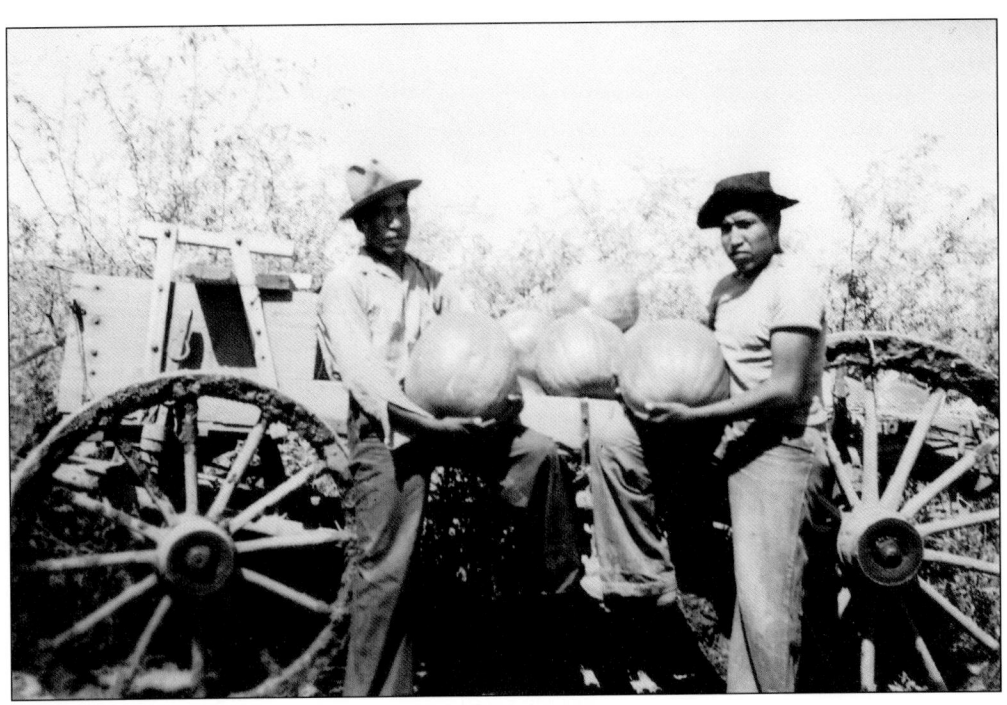

In 1937, the Tohono O'odham began hosting the Papago Indian Fair and Rodeo in Sells. The fair included prizes for agriculture, livestock, sports, and baby contests. During the fourth annual fair in 1941, two Tohono O'odham men brought pumpkins grown on the reservation to the fair, pictured above. The pumpkins were likely brought in for the agricultural competitions. Below, a young Tohono O'odham couple enjoys a ride on the Ferris wheel during the 1939 Tohono O'odham Fair at Sells. (Above, AHS 10009; below, AHS 10011.)

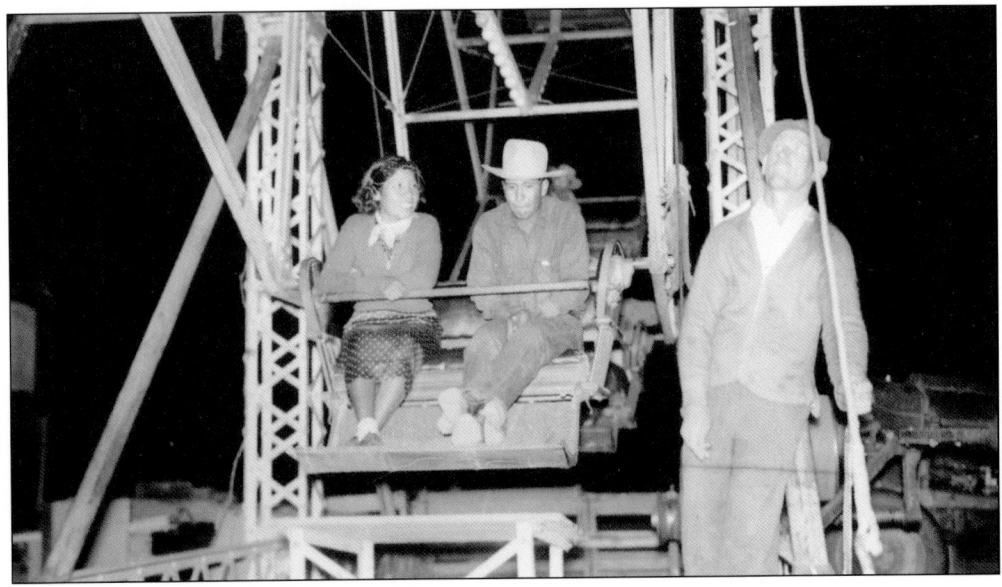

27

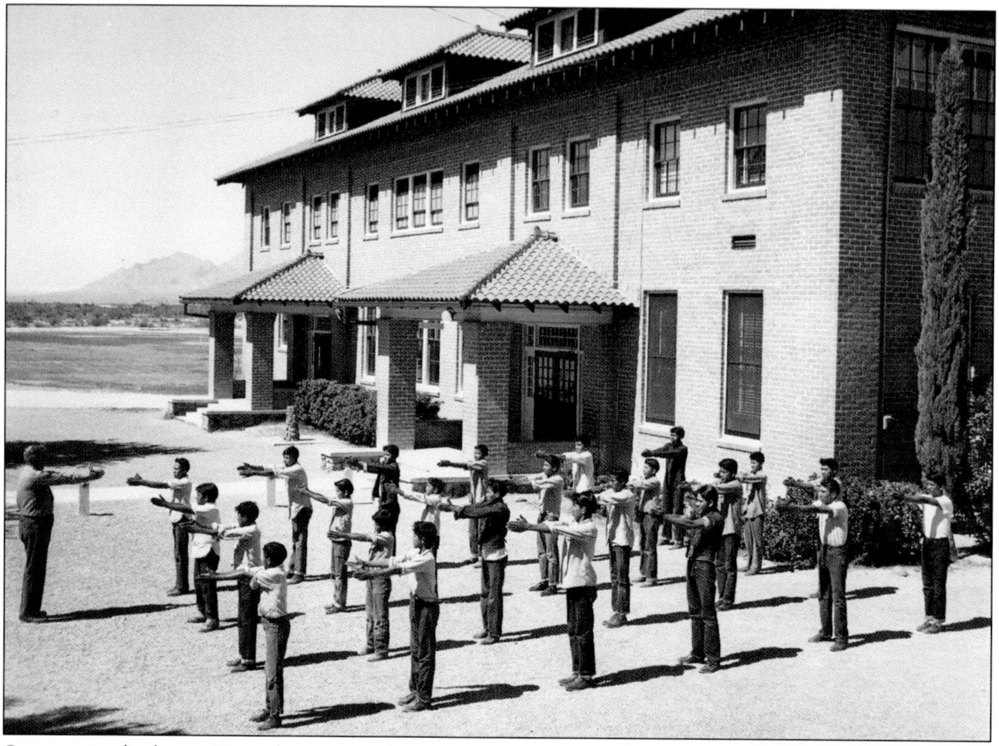

Starting in the late 1880s, a boarding school system was established by European American reformers to "assimilate" and "civilize" the Native American population. The Tucson Training Indian School opened its doors in January 1888 and ran for 72 years until it closed in 1960. Throughout its history, students from 20 Southwestern tribes were represented on campus. The students participated in farming, sports, sewing, and academics at the *escuela* (school). Above, students participate in an exercise outside of the school. Below, young Tohono O'odham students stand in front of Mission San Xavier del Bac with two priests. (Above, AHS MS1255f.393m; below, AHS B109090.)

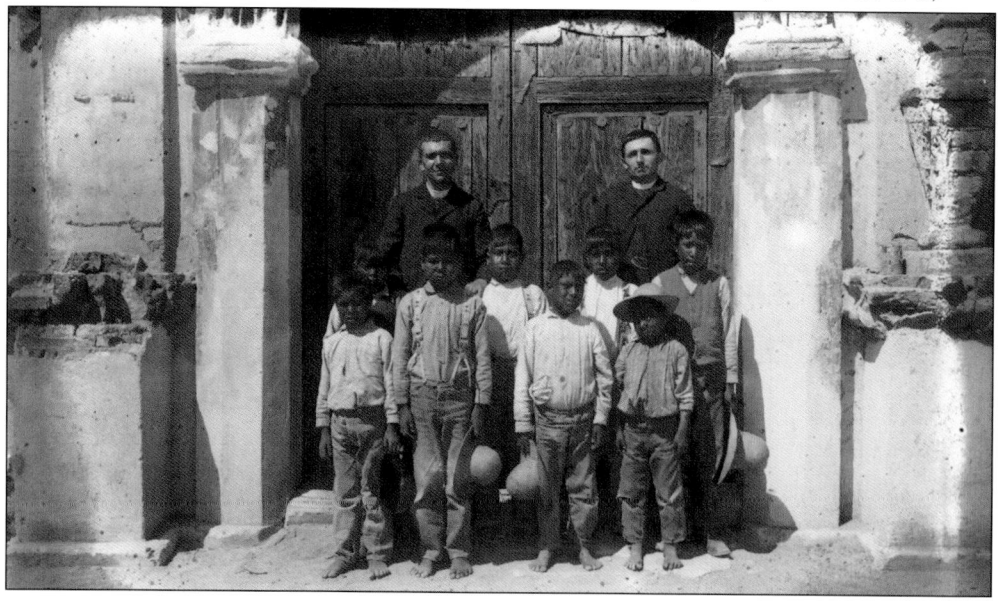

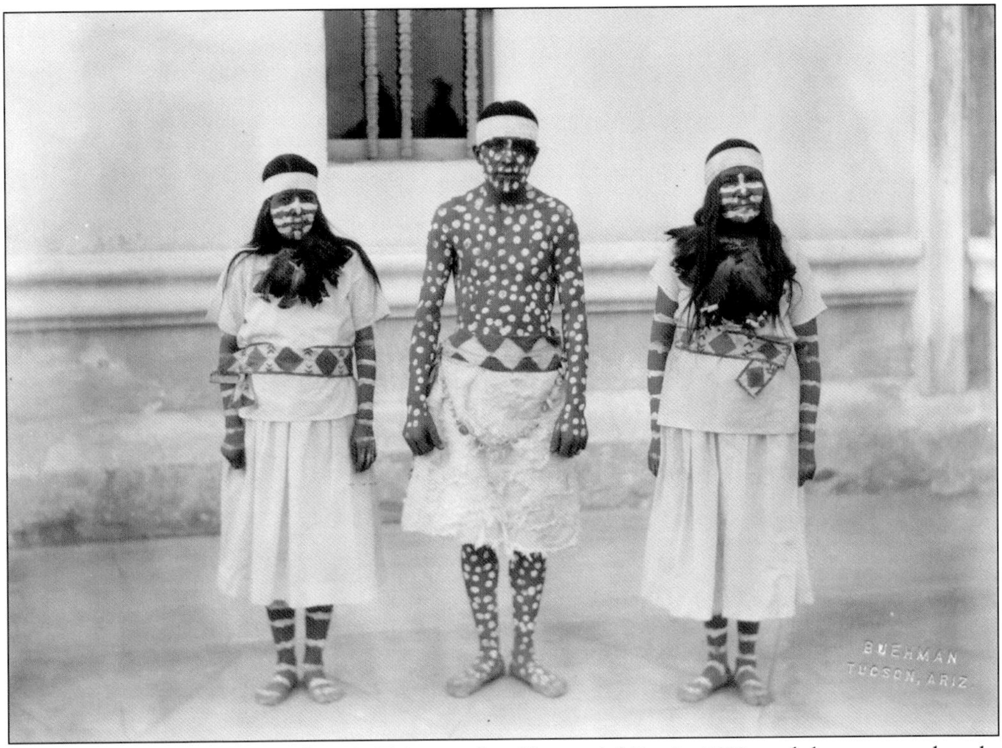

Missionary Fr. Eusebio Kino founded Mission San Xavier del Bac in 1692, and the current church, pictured below about 1904, was constructed between 1783 and 1797. Photographer Henry Buehman visited San Xavier around 1890 and took images of several Tohono O'odham *celkona* dancers, pictured above. Adorned with seashells and feathers, the man and two women pose wearing white fabric, headbands, and paint. San Xavier continues as a church for the local Tohono O'odham community and is visited by approximately 200,000 visitors each year. (Above, AHS BN94161; below, AHS BN201709.)

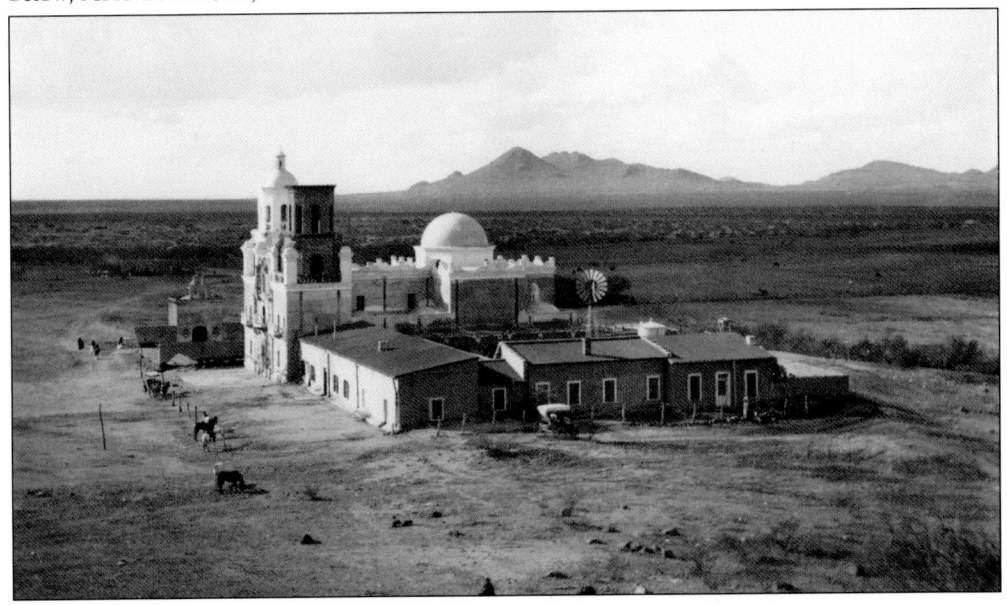

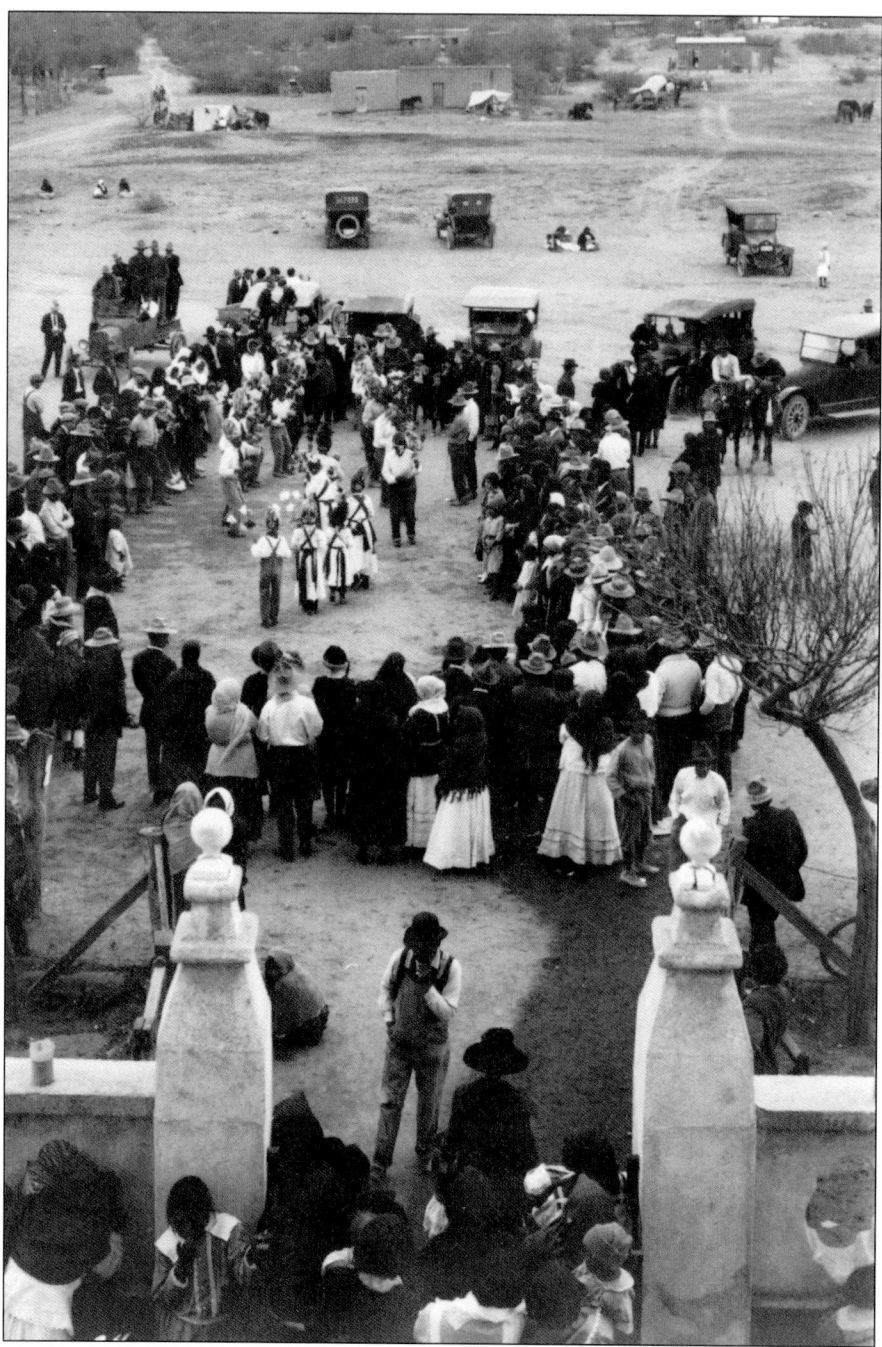

Although their history in the Sonoran Desert dates back to at least 552 CE, the Pascua Yaqui tribe did not become a federally recognized tribe until September 18, 1978. Yaquis faced subjugation and persecution throughout their history. During the late 19th century and the early 20th century, many Yaquis relocated between the United States and the Mexican state of Sonora. The Yaqui culture is based on a unique blend of ancient beliefs and the religious teachings of Jesuit missionaries. Pictured here are Yaqui dancers, shown from a distance, at Mission San Xavier del Bac. A crowd of spectators came to watch the scene. (AHS BN116562.)

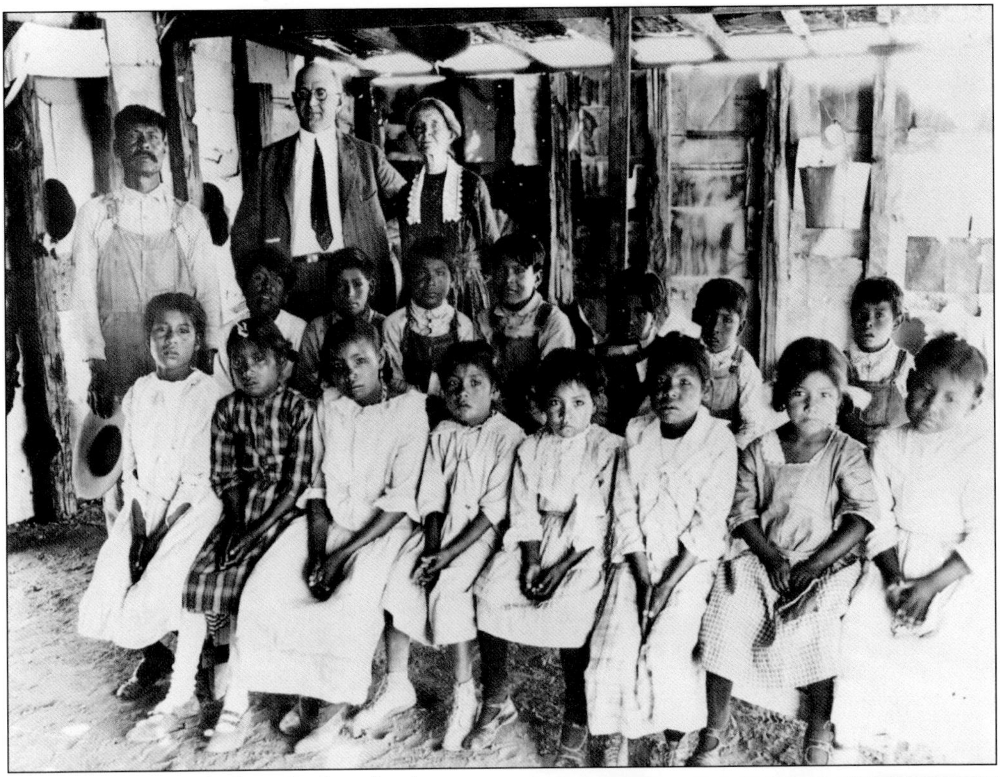

Starting in 1923, Thalmar Richey (back, third from left) taught school for Pascua Yaqui children in Tucson. The school building was a simple structure with no permanent wall on one side that also doubled as a church. The photograph above was taken in 1928 showing the 15 students at the school with the girls in the front row and the boys in the back. Also pictured is the superintendent of schools, C.E. Rose, standing to the left of Richey. At right, a Yaqui family is photographed making tortillas. The Pascua Yaqui Reservation is located about 15 miles southwest of downtown Tucson on 1,152 acres. (Above, AHS 30; right, 9641.)

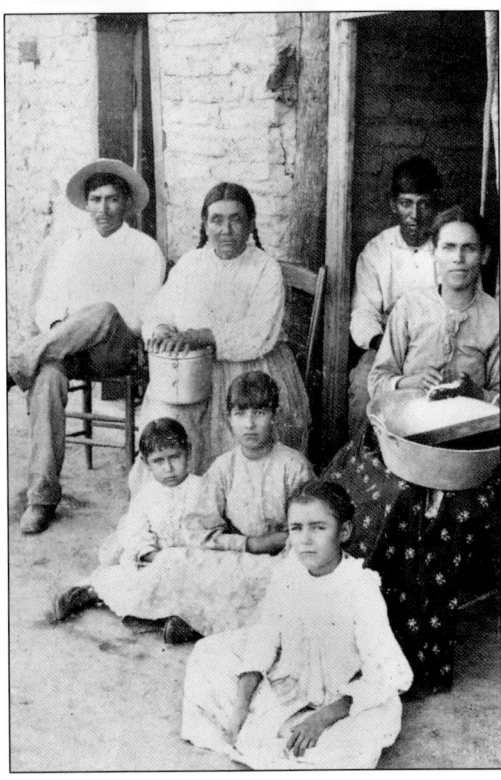

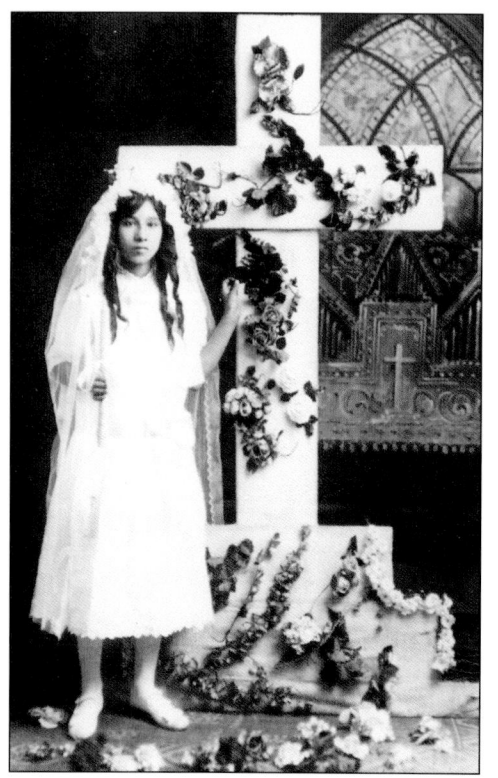

Catholicism has played an important role in the religious lives of many across Pima County. At left, Rita Lopez had her portrait taken to mark her First Holy Communion on April 28, 1916. The daughter of Mexican-born parents, Juan and Cruz Lopez, Rita grew up in Helvetia with her four siblings. Her father worked as a rancher and her older brothers worked in the mining industry. Below, St. Augustine Cathedral on Stone Avenue in Tucson has been the location where thousands of young children attended their First Holy Communion ceremonies. (Right, AHS 66004; below, AHS PC174f7a.)

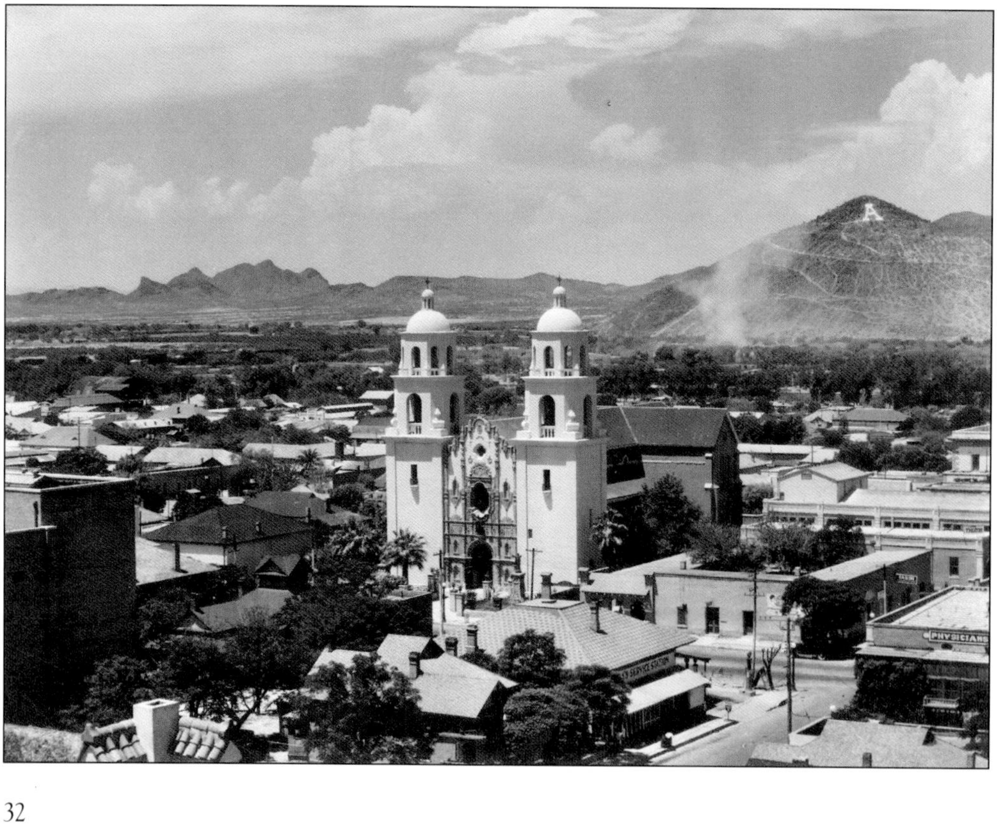

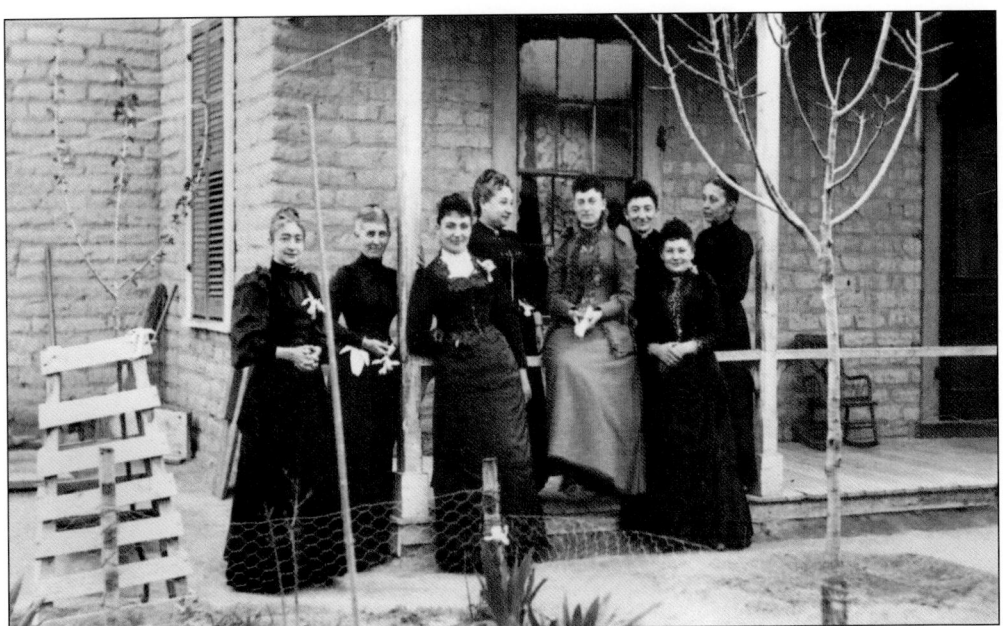

In 1892, the Sorosis women's club of Tucson included some of the earliest Jewish women to call Pima County home. The name of the group likely had its origins with the Sorosis women's group formed in the 1860s for professional women on the East Coast. From left to right are Eva Mansfeld, Harriet Wright, Jenny Drachman, Gertrude Florsheim, Bettina Steinfeld, Freda Katzenstein, Doris Goldschmidt, and Mrs. Graves. (B113425.)

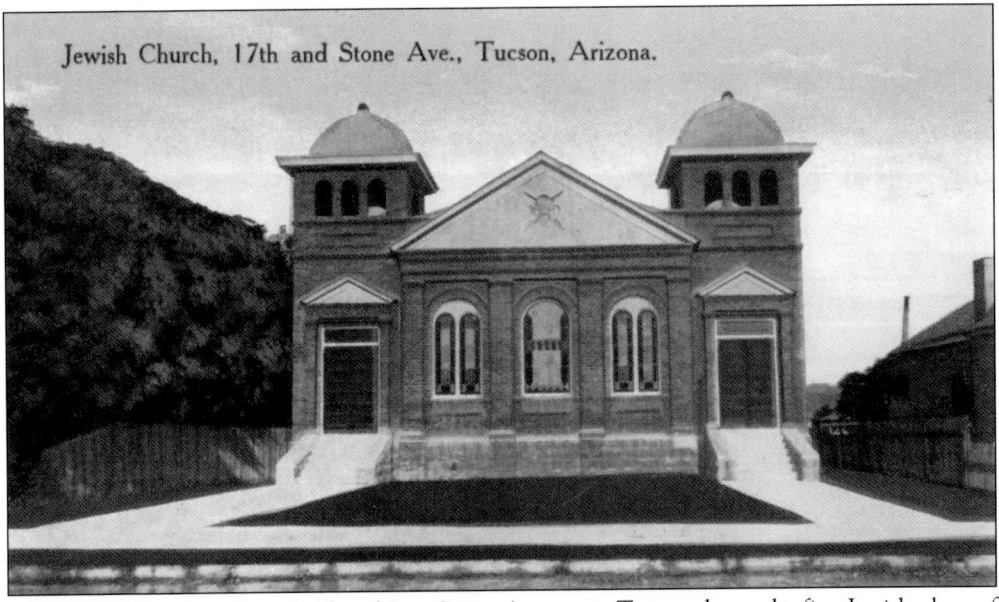

This postcard for the "Jewish Church" on Stone Avenue in Tucson shows the first Jewish place of worship in the Arizona Territory. Opened in 1910, it was built with funds raised by a local Jewish women's organization called the Hebrew Ladies Benevolent Society. On September 6, 1949, the congregation moved out of the building, and the temple went through several owners until it was reopened as the Jewish History Museum in 2008. This 1914 postcard is the earliest known image of the temple. (UA Photograph Files.)

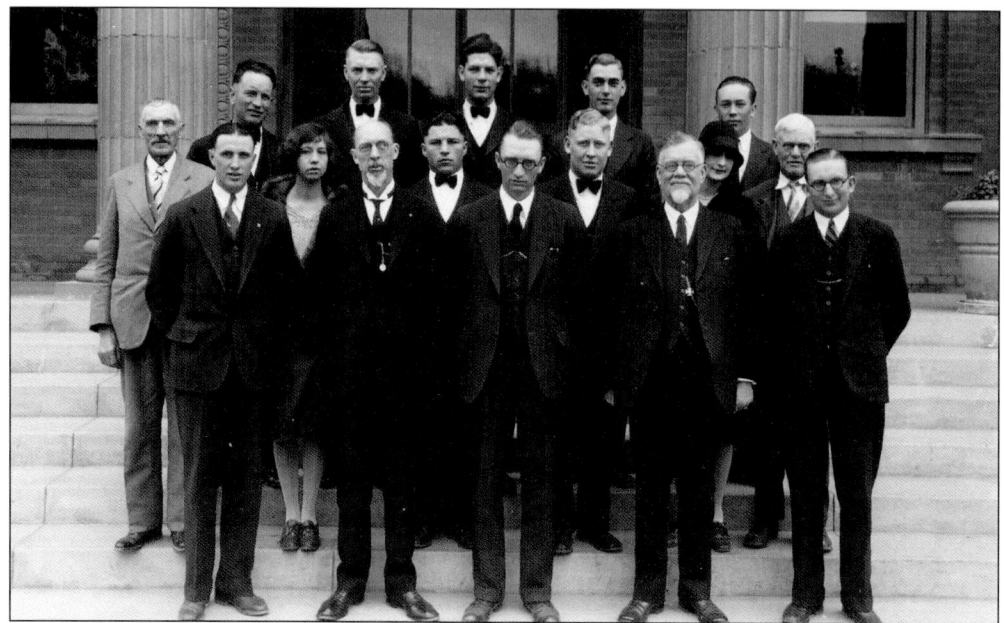

The Latter-Day Saints established settlements across Arizona, including the Binghampton community north of Tucson near the Rillito River in the late 1890s. As the city of Tucson grew around the Binghampton area, the Mormon community maintained strong ties in Pima County. Pictured here is the Mormon Mission Society Boys Group, photographed by the Buehman Studios around 1930. (AHS BN202891.)

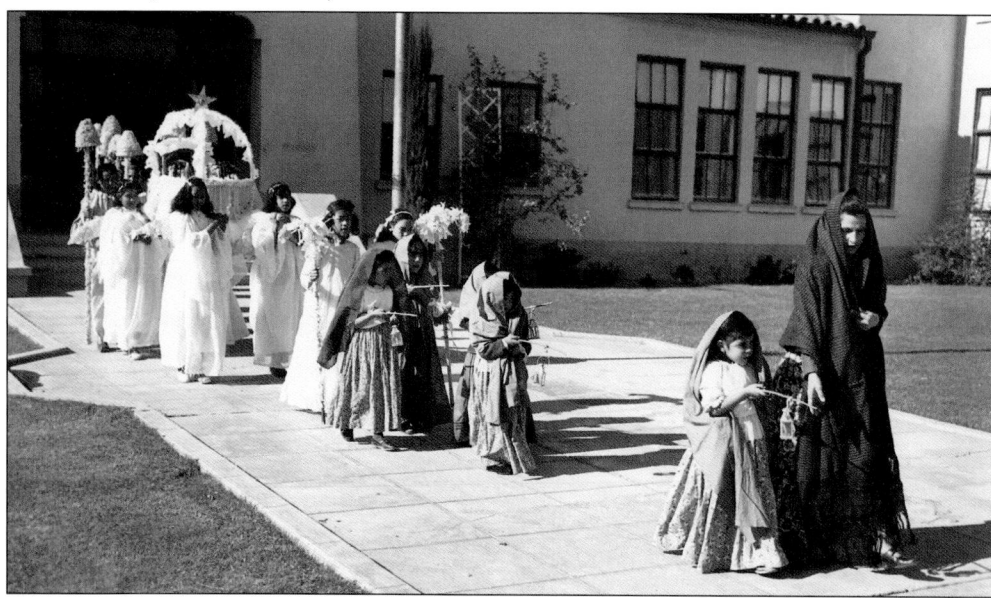

The annual Las Posadas procession at Carrillo School has been a Tucson tradition since the 1930s. Started at the school by teacher Marguerite Coulier, Las Posadas is a Mexican custom with origins in the 16th century. Las Posadas, meaning "lodging," dramatizes the Bible story of Joseph and Mary's journey to Bethlehem on the eve of Jesus's birth. The costumed students sing and seek shelter at several locations, being turned away. Finally, at the last stop, they are welcomed. (AHS MS1255f.344e.)

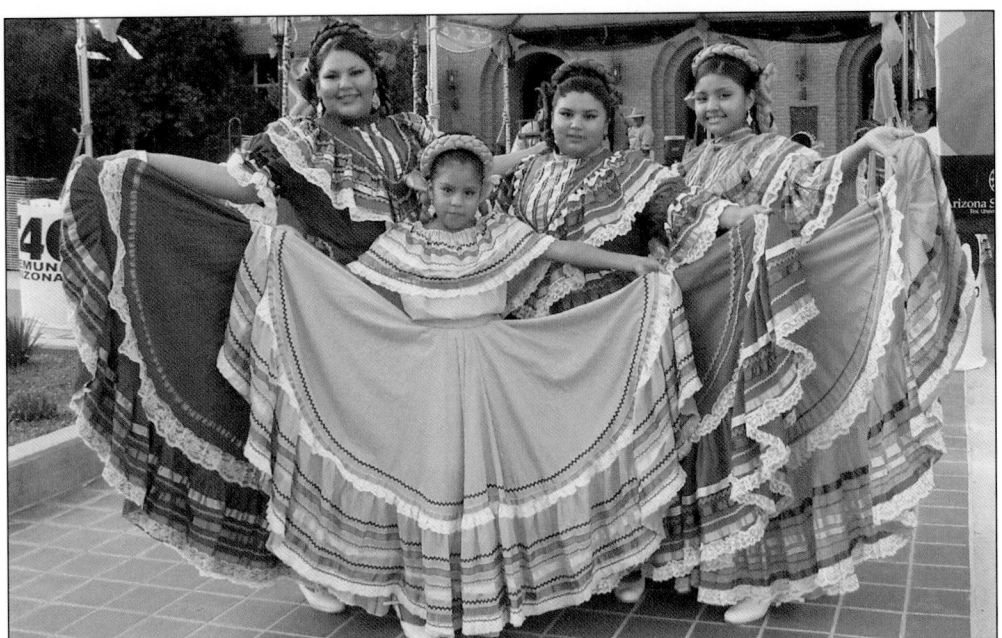

Diverse musical traditions have been passed on through the generations in Pima County. During the third annual ¡Viva Arizona! Hispanic Performing Arts Conference in 2008, four young women in *folklorico* dresses paused for the camera. The conference consisted of three days of workshops that taught flamenco, salsa, and folklorico dancing as well as musical instruction in mariachi. The workshops ended with performances to celebrate the "role of Hispanic culture, music, and dance in Tucson's history." (Photograph by Jill McCleary.)

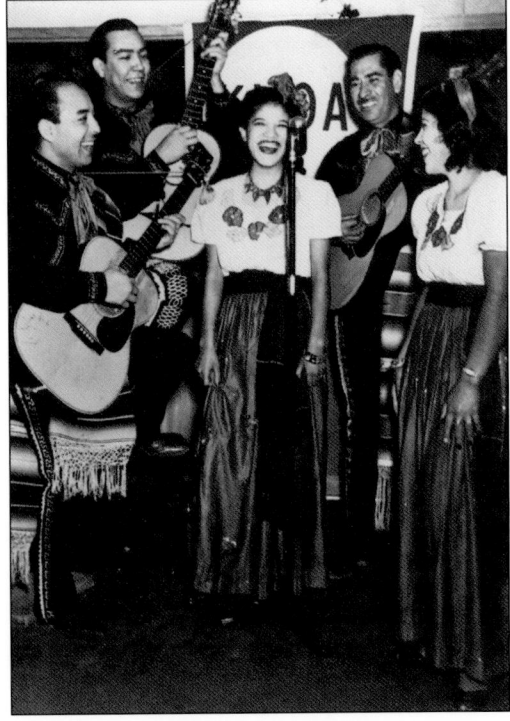

Often referred to as the "Father of Chicano Music," Lalo Guerrero grew up in Tucson's Barrio Libre. He went on to entertain listeners for decades, writing hundreds of songs that reached out to Latin audiences. He was declared a National Folk Treasure by the Smithsonian Institution and received the National Medal of Arts. Guerrero passed away in 2005 at the age of 88. Pictured here, Lalo Guerrero (second from the left) performs with a musical group at the KVOA studios in Tucson. (AHS 64453.)

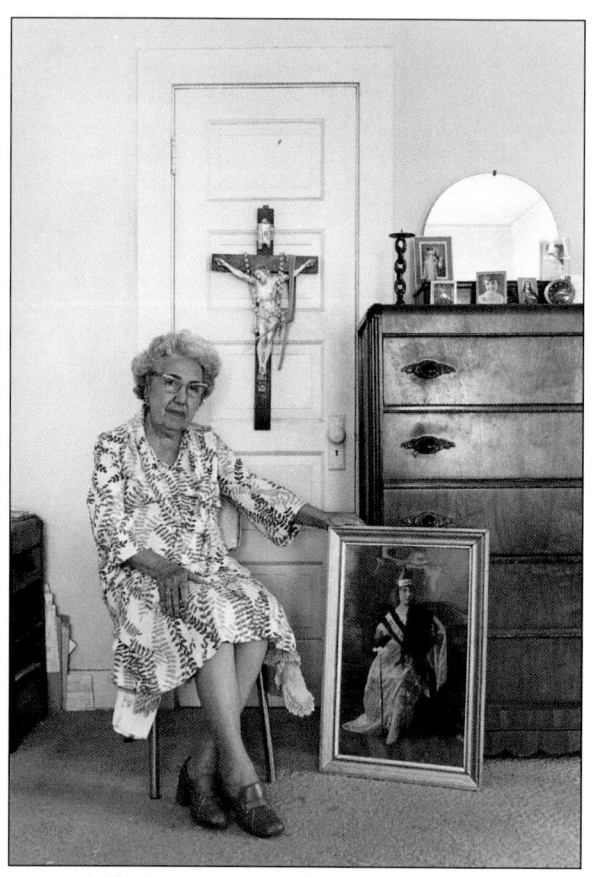

Celebrations commemorating Mexican Independence Day are a long-standing tradition reflecting southern Arizona's deep Mexican roots and shared cultural heritage. Festive parades, speeches, fireworks, music, and dancing have long been enjoyed by Tucsonans of Mexican, Anglo, and Native American descent each September 16 in commemoration of the 1810 start of Mexico's war for independence from Spain. In the photograph at left, María Soto Audelo poses in her Tucson home in 1981 next to a portrait taken of her 64 years earlier during Tucson's September 16, 1917, celebrations. The 1917 portrait shows the young María adorned in a sequined dress (made by her mother), which included a sash reading "Mexico" and a headdress proclaiming "Liberty." The c. 1910 photograph below shows an elegantly arrayed group of Tucsonans waving both flags of Mexico and the United States at a Mexican Independence Day gathering. (Left, AHS 72122; below, AHS 69475.)

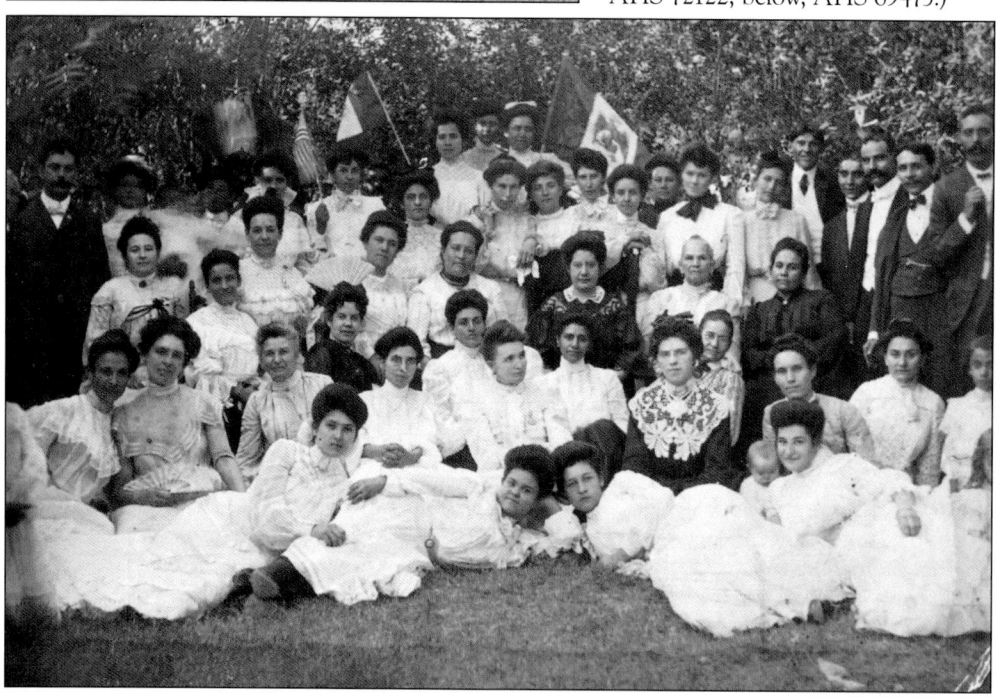

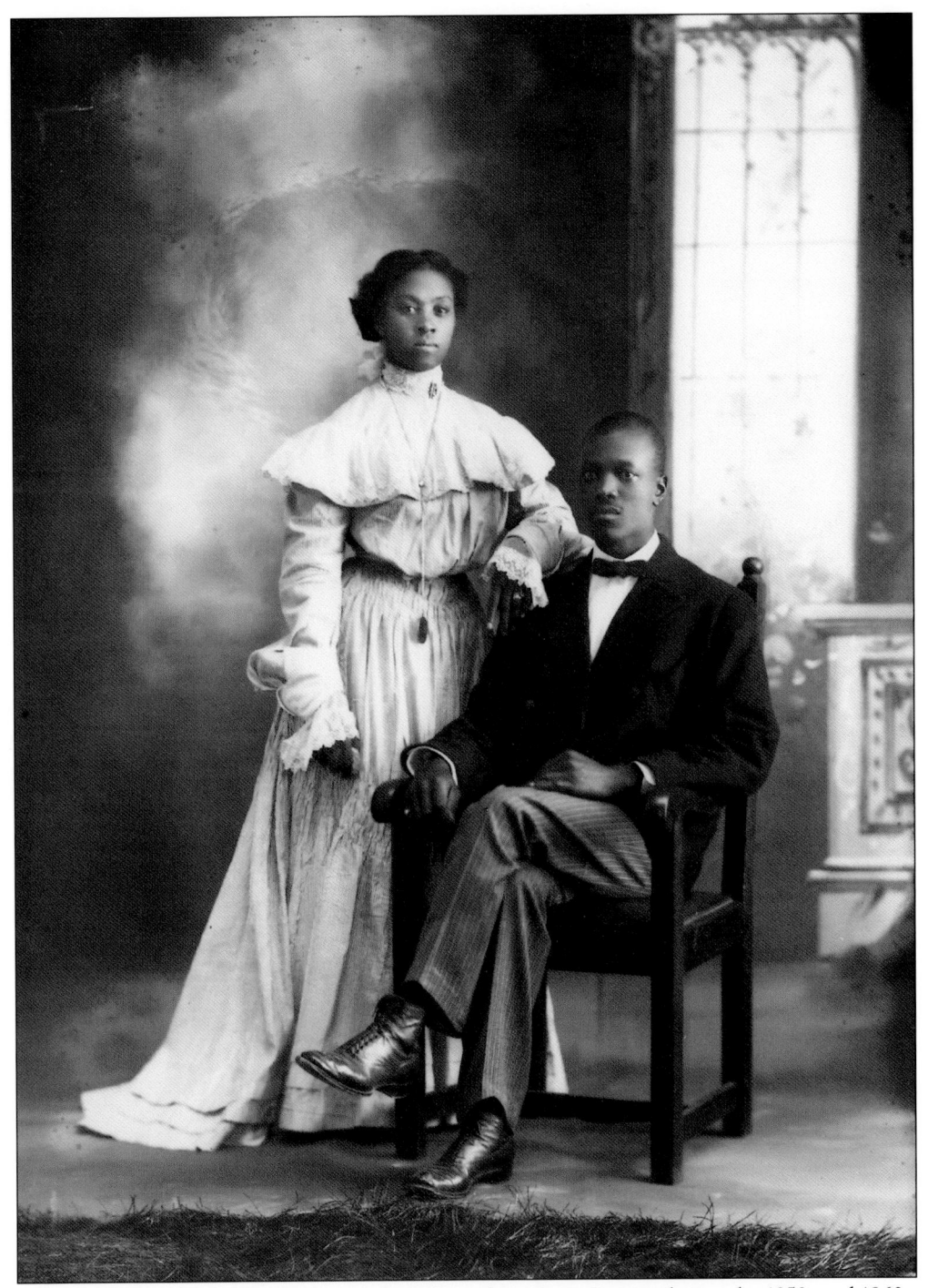

African Americans first began to permanently settle in Pima County during the 1850s and 1860s. Years later, this wedding photograph of Mr. and Mrs. Clark was taken at the Buehman Studio in Tucson around 1910. At the time, the number of African Americans in Arizona represented less than one percent of the state's population. Some of the early occupations held by African Americans included barbers, cooks, maids, janitors, and waiters.

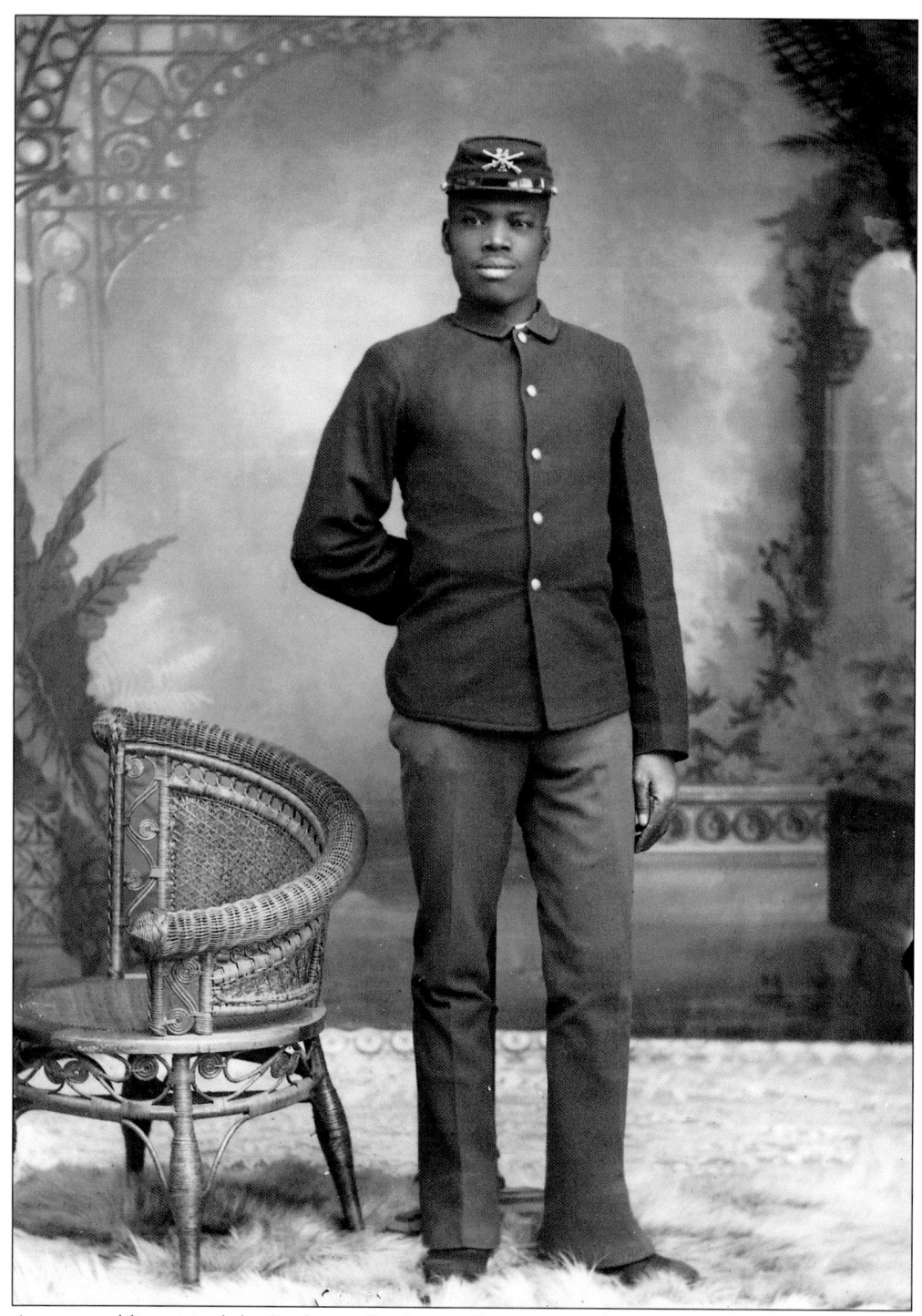

A young soldier visited the Buehman Studios in Tucson around 1892 to have his portrait taken. The unidentified soldier's cap indicates that he was with Company A, 24th Infantry. The all-black 24th Infantry was created on March 3, 1869, and served in Arizona beginning in 1888. Company A arrived in Tucson in December 1891. (AHS BD109357.)

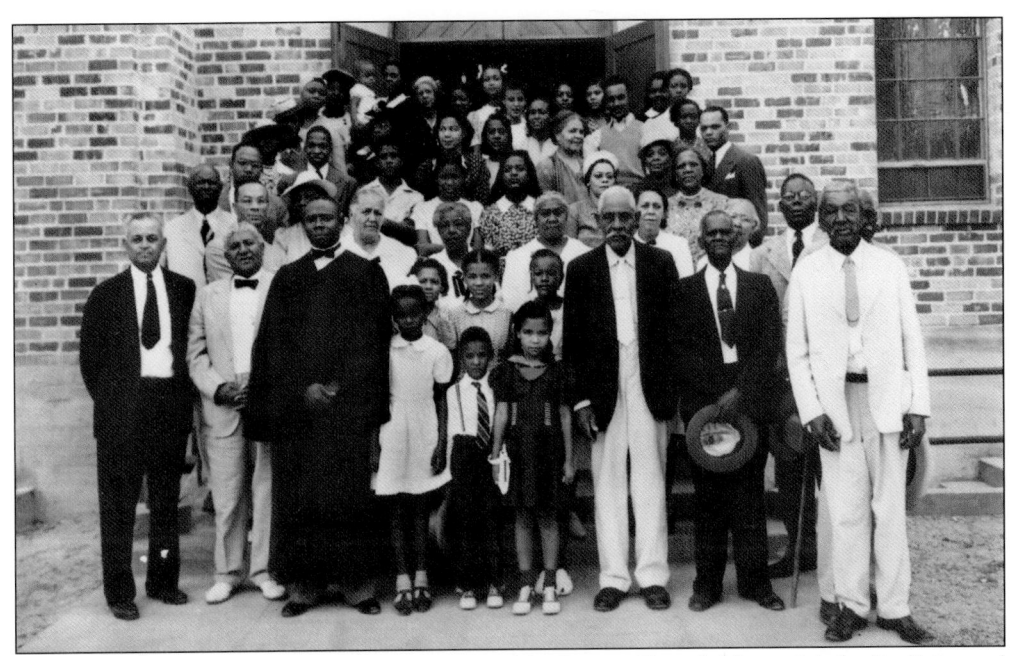

Dressed in their Sunday best, the congregation of the Prince Chapel African Methodist Episcopal Church poses for the camera around 1941. Organized in 1905, when the African American community in Tucson was estimated to be less than 100, the church was formed in the kitchen of the church's first minister, Rev. W.A. Ratcliffe. Under the direction and planning of Rev. Jessie Carter (first row, third from left), this building at Seventeenth Street and Stone Avenue was built by well-known Tucson architect Henry O. Jaastad and dedicated in the early 1940s. (AHS 78499.)

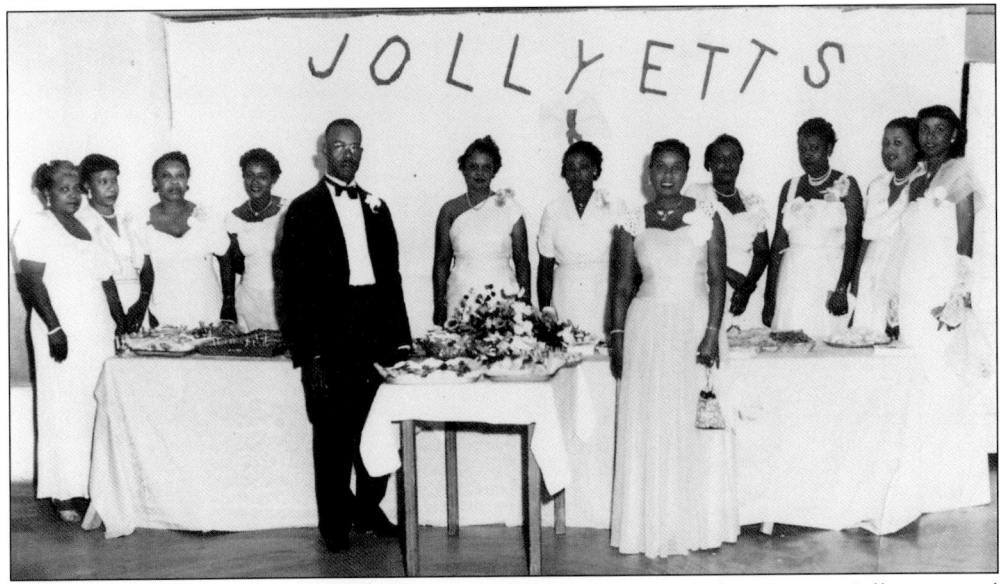

Frank C. Johnson and his wife, Bernice, stand in front of a group of women at a Jollyetts social club event. The Johnsons moved to Tucson from Texas in 1936 and were involved with the Prince Chapel AME Church and several social organizations. Frank was a World War II veteran and became the first full-time African American deputy in the Pima County Sheriff's Department in 1948. He worked for the department for over 20 years before he retired in 1969. (AHS 78496.)

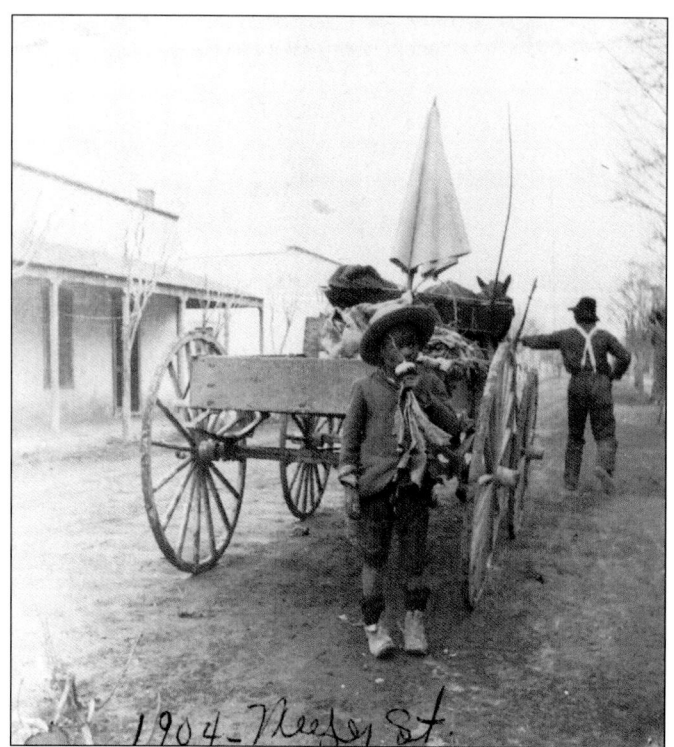

Making daily rounds from house to house in wagons selling fresh vegetables grown on the banks of the Santa Cruz River, Tucson's Chinese truck farmers found a means to survive after other areas of employment, such as mining and laundry, were forbidden to them. Tucson's Chinese truck farmers were known to frequently offer neighborhood children small samples of their produce, as shown in this photograph taken in 1904 on Meyer Street. Truck farming eventually gave way to more permanent business establishments such as grocery stores. (AHS 25728)

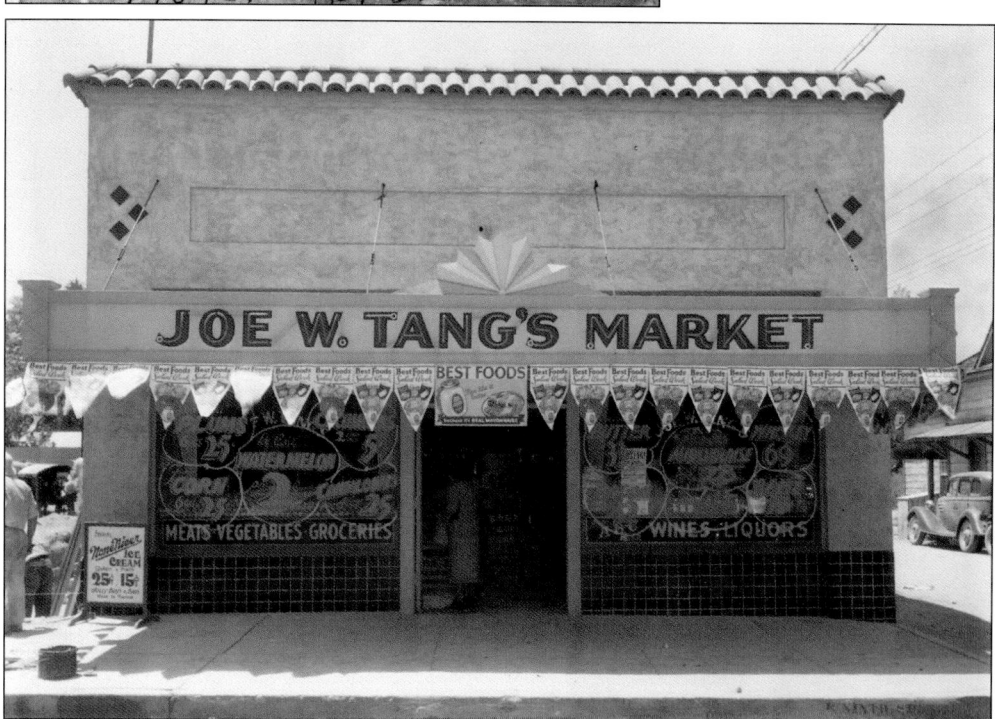

Joe W. Tang was one of several successful Chinese business owners in Tucson. Opened around 1931, Joe W. Tang's Market was located at 526 East Ninth Street and sold everything from corn and cantaloupes to whiskey and ice cream. The store closed in the mid-1950s. (AHS BN202111.)

As the railroad was built across Arizona in the late 1800s, the number of Chinese workers arriving in Arizona boomed. In May 1893, Tucson resident Ah Chung received this certificate of residence, establishing that he was a legal immigrant in the United States. After the passage of laws such as the Chinese Exclusion Act of 1882, individuals like Chung had to register with the government to prove their residence. While Chinese individuals faced discrimination in Pima County, their population continued to grow as they established significant roles in the community. (AHS 78649.)

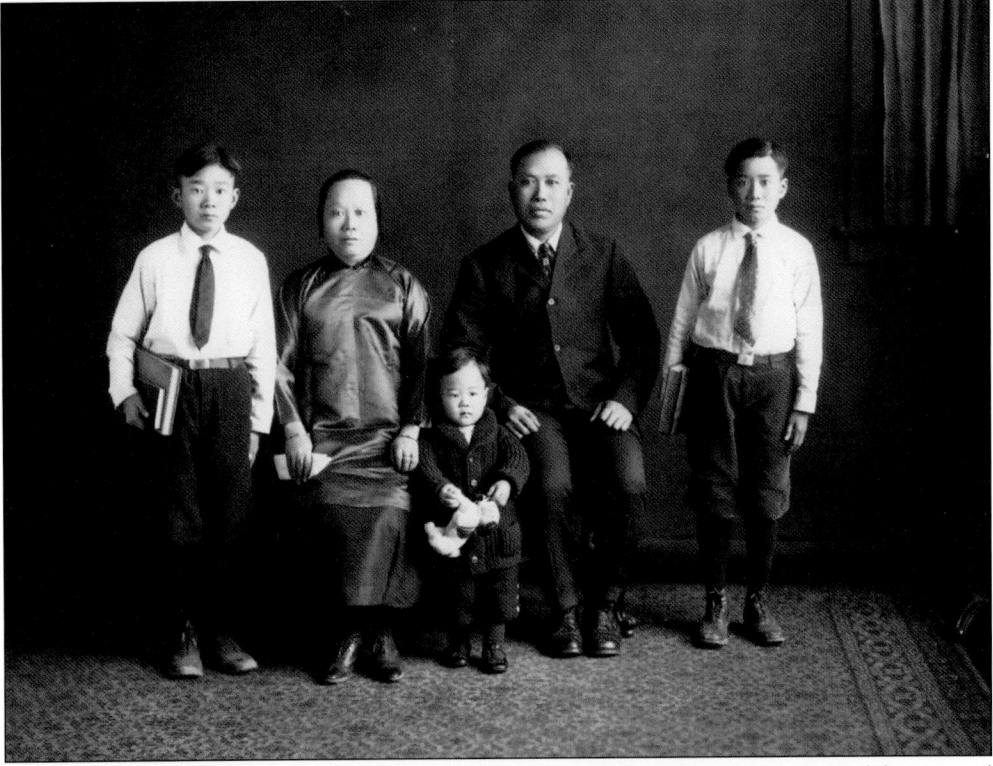

The Wong family poses for a family portrait around 1926. Yan Wong, born in California, and his wife, York Lang Mock, born in China, worked as clerks in a Tucson grocery store. They had three sons, from left to right, Bing Kenn Wong, Bing Susa Wong, and Bing Gan Wong. The youngest, Bing Susa, better known as "Jim," holds a stuffed dog. Jim later worked as a farmer in Marana. (AHS MS1242f.73h.)

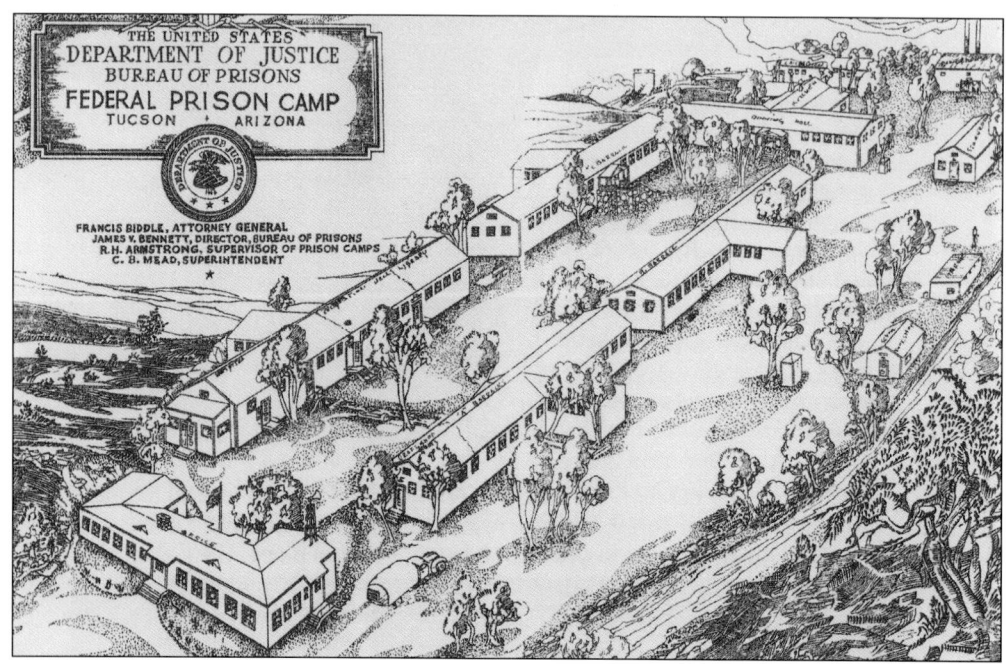

The desire for easy access into the Santa Catalina Mountains led to the approval of a federal prison camp on March 3, 1933. Prisoners were sent to the prison to be "rehabilitated" through the labor of building the Catalina Highway, a road that would allow for a safer and more direct route up the mountain. The prison opened in June 1933 and held over 8,000 inmates over the next 18 years. The most famous inmate was Gordon Hirabayashi, a Japanese American who openly refused to relocate to a Japanese internment camp during World War II. Some 45 Japanese Americans who refused to enter the draft were also incarcerated. These men formed a tight relationship and met frequently after being released. The group called themselves the "Tucsonians," pictured below. Today, the location of the prison is known as the Gordon Hirabayashi Recreation Site. (Both, courtesy of the Coronado National Forest.)

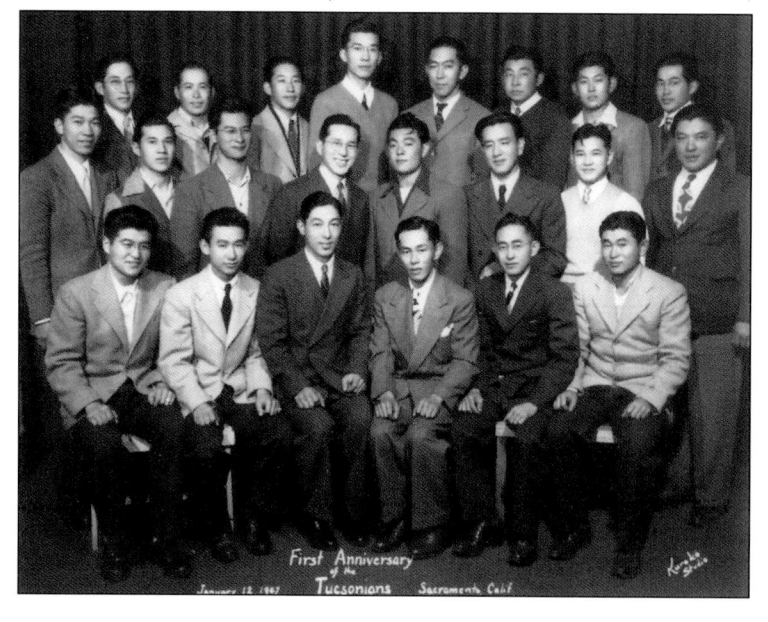

Three

PLACES TO LIVE, WORK, AND PLAY

In Pima County, the principal routes of travel were south and north along the Santa Cruz and San Pedro Rivers where Native American farming communities first flourished. In 1540, the first Spanish conquistador, Francisco Vásquez de Coronado, ventured north through the region seeking reported "cities of gold" and opened routes for conquest and later settlement. Coronado and those who followed brought with them new foods, livestock, religions, traditions, technologies, work habits, and even new ways to play.

Through time, the Santa Cruz River has sustained a succession of Native American, Spanish, Mexican, and American farmers who cultivated the fertile floodplain and produced food for their growing populations. The introduction of cattle, horses, and new food crops by the Spanish brought a new ranching industry established at mission communities and on land grants given to civilians at La Canoa, El Sopori, and Aribac. Following the Civil War, cattle ranching greatly expanded, and two of the grandest and most extensive cattle ranches, the Empire Ranch and Canoa Ranch, dominated the region. Today, the cattle industry continues to be a mainstay of rural Pima County.

Other than ranching and farming, mining for gold, silver, and copper has been one of the most important industries in the region. The discovery of gold in California in 1849 brought a flood of miners and fortune-seekers, effectively opening the West and prompting the Gadsden Purchase in 1854. Repeated rushes for gold and silver created mining camps and boomtowns that flourished for a time and then were abandoned. Today, old mines and towns like Total Wreck, Cerro Colorado, Sasco, Olive Camp, Quijotoa, Cababi, Rosemont, Greaterville, Helvetia, Kentucky Camp, and Ruby dot the landscape. After 1900, copper mining became dominant, and active mines continue at Silverbell, San Xavier, Pima Mine, Twin Buttes, and Ajo.

Leisure time might be spent at Sabino Canyon, Fuller's Agua Caliente Hot Springs Resort, Carrillo's Gardens, Levin's Park, the opera, horse races, and during saint's day celebrations or at the many saloons and "sporting houses" found in nearly every town and camp.

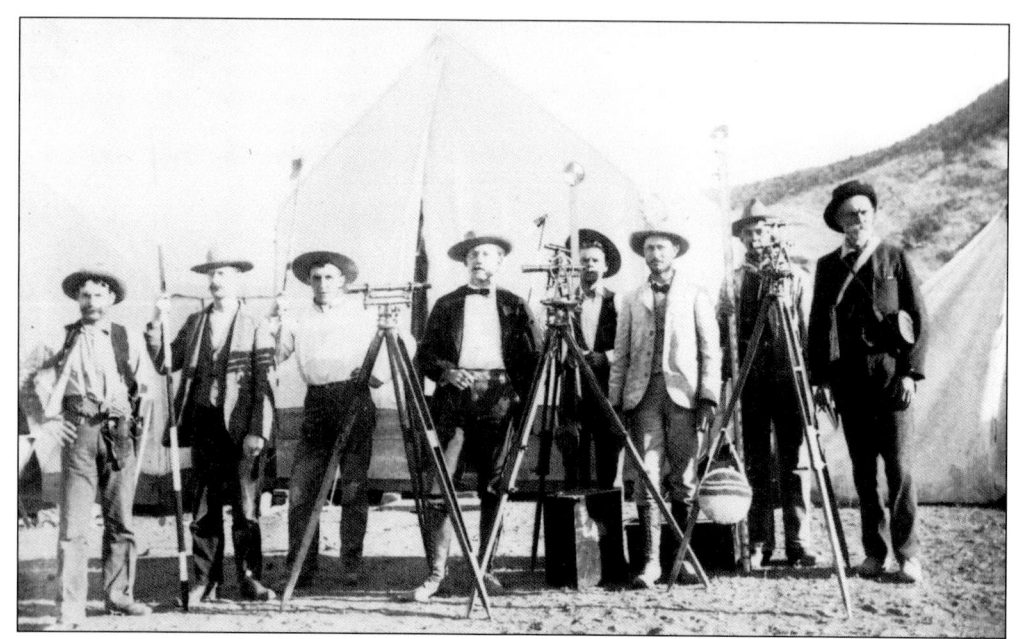

George Roskruge (far right) and his surveying team are shown here in Helvetia around 1902. Roskruge arrived in Tucson in 1874 to accept the position of chief draftsman and went on to become Pima County surveyor and surveyor general for Arizona. His job allowed him to document much of Pima County through his camera's lens. Today, Roskruge School in Tucson is named after him. (AHS PC142 92807.)

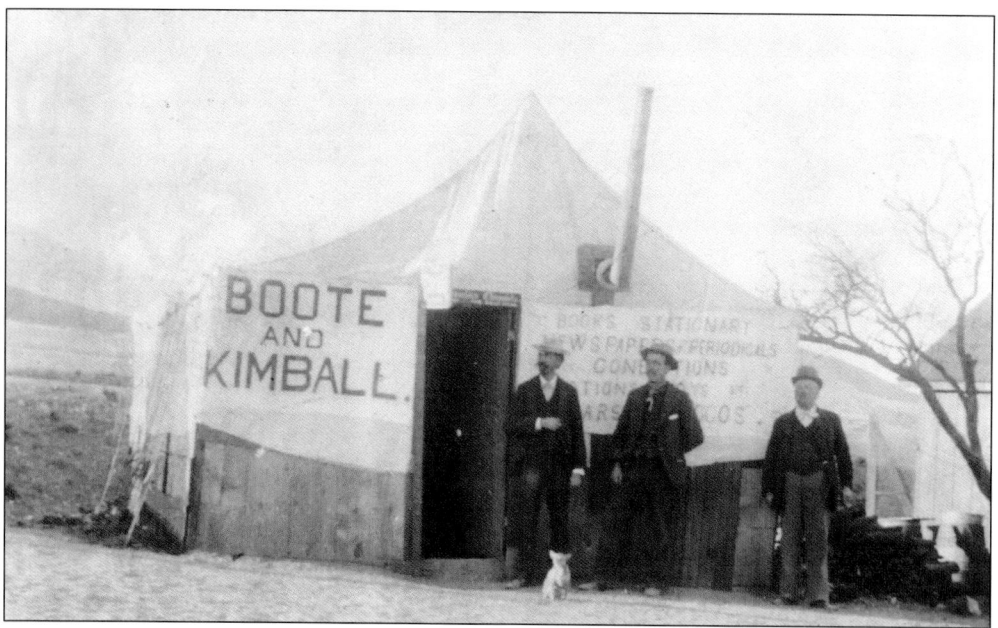

The Boote and Kimball store in Helvetia allowed locals to buy books, stationery, newspapers, confections, toys, and cigars. The simple tent structure was photographed around 1900, when Helvetia was a booming mine town. One of the shop's owners, Frederick Kimball, came to Tucson in 1899 and also owned a bookstore in Tucson. Once a week, Frederick would ride his bicycle 35 miles to Helvetia and return to Tucson the next day. (AHS PC220f.6 11221.)

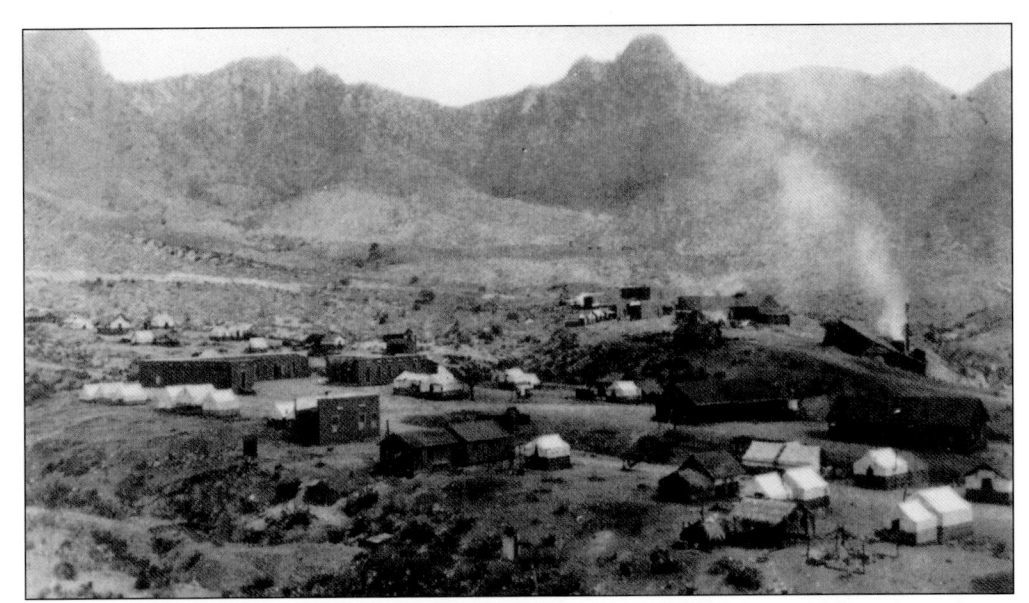

As early as the 1870s, the land surrounding Helvetia was mined for copper. When the Helvetia Copper Company of New Jersey bought many of the area's mining claims in 1891, the community began to grow. A post office was established in 1899, and at the turn of the century, Helvetia was a developing, prosperous mining town, pictured above around 1900. The town boasted dozens of tent houses, a schoolhouse, carpenter shop, and blacksmith shop. As with many mining towns in Pima County, Helvetia's boom years came to an end. The post office closed in 1921, and almost nothing of the town remains today. Below, a woman rides a horse among the dwellings of Helvetia about 1902. (Above, AHS 44966; below, AHS PC220 5324.)

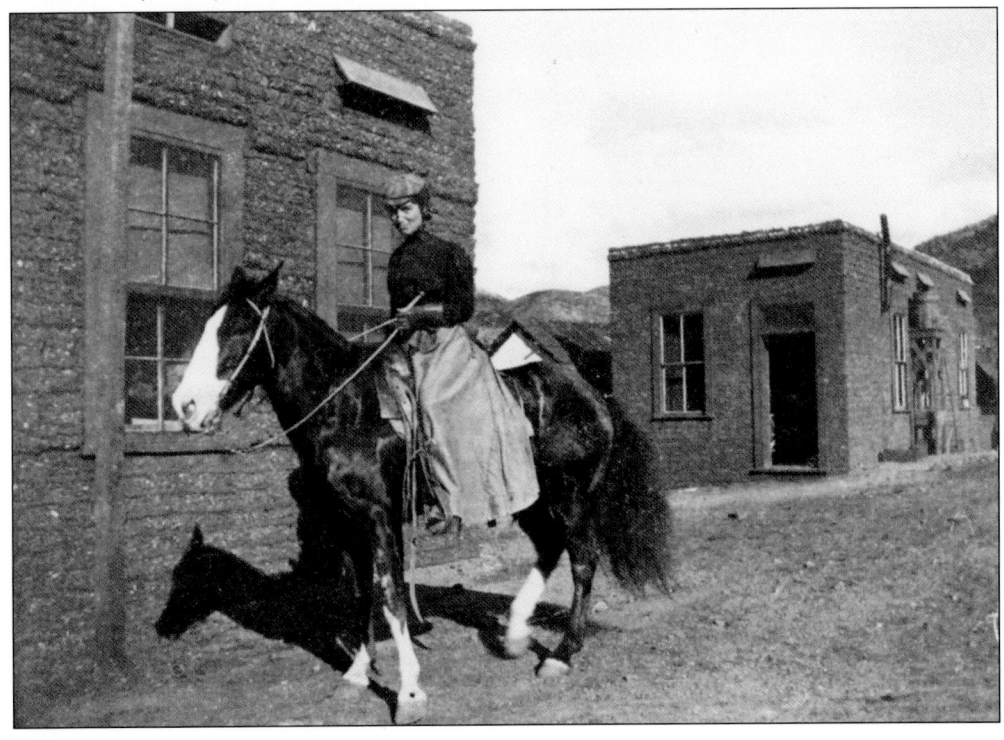

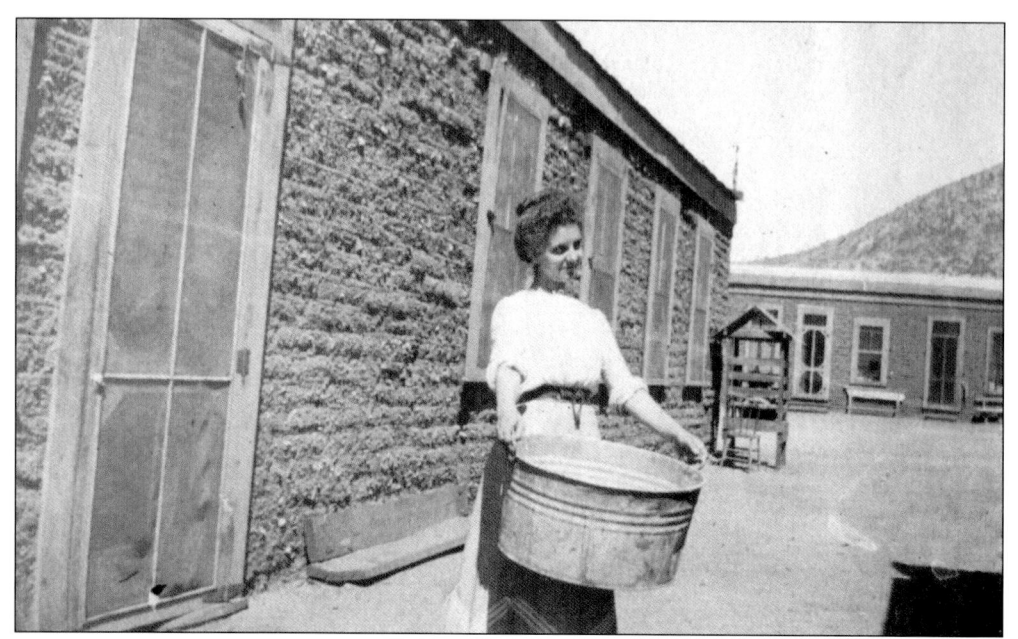

Helvetia was in the midst of growth when Edith Stratton moved to the mining town to work as a teacher around 1901 at the age of 22. Above, Stratton is pictured next to the boardinghouse where she likely lived, with the dining hall to her left. A graduate of the Los Angeles Normal School, now UCLA, she was photographed with her class at the schoolhouse in Helvetia around the same time. Stratton left Helvetia in 1903 to teach in Tucson, where she met her husband, George Farwell Kitt. She later became the secretary of the Arizona Historical Society, where she worked to preserve her native state's history for over 20 years. (Above, AHS PC27 618; below, AHS 3103.)

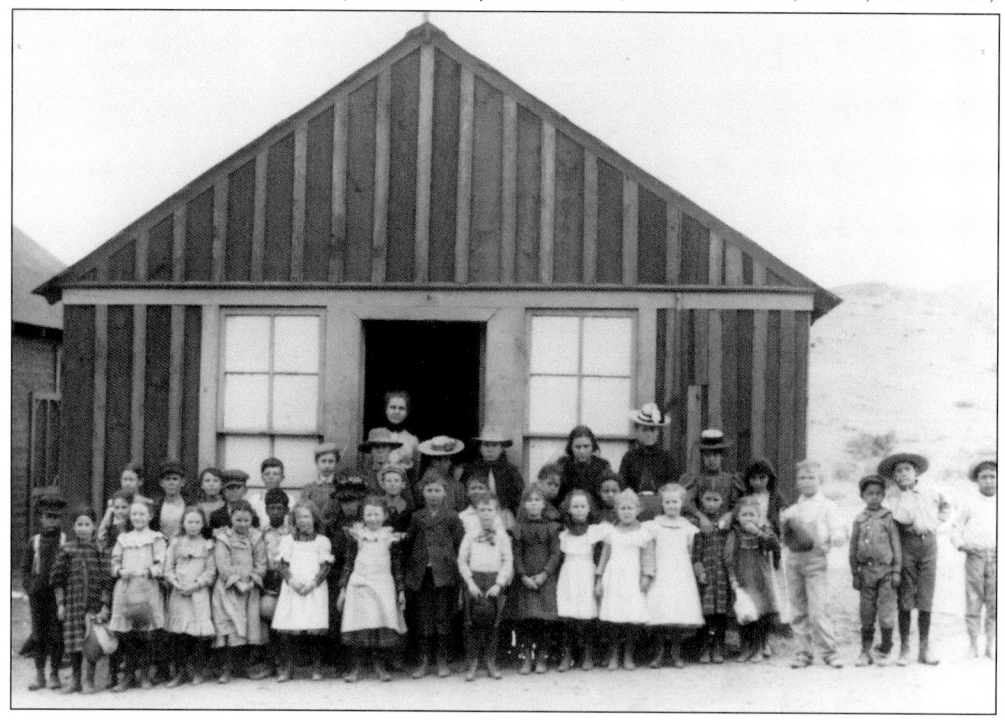

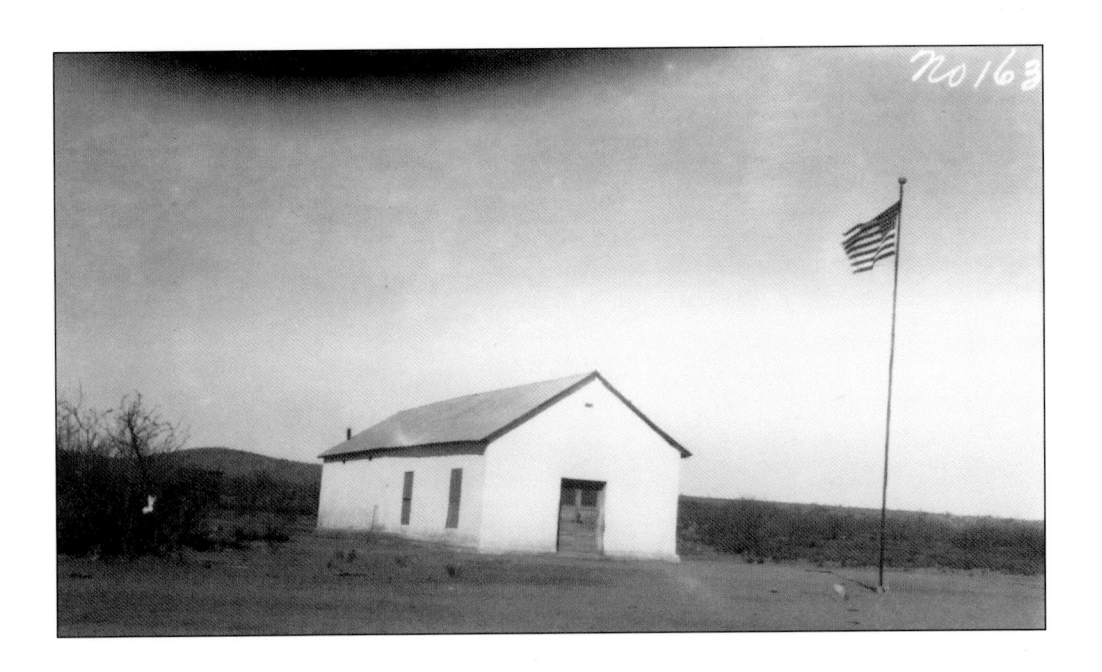

The Arivaca schoolhouse, pictured above, was built in 1879 with funding from Don Pedro Aguirre, a prominent man in the freighting business in Arizona. Over 50 years after the school's establishment, Evalyn A. Bentley visited the schoolhouse for a health assessment and snapped the image below. Bentley was involved in the Keep Growing Project, a program that monitored the health of students across Pima County. For the photograph, Bentley had students that received health awards stand, while those that did not meet the standards were told to sit. Similar pictures were taken at schools all across Pima County. Today, the schoolhouse is still used as a community center and is the oldest standing schoolhouse in Arizona. (Both, UA Photograph Files.)

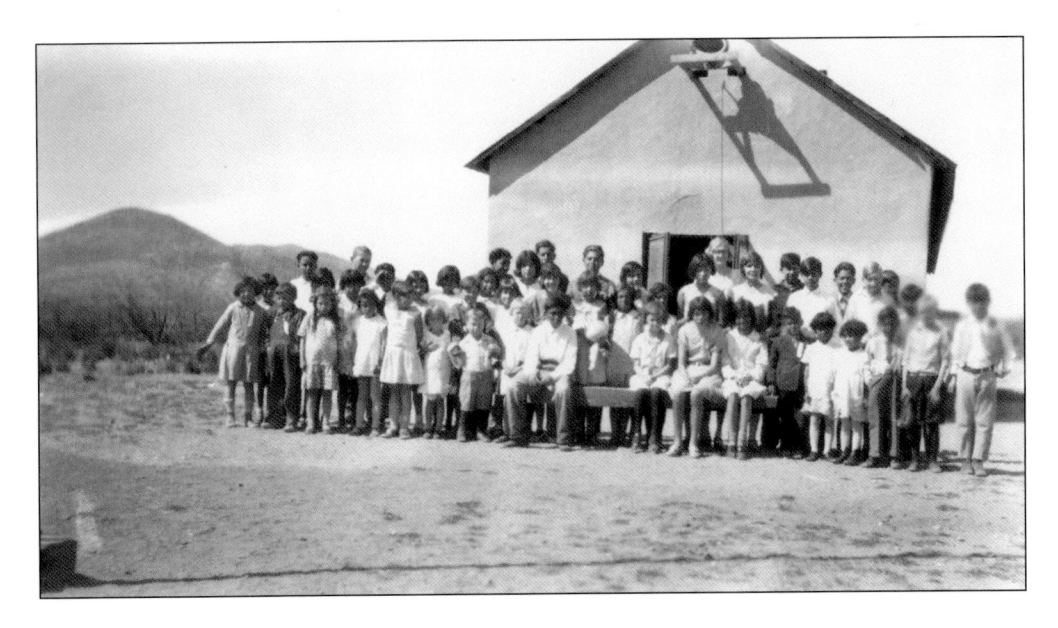

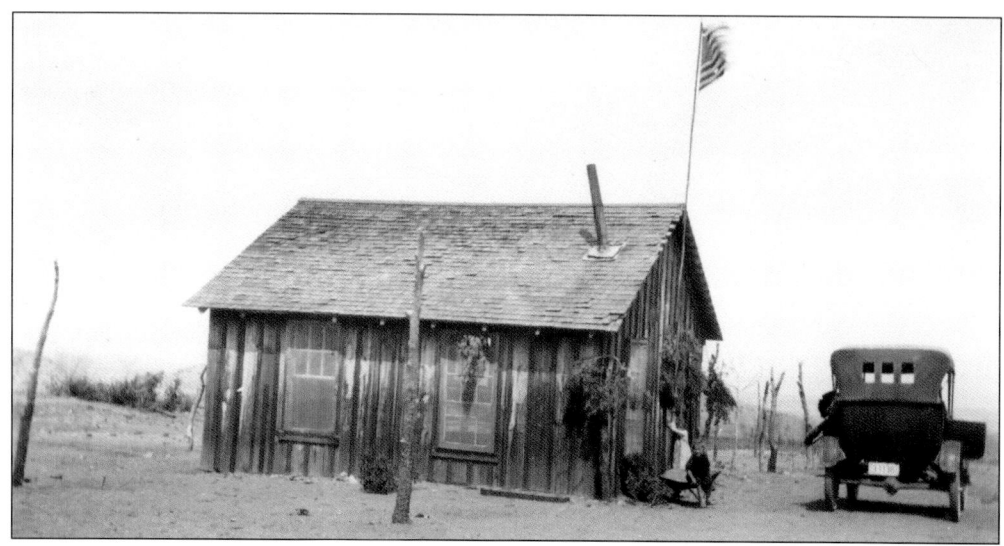

The US flag waves over the Sierrita schoolhouse in this image taken in 1922. Two young girls can be seen near the entrance of the building across from the automobile. Ten years after this image was taken, the county school superintendent had the rural school closed, saving the school system $1,500 a year. The 13 children enrolled in the one-room schoolhouse were enrolled in Twin Buttes School instead. (UA Photograph Files.)

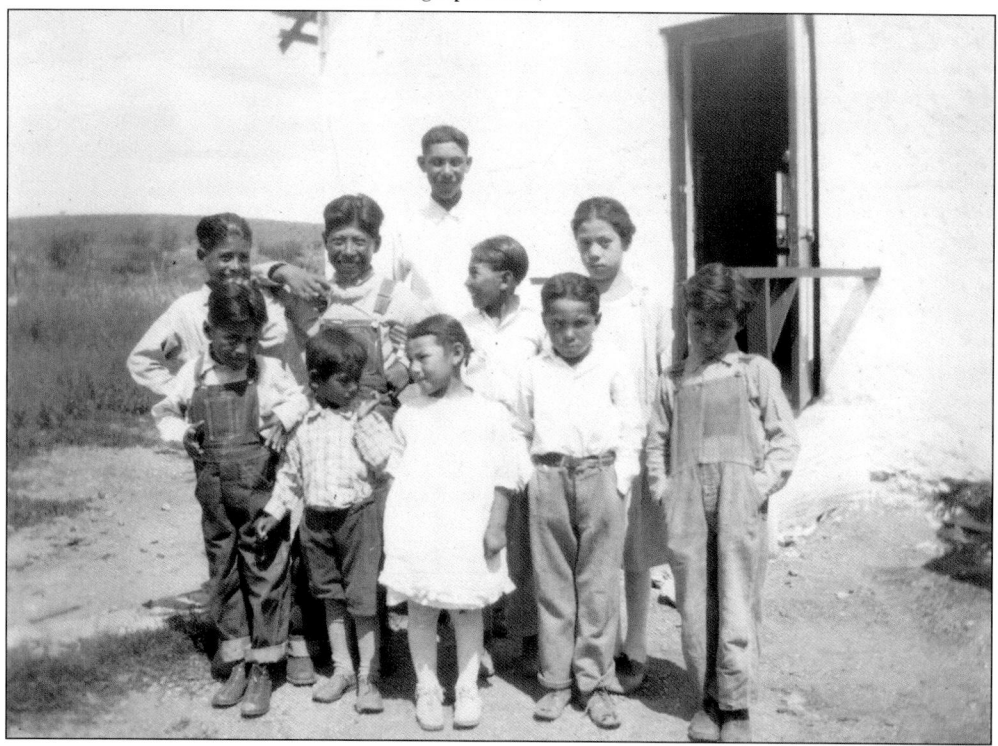

The school of Greaterville, pictured above in 1929, was established in 1882 and served the small mining community for 70 years. Enrollment numbers followed the population fluctuations of the town, with a high of 31 students in 1886 and only five students when it closed in 1952. (UA Photograph Files.)

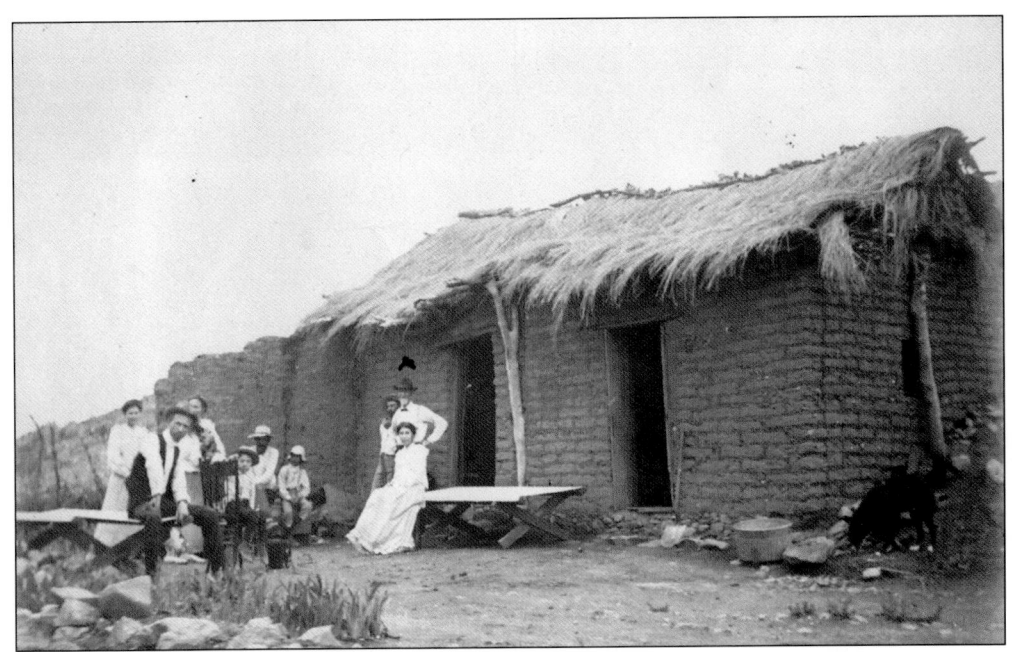

A group poses outside Fred Hughes's Greaterville home. Hughes distinguished himself in the 1st California Infantry, the Arizona legislature, and the Tucson Board of Supervisors. In 1897, he fell from grace when he embezzled $3,000 from the Arizona Pioneer's Historical Society (now called the Arizona Historical Society) then lost it all gambling. Hughes was a fugitive for several months before being tried and sentenced to five years in prison. (AHS PC27 449.)

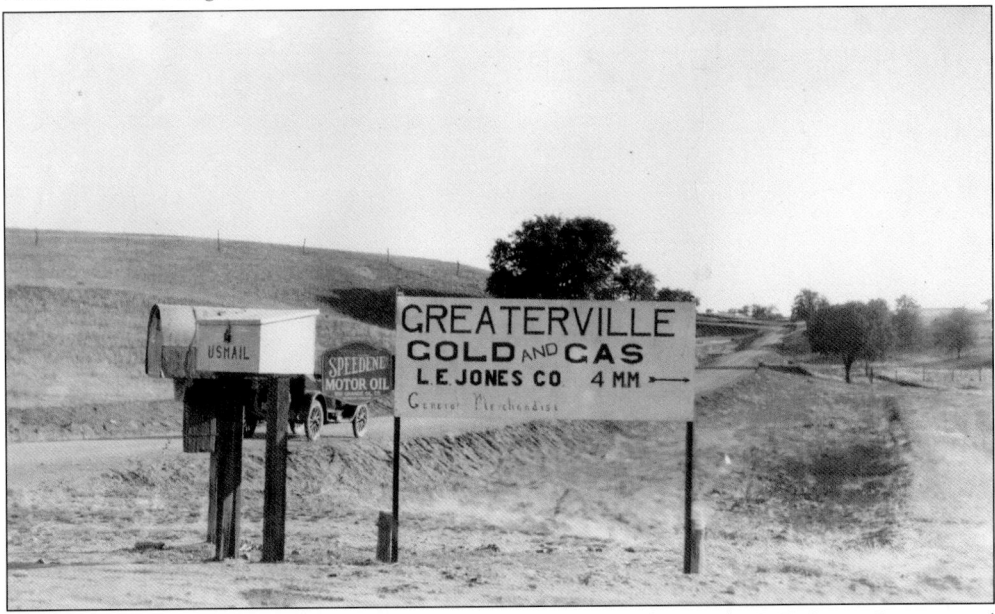

A sign advertising "gold and gas," as well as general merchandise at the L.E. Jones Co., greeted motorists passing through the junction of the Patagonia and Greaterville Highways. The town of Greaterville is known for the placer gold found there in 1874 and for its location along the "Renegade's Route," a path outlaws used to flee to Mexico. The town's population probably never exceeded 500. (AHS PC27 471.)

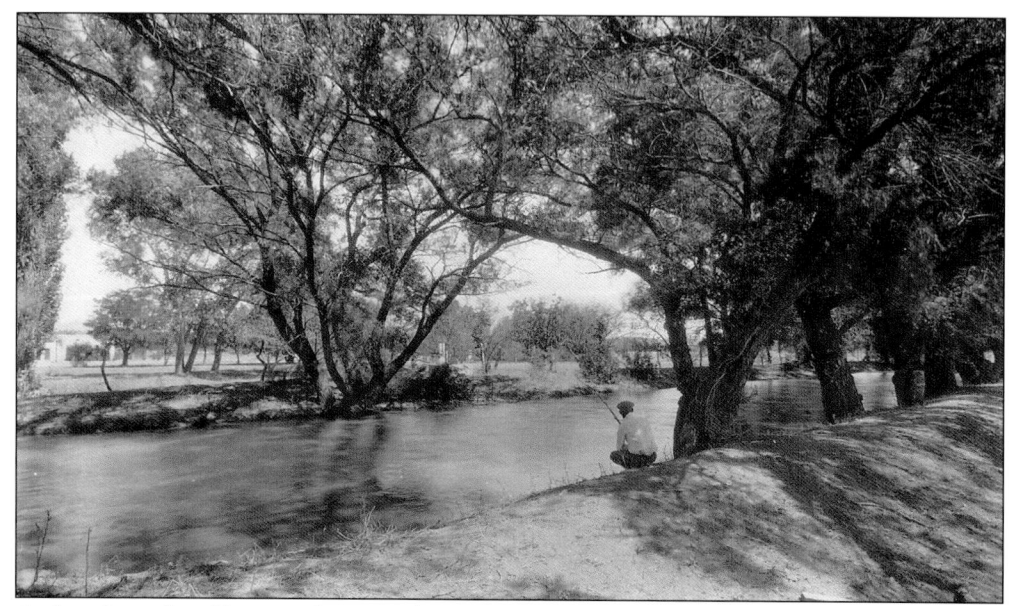

Archaeological and historical sites in the Canoa area, south of Tucson, have been found dating from the Archaic, Hohokam, Piman, Spanish, Mexican, and Territorial periods. Canoa Ranch was established in 1820 as part of the San Ignacio de la Canoa Spanish land grant and is one of the oldest historic ranches in Pima County. The ranch was purchased by Levi Manning in early 20th century and had a worldwide reputation for its cattle. Pima County purchased the ranch in 2001 to restore and conserve the area as part of the Sonoran Desert Conservation Plan. Above, a man fishes at the Canoa Canal around 1925. Below, a calf sits in the shade of a ramada at Canoa Ranch. (Both, courtesy of Deezie Manning-Catron.)

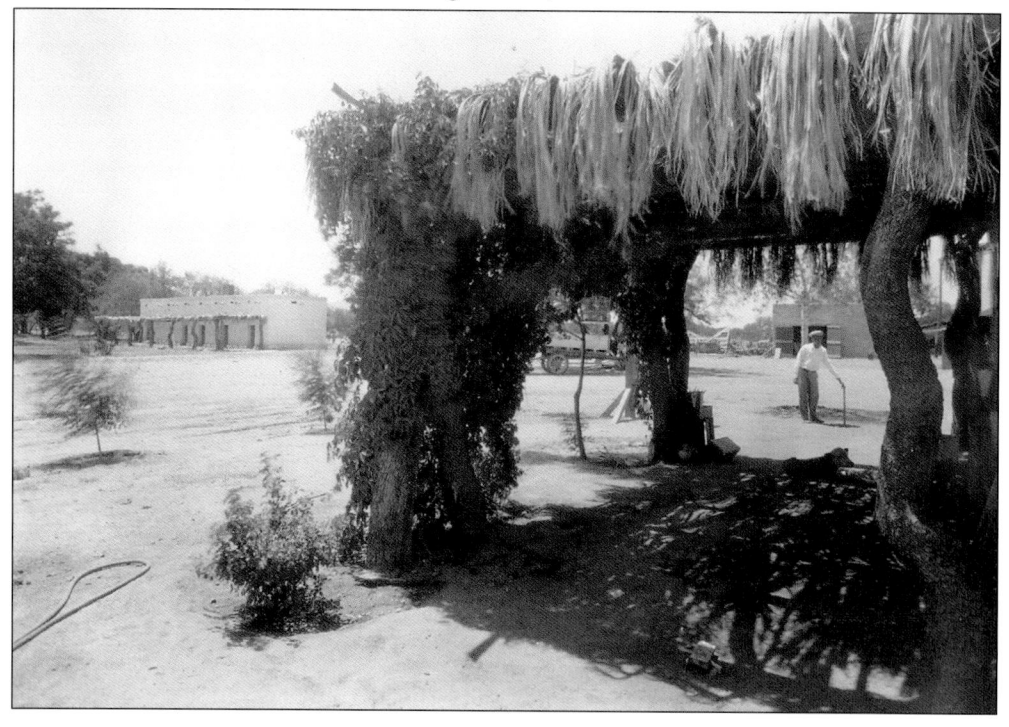

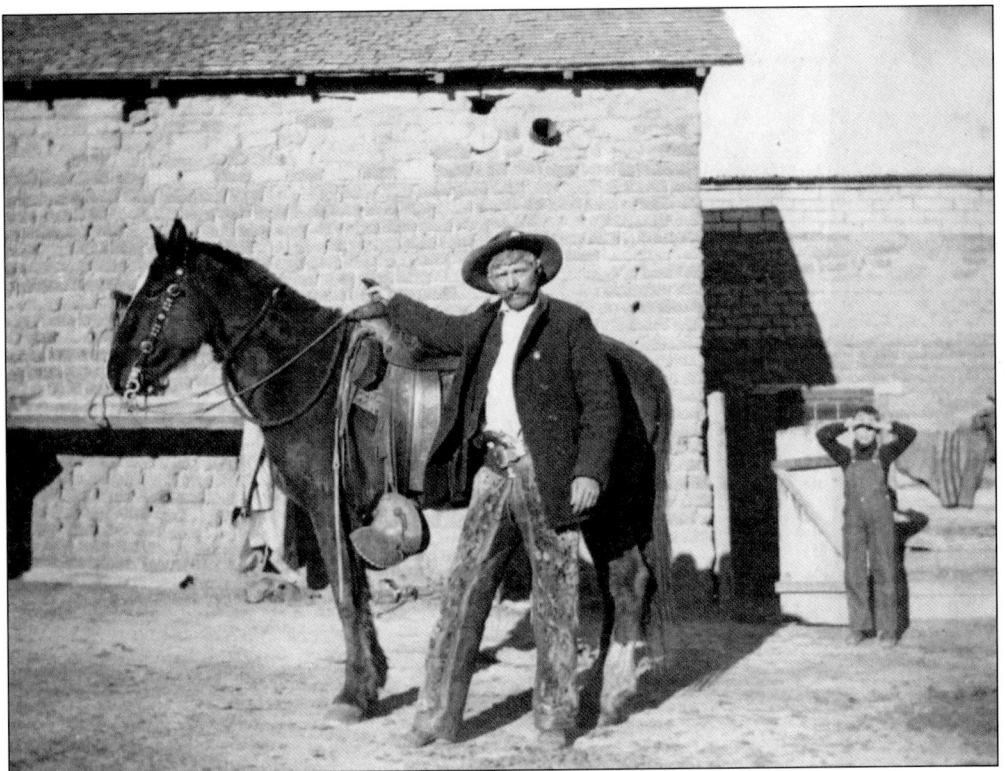

Hadden McFadden stands next to a horse during a visit to the Empire Ranch in 1900. McFadden, a native of California, came to Arizona in the 1890s and was living in Greaterville when this picture was taken. The Empire Ranch was originally homesteaded on 160 acres by William Wakefield and went through several owners until it was solely in the hands of Walter Vail in 1881. By the time Walter died in 1906, the ranch covered almost one million acres. (AHS PC27 487.)

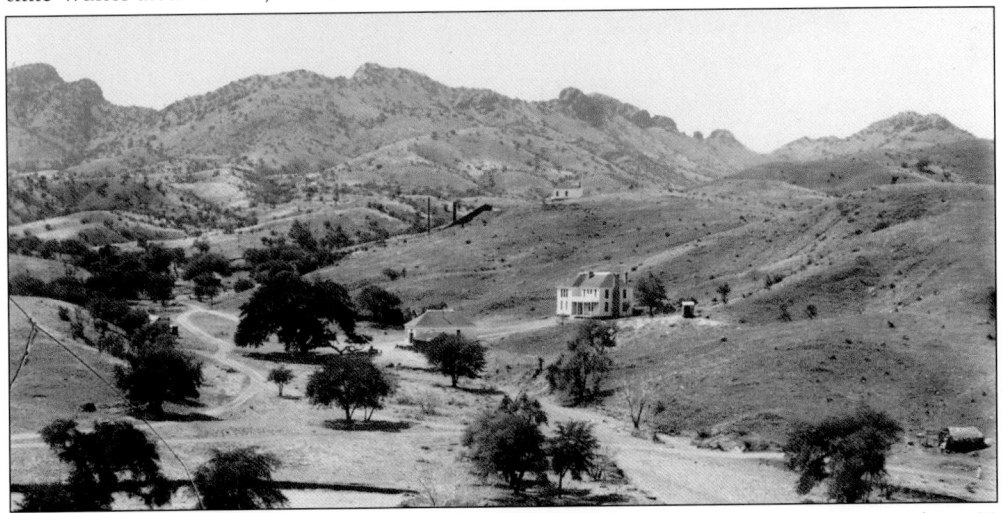

Taken in 1896, this photograph shows a striking view of Old Rosemont, a mining camp about 30 miles southeast of Tucson. In the foreground are a store and warehouse with a large hotel just up the mountain. In the background, the smelter and assay office are visible. Old Rosemont was an active community between 1894 and 1910. (UA Photograph Files.)

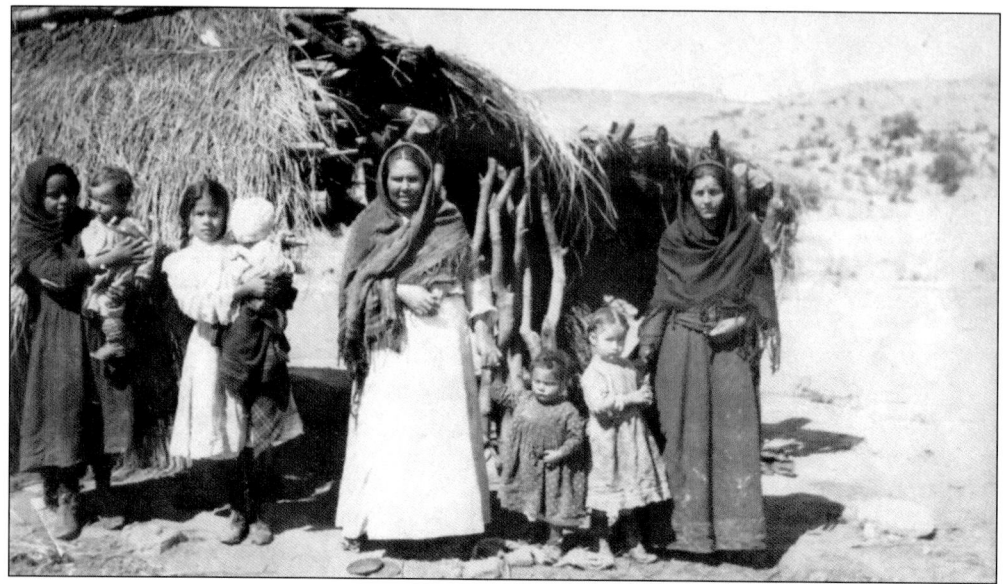

Although the railroad had arrived almost 15 years earlier, Tucson was still a small town when Loretta Lowell took this photograph in 1894. Dwellings like this one were a common sight. The materials used to build local structures often came from saguaro ribs, cholla cacti, grasses, soil, mesquite, and palo verde trees. (AHS 5385.)

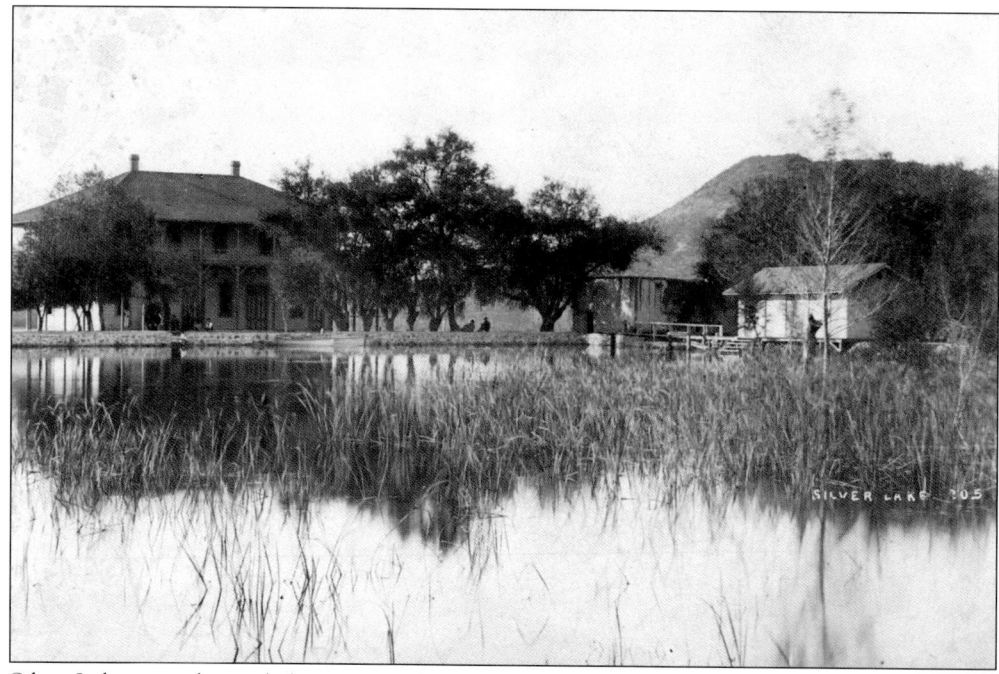

Silver Lake, once located about two miles south of downtown Tucson, was formed after a dam was built on the Santa Cruz River to provide power for a mill. By the 1880s, the lake had become a resort area for locals. The 1881 *Tucson City Directory* described activities available at the lake, which included "several boats for sailing or rowing up the river" and a "stout rope" for new swimmers to grasp while learning to swim. Over time, floods washed away the dam and removed the lake. (UA Photograph Files.)

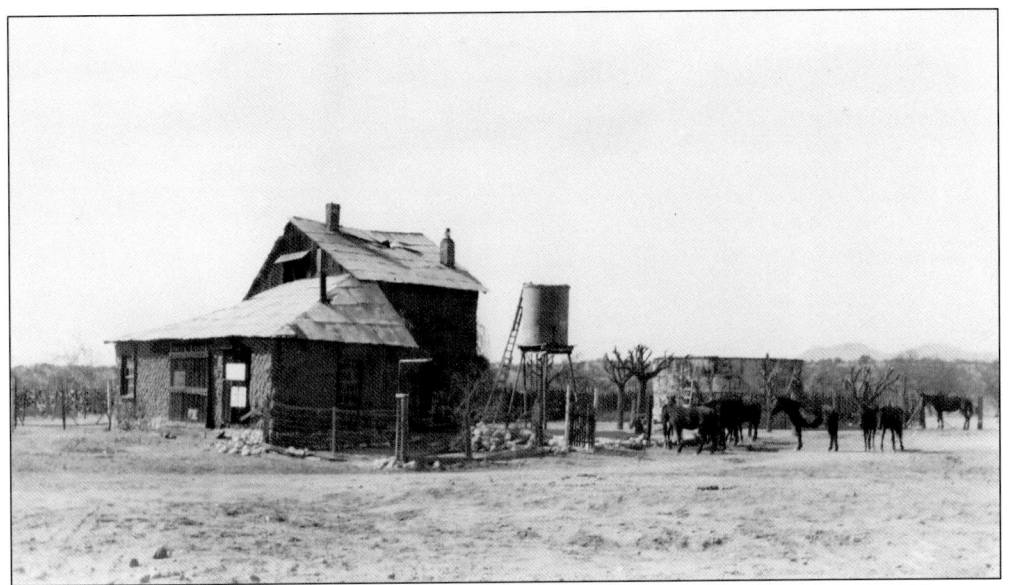

In 1874, a German immigrant named George Pusch established the Steam Pump Ranch in the area that would later become Oro Valley. The name "Steam Pump" was given because it was one of the few ranches in the Arizona Territory to use a steam pump to draw water from the ground. (AHS 3117.)

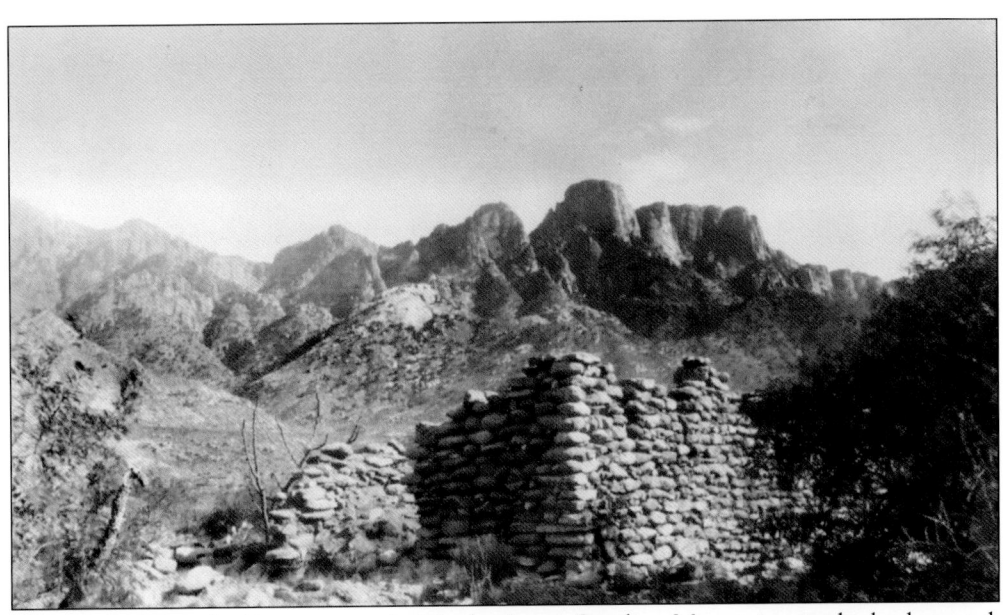

The ruins of Rancho Romero stand with the Santa Catalina Mountains in the background. Located in what is today Oro Valley in northern Pima County, the land was purchased by Francisco Romero in 1844 and developed by his son Fabian, who is credited as the founder of Rancho Romero. The area where the ranch buildings once stood is now part of Catalina State Park. (AHS PC27.)

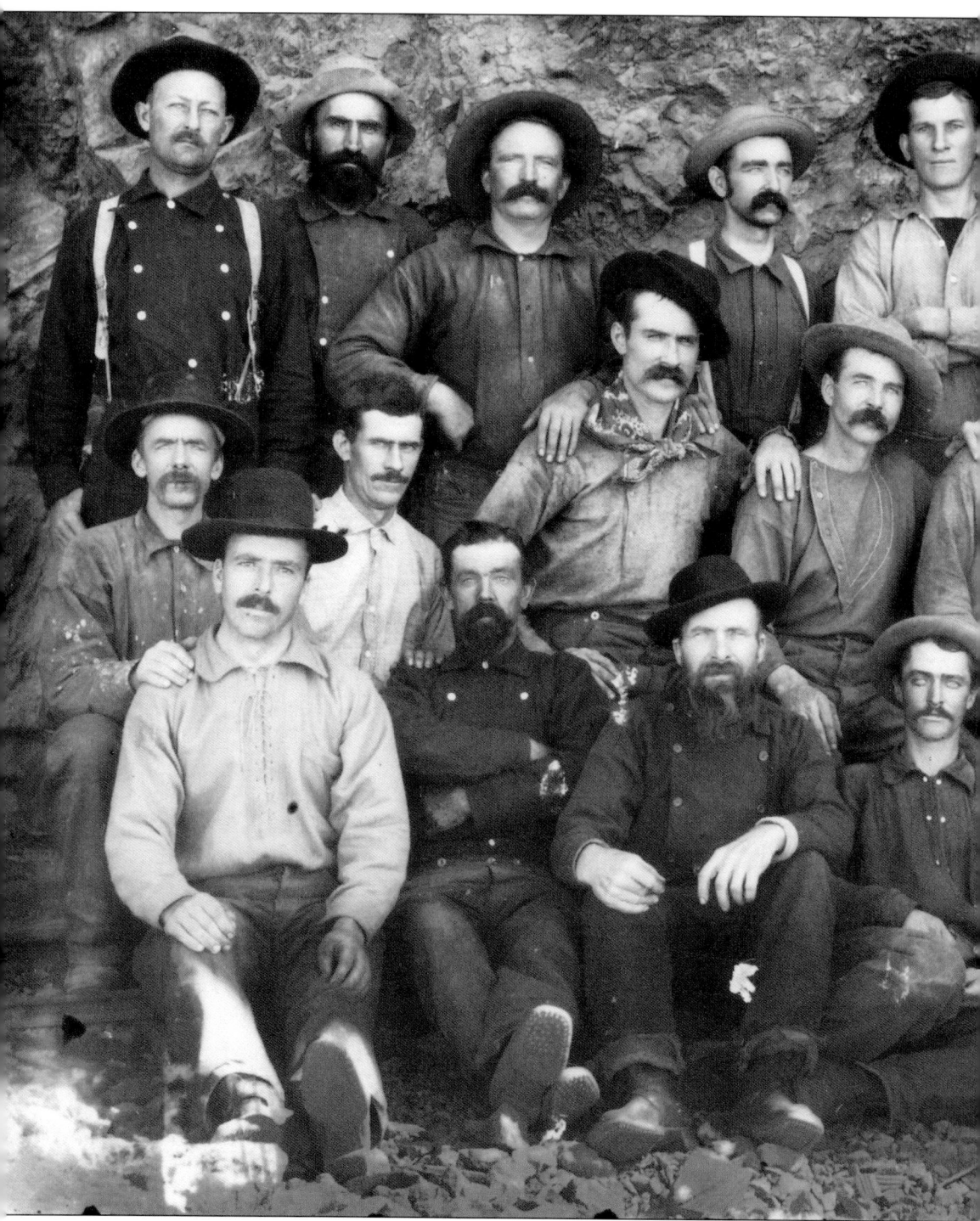

Quijotoa, a Tohono O'Odham word meaning "carrying-basket mountain," enjoyed one of the biggest, and shortest, mining booms in Arizona. Scotsman Alexander McKay's discoveries in 1883 on what would later be called Ben Nevis Mountain, as well as the arrival of millionaires James G. Flood and John W. Mackay (also known as the "Bonanza Kings"), stirred up a great deal of excitement in Quijotoa's mining prospects. In less than five months, the town's boom was bust, though some mining activity did continue. In this photograph, a group of miners poses outside an unidentified Quijotoa mine. (AHS B109165, B89331.)

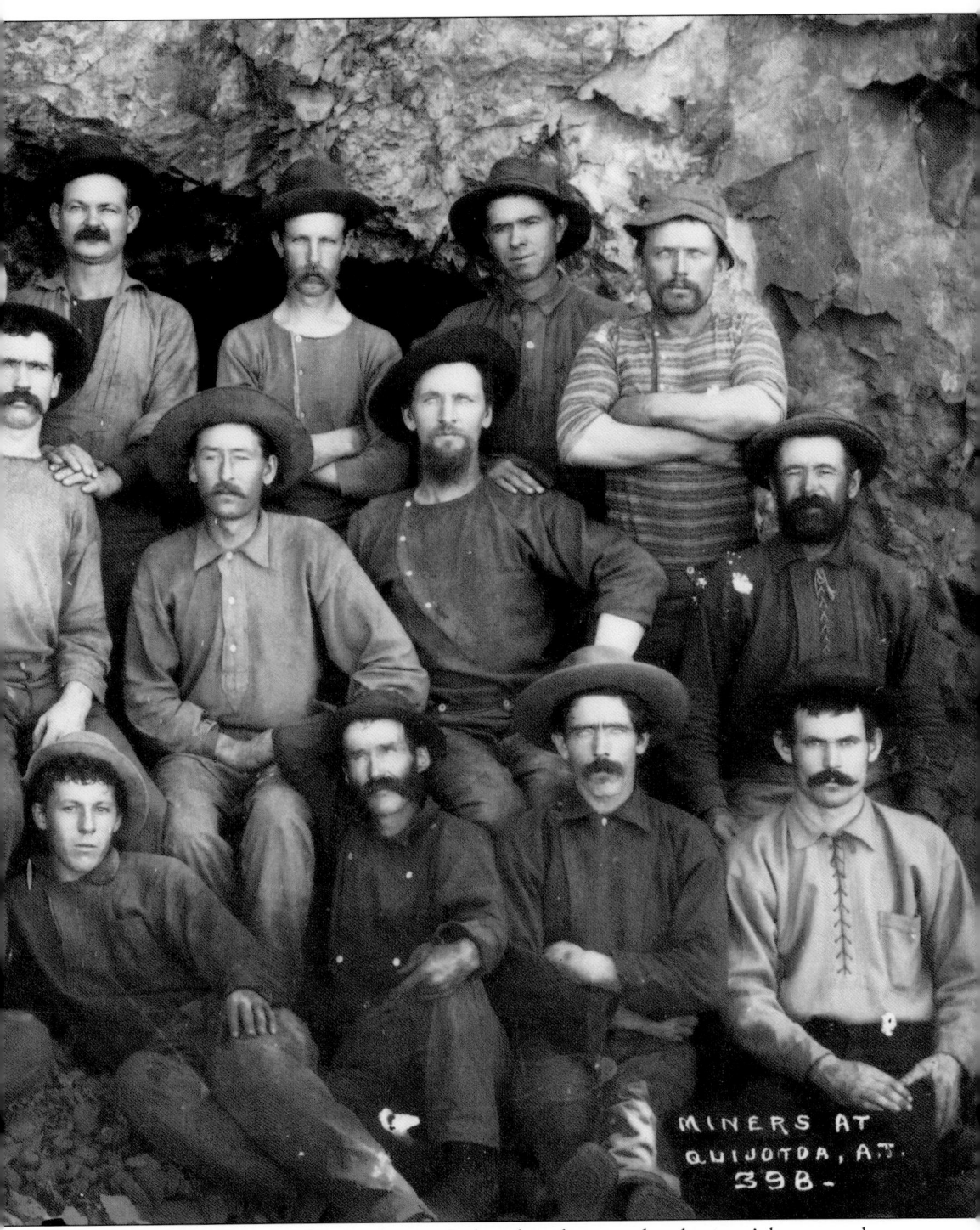

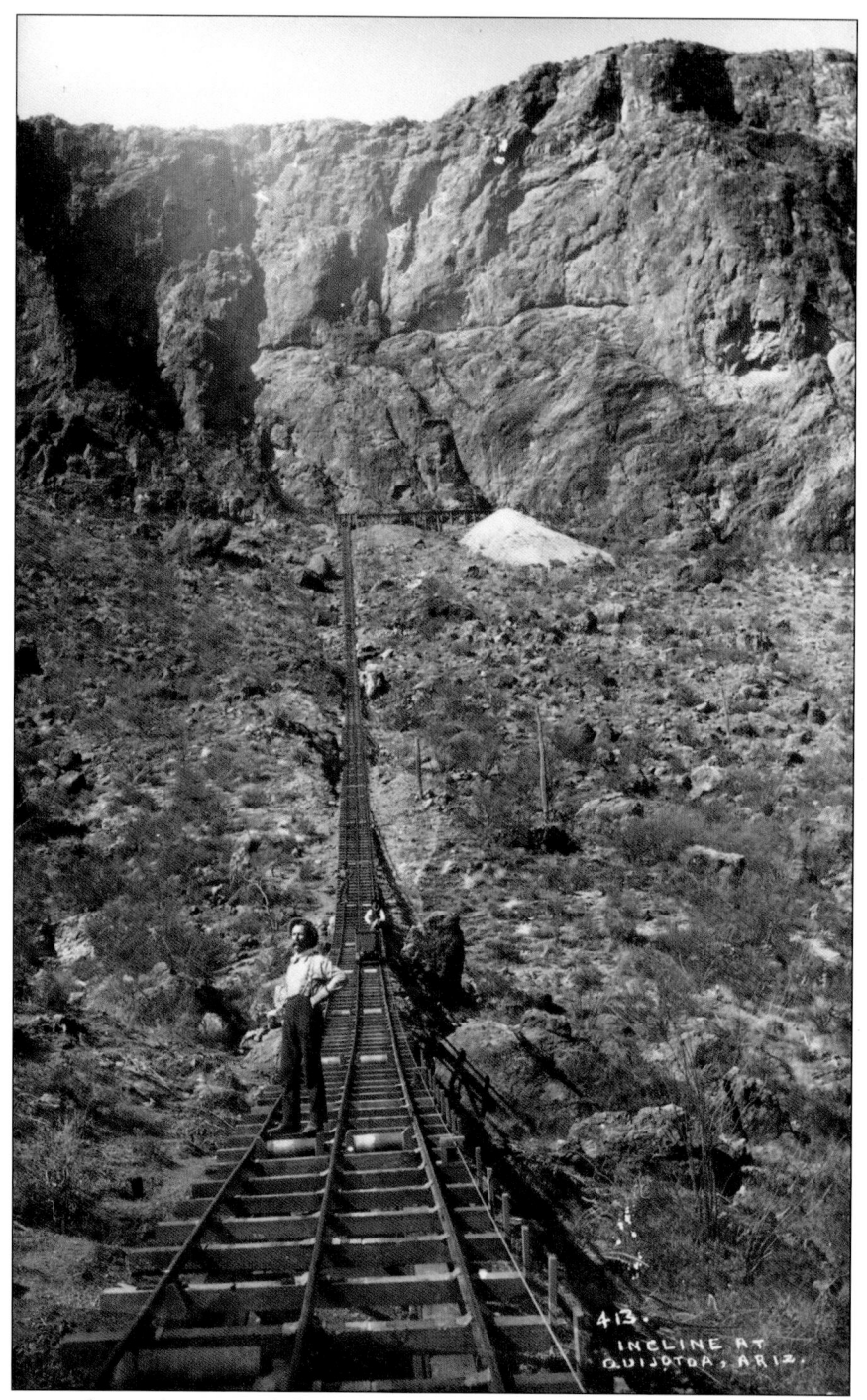

This steep-incline railway served the mine in Quijotoa and demonstrates the difficulty miners encountered in pursuit of silver. Before the boom at Quijotoa, one such mountain looked so daunting that all but Scotsman Alexander McKay refused the challenge. After McKay returned with very promising ore samples, the boom began. An *Arizona Citizen* reporter later named the mountain Ben Nevis after the famous landmark in McKay's homeland. (AHS B68747.)

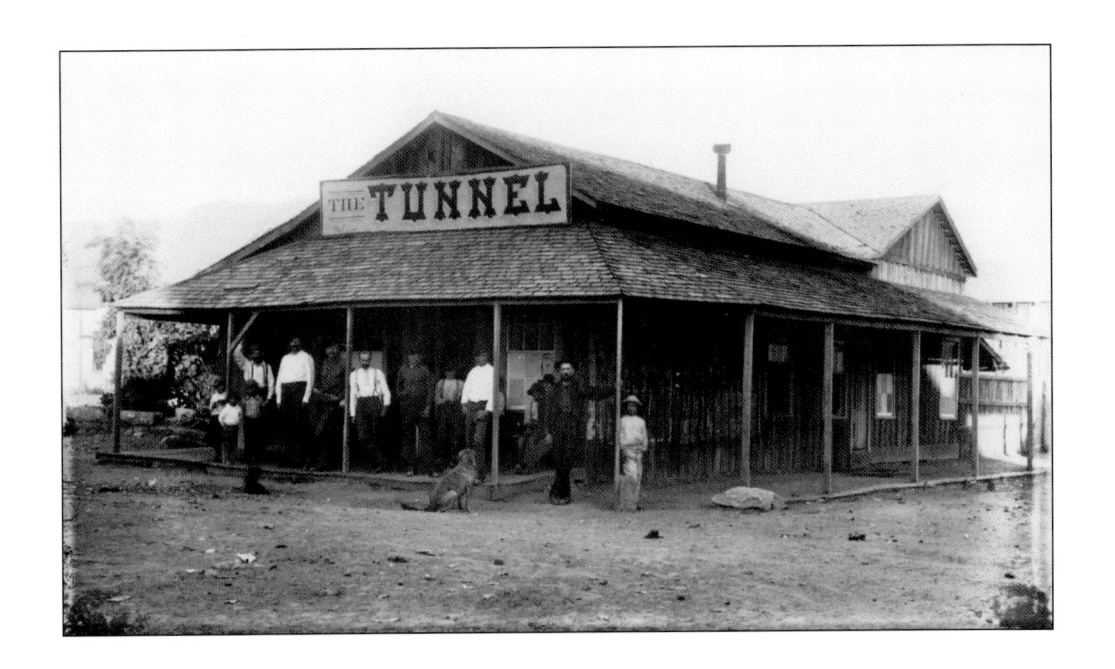

During Quijotoa's boom in 1884, approximately 20 saloons provided food, drink, and entertainment to miners from the area's four townships. Pictured above, The Tunnel's name reflects the mining activities in the area and was possibly named after a locally famous tunnel discovered 100 years prior. The Star Hotel, below, was operated by Mrs. L.A. Henry. Situated on the main street, Logan Avenue, Mrs. Henry converted her hotel first into a boardinghouse and later a restaurant as the population shrank. In its prime, the Star Hotel's restaurant was the area's most popular gathering place. (Above, AHS B111394; below, AHS B89932.)

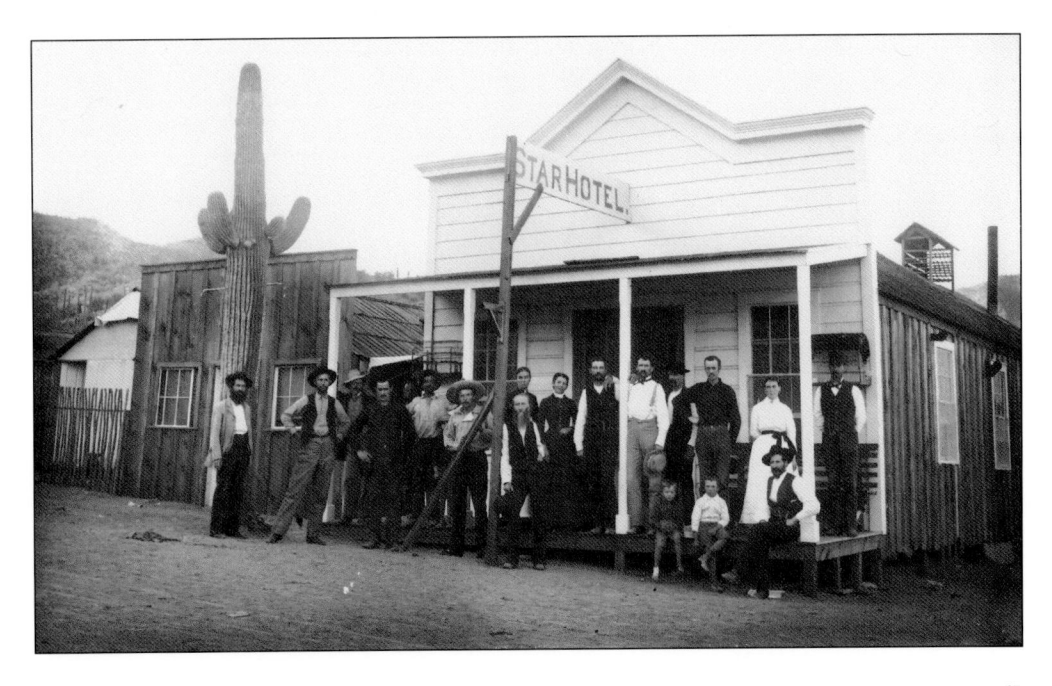

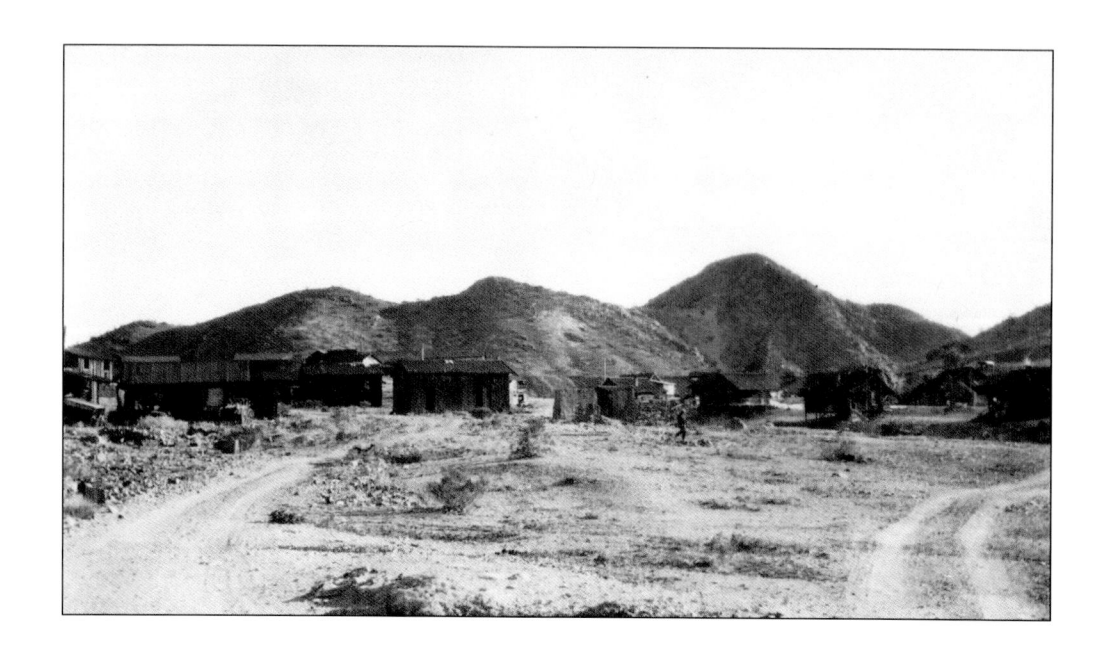

Copper mining was the backbone of the town of Silver Bell (also written as Silverbell), whose hills never had enough silver to be profitable. Mining operations and the town's population waxed and waned; during the profitable years, it was known as a "lively place" and "the toughest town in Pima County." In the photograph below, a Silver Bell citizen rests on the front porch of his home. Above, a figure walks past abandoned homes during the declining years after World War II. The next upswing would not occur until 1951. Silver Bell faded into a ghost town in 1983, when Arizona Smelting and Refining Company (ASARCO) shut down operations. (Above, UA Photograph Files; below, AHS PC27 627.)

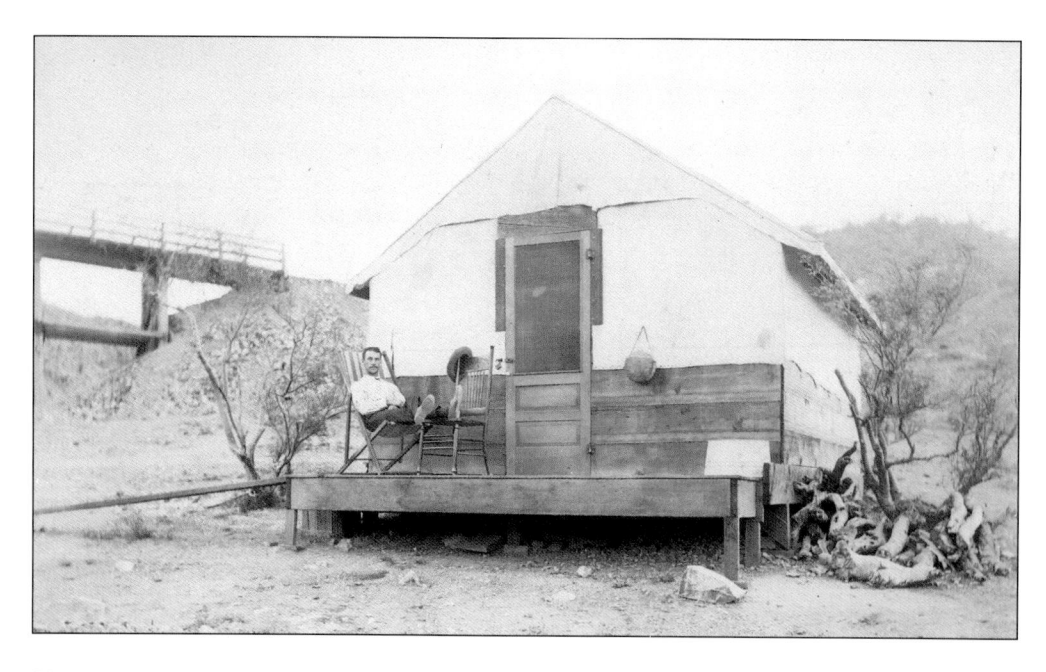

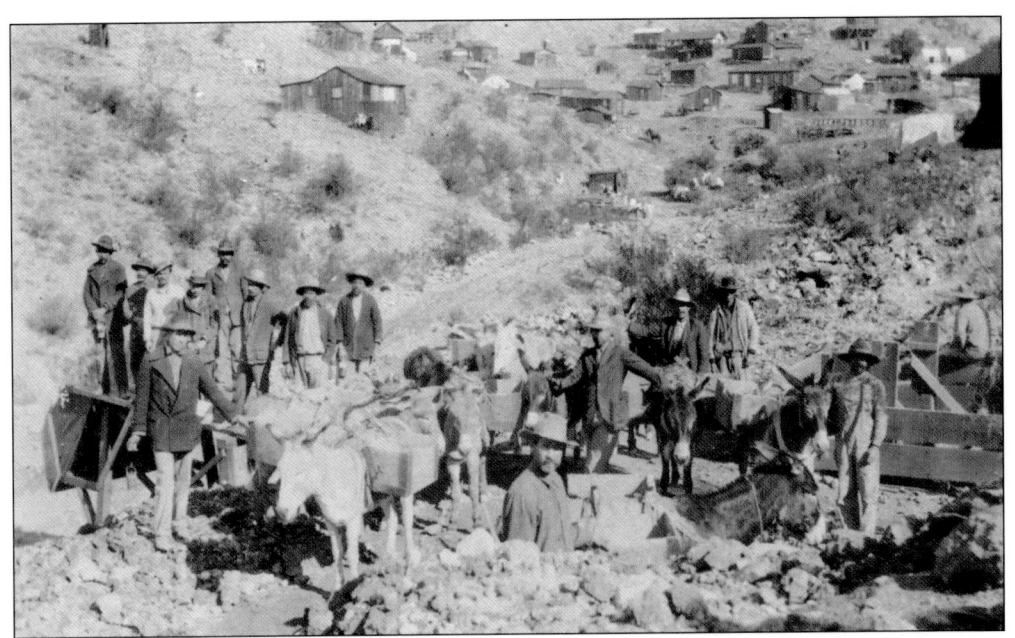

Mining operations in the town of Silver Bell slowed to a trickle in the 1910s. The Development Company of America, which owned the Imperial Copper Company in Silver Bell, went bankrupt after water infiltrated its mines in Tombstone. That, compounded with the lack of silver found in the Silver Bell area, choked the industry nearly to death. Below, the miners shown in this 1918 photograph at El Tiro Mine may have been among those who participated in three fundraisers that year to support American soldiers fighting in and returning from World War I. On April 30, the *Arizona Daily Star* reported, "Patriotic activities in Silver Bell have flourished like the proverbial Green Bay tree of late." El Tiro was later transformed into an open mine pit and, as late as 1981, helped process 600 tons of ore per hour. (Both, UA Photograph Files.)

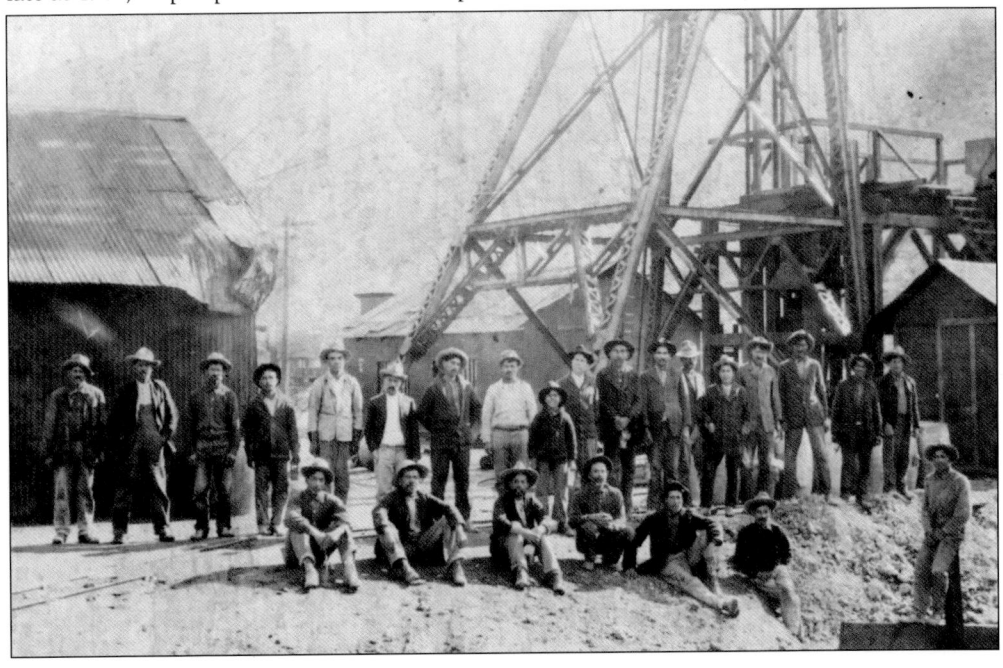

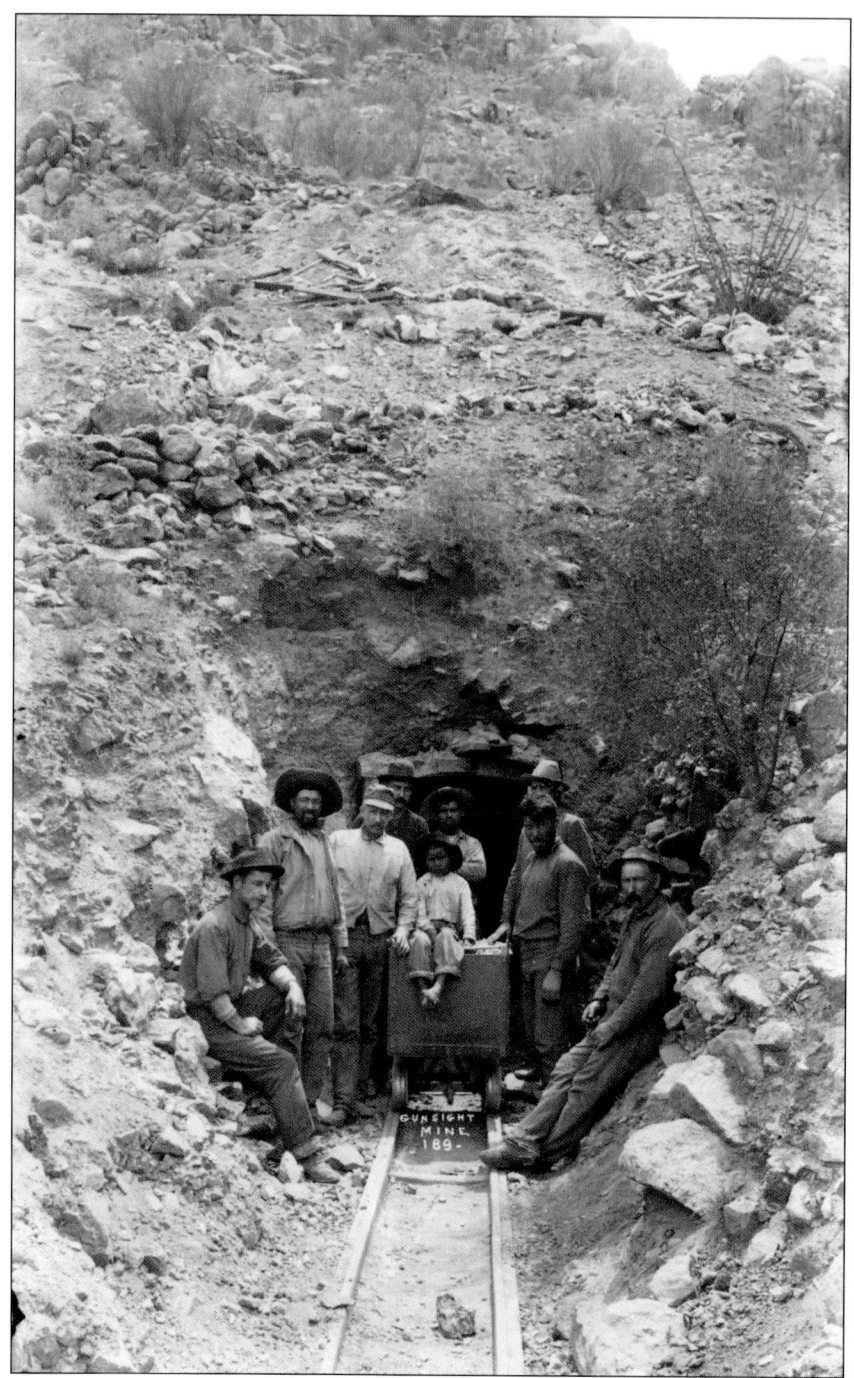

A group of miners, including a small child, pauses for a photograph outside the Gunsight Mine around 1890. The town of Gunsight, about 125 miles east of Tucson, was started in September 1878, and a post office was officially established in 1882. At the town's peak, the community boasted a population of around 1,500. Like many Pima County mining communities, the town's boom was short lived. The post office closed only 14 years after its opening, and little remains of Gunsight today. (AHS B91740a.)

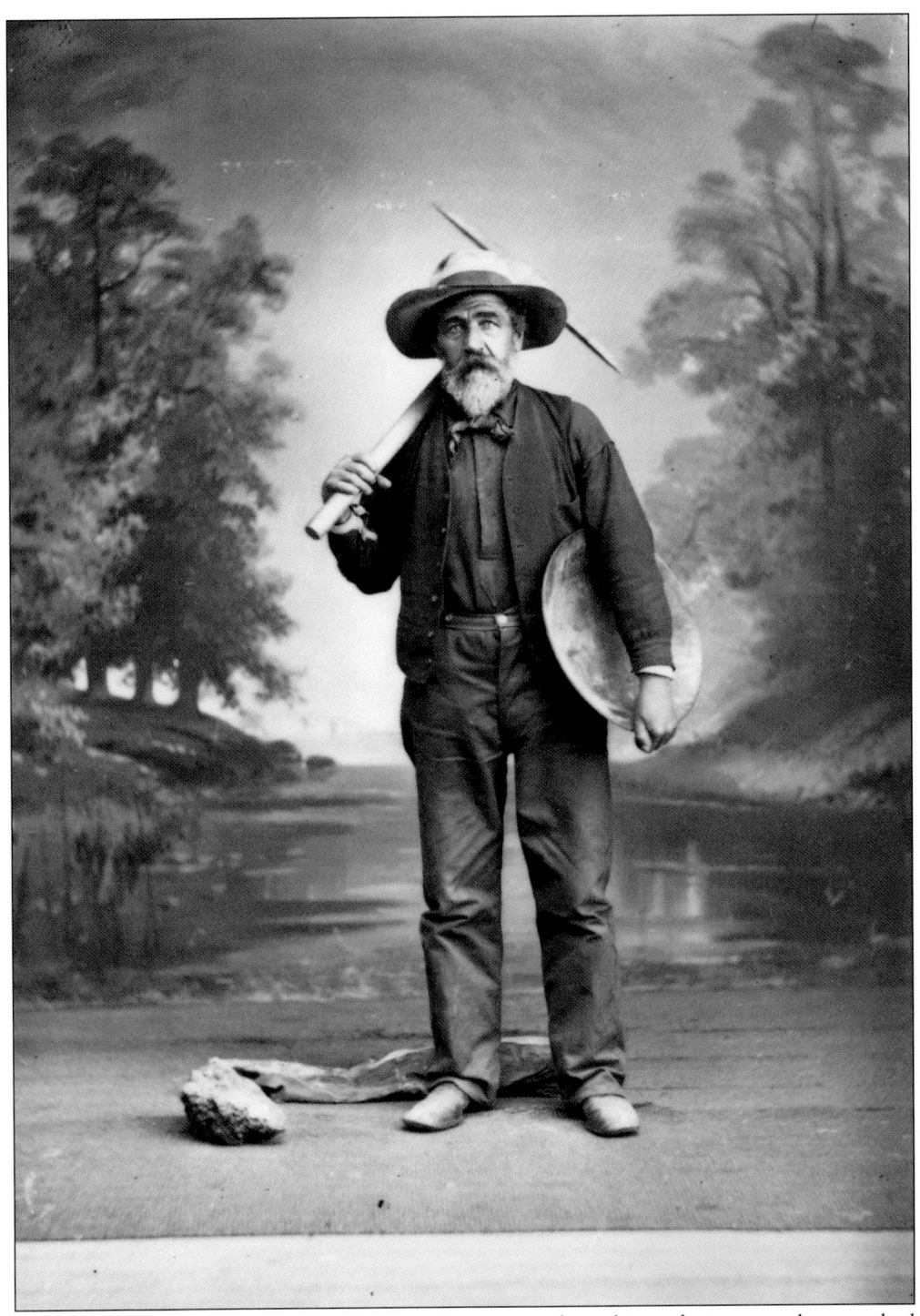

This unidentified miner, dressed in clothes and props to indicate his profession, was photographed at the Buehman Studios in Tucson around the turn of the century. The studio simply labeled the photograph as "Wenkle Man." Whether the description was a reference to his name or to the town of Winkleman, Arizona, is unknown. (AHS B8438.)

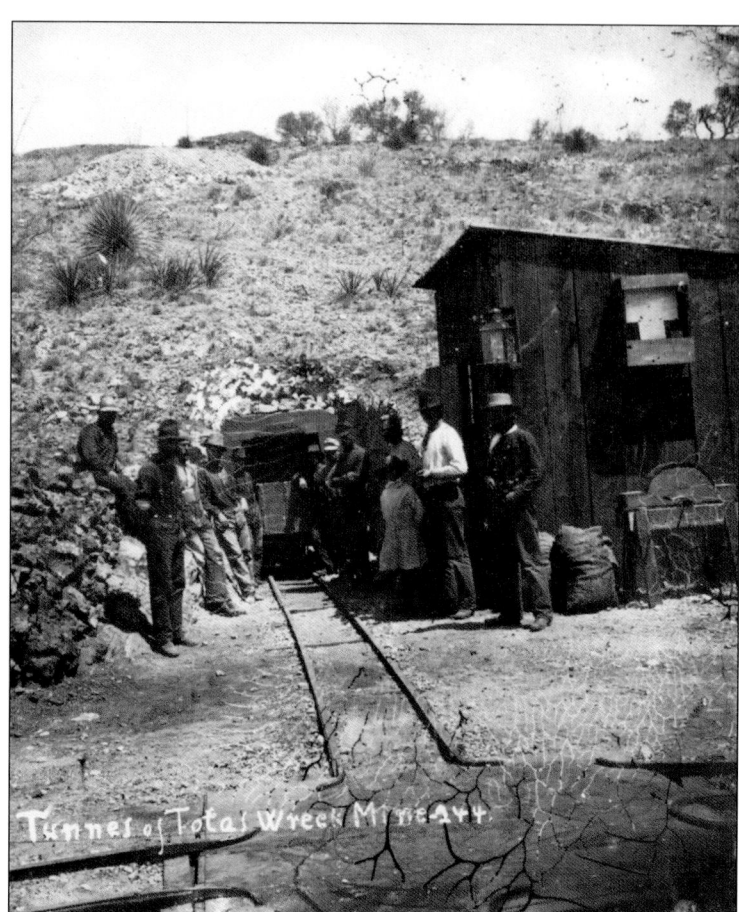

The uniquely named Total Wreck Mine was located about 30 miles southeast of Tucson. It was discovered in 1879 by John T. Dillon, who reportedly described the mineral formation as a "total wreck," and the name stuck. A post office was established in August 1881, and mining for silver ore followed. However, the town's boom was short lived. Its post office closed in 1890, and mining stopped around 1911. (AHS B109171.)

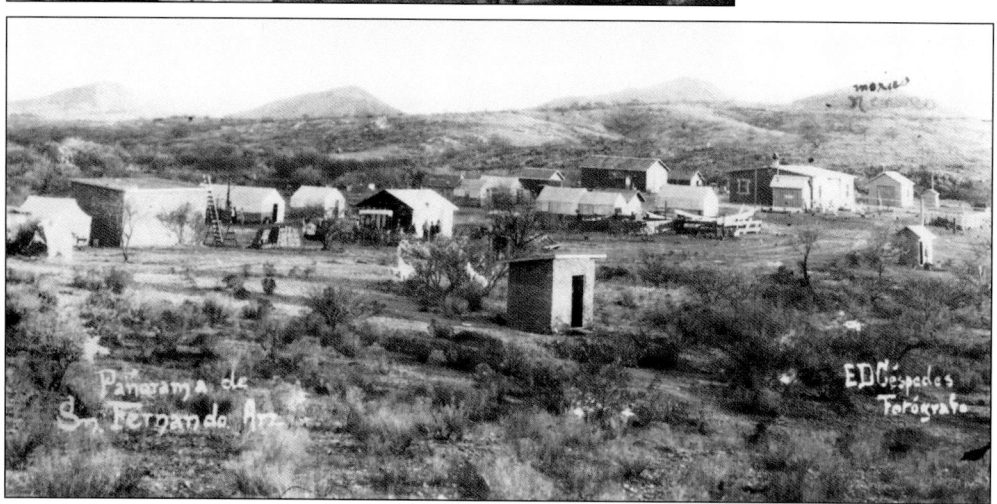

Labeled as a "panorama de San Fernando," this image shows the border town of what is now known as Sasabe, Arizona, located about 40 miles west of Nogales. A post office first came to the area in 1892 to meet the needs of the La Osa and Buenos Ayres Ranches. To show the close proximity to Mexico, a line was drawn on the photograph to signify the international boundary. (AHS 66472.)

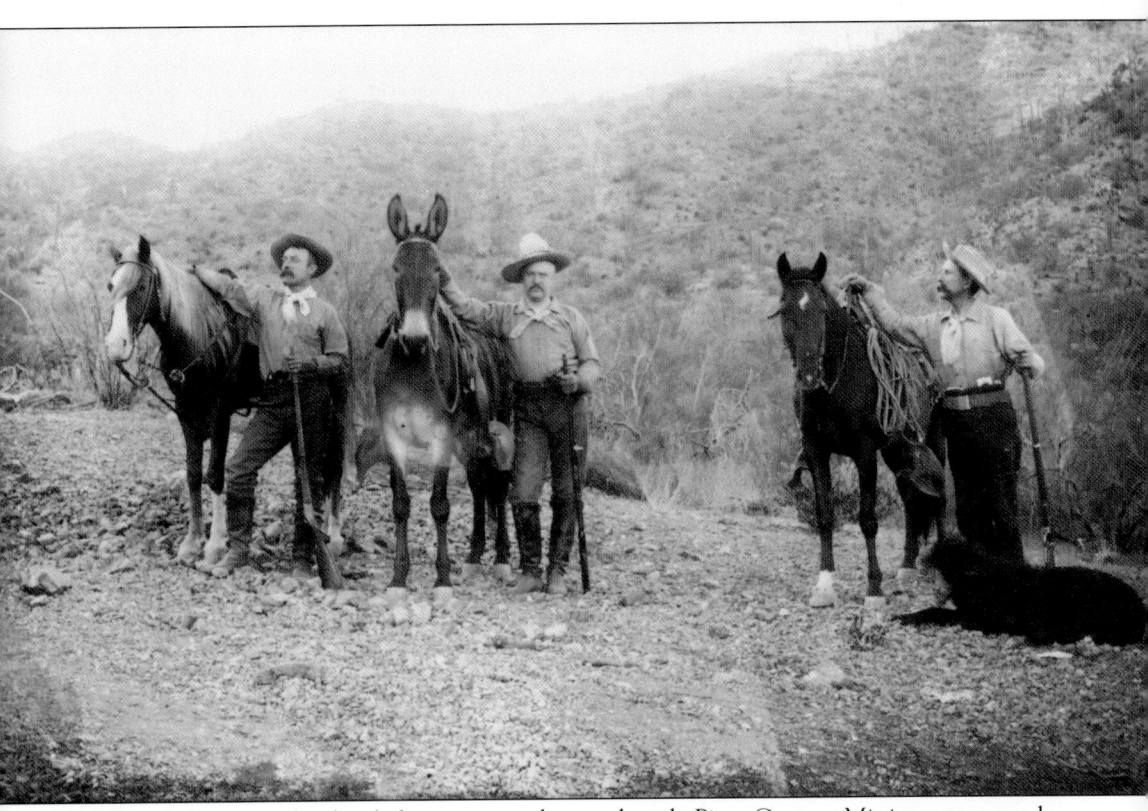

The search for mineral riches led many to explore and settle Pima County. Mining camps, such as Ajo, Olive, Total Wreck, Helvetia, Greaterville, and Cerro Colorado, appeared as the result of successful explorations. Many of these once-bustling camps have now turned into ghost towns as silver and gold resources ran out or economic factors caused mines to close. The three men pictured here stopped near Quijotoa in western Pima County around 1885. (AHS B89931.)

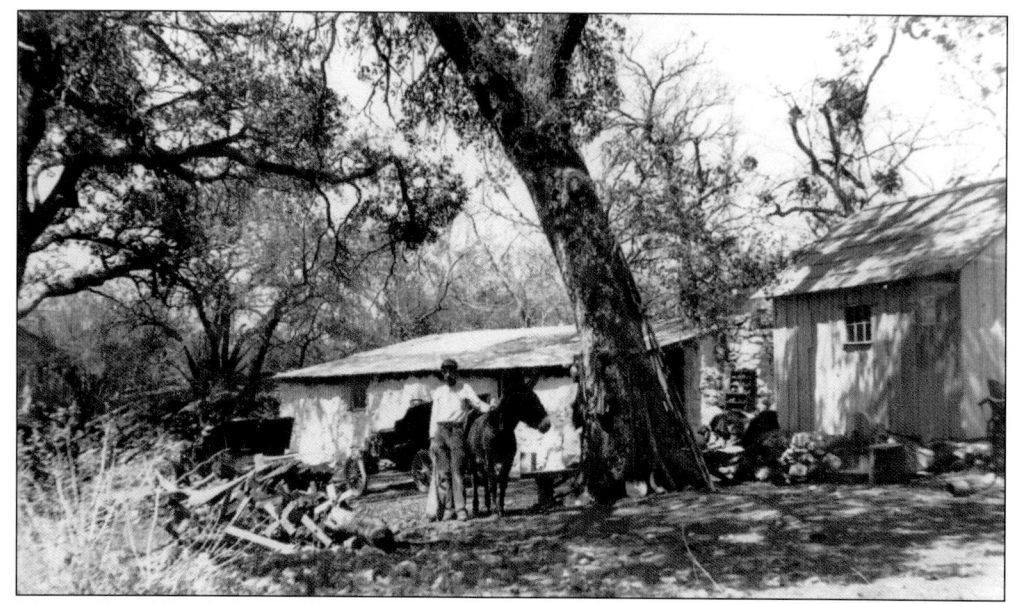

Mining for gold and silver in the Santa Rita Mountains has given rise to places such as Greaterville, Kentucky Camp, Helvetia, Rosemont, Alto, and Salero. One of the largest ventures occurred in 1902 under the Santa Rita Water and Mining Company, created by George Bird McAneny, a wealthy businessman with ties to Comstock Mines in Nevada and the Contention Mine in Tombstone. This photograph of a miner outside his cabin in the Santa Rita Mountains was taken during that same time period. (AHS PC142 62312.)

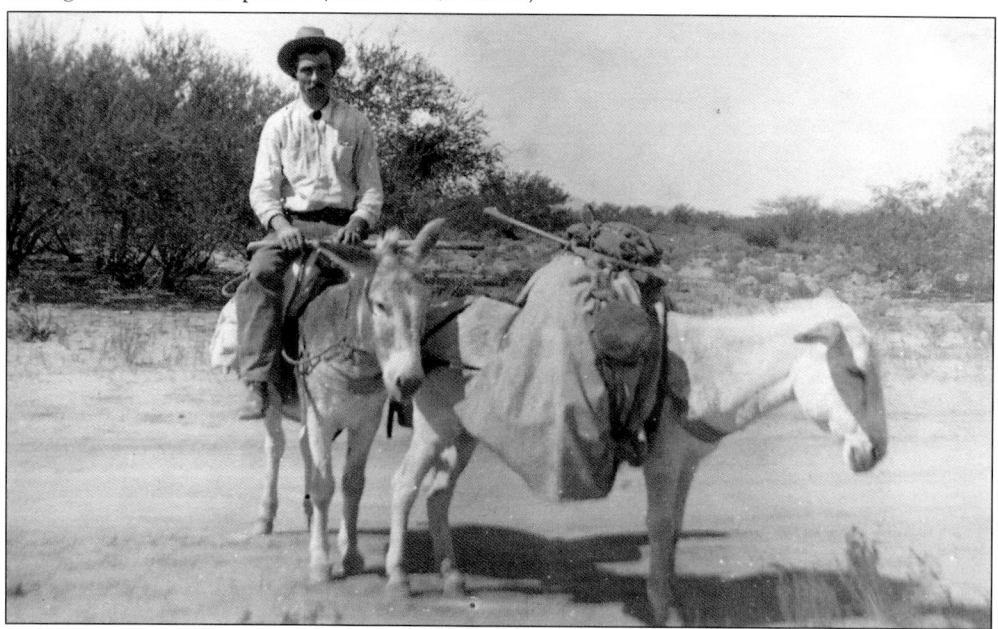

Camile Pierrel, a prospector hoping to strike it rich in the Santa Catalina Mountains, was photographed in Tucson on October 17, 1899. Born in France in 1864, Pierrel immigrated to the United States in 1882. A year after this photograph was taken, Pierrel was already looking for minerals elsewhere. He moved out of Pima County and worked as a miner in Prescott, Arizona. (AHS PC120 AQ.)

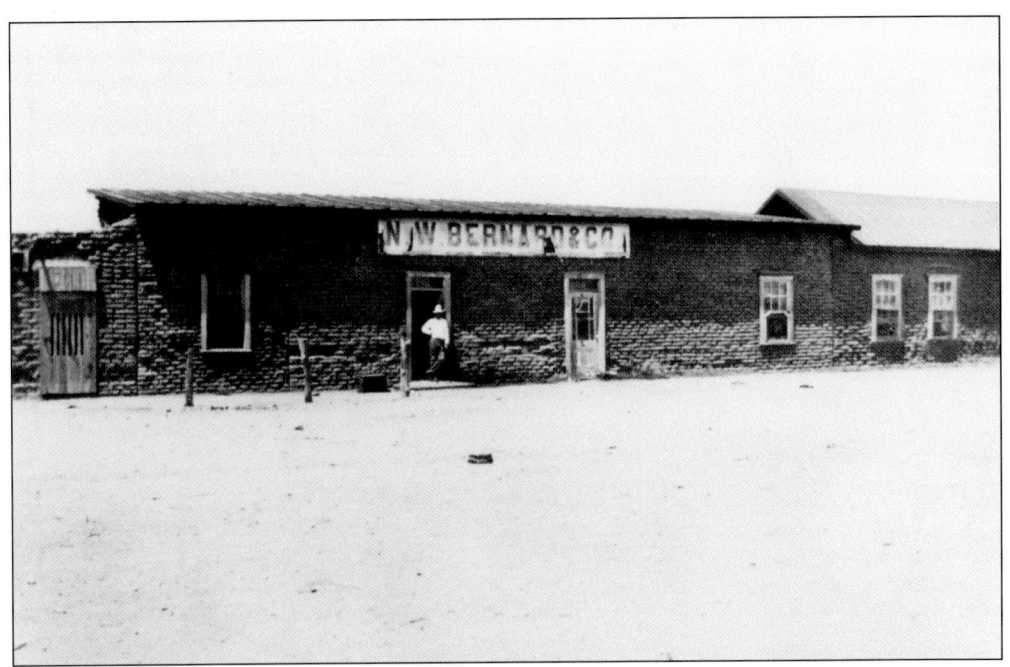

The N.W. Bernard & Company store opened for business on the main street of Arivaca in the 1870s. Owned by Noah W. Bernard and his partner J.E. Curry, the store carried general merchandise for the town's population, which depended heavily on mining and ranching. Customers could pick up food, books, knives, pipes, soap, and shirts. The image was taken in 1907 with Les Farrell in the doorway. (AHS 74062.)

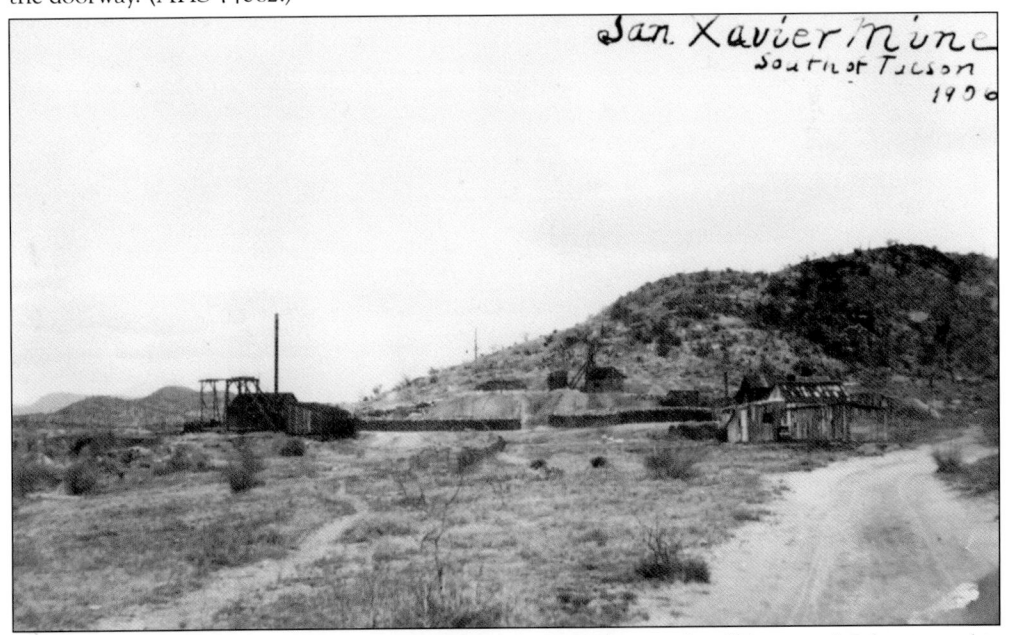

The San Xavier Mine was located approximately 20 miles south of Tucson. At the time this photograph was taken in 1906, the mine was already 26 years into production. The mine closed after prices for zinc and lead fell in the mid-20th century, leaving over 300 workers without a job. (AHS PC142 62306.)

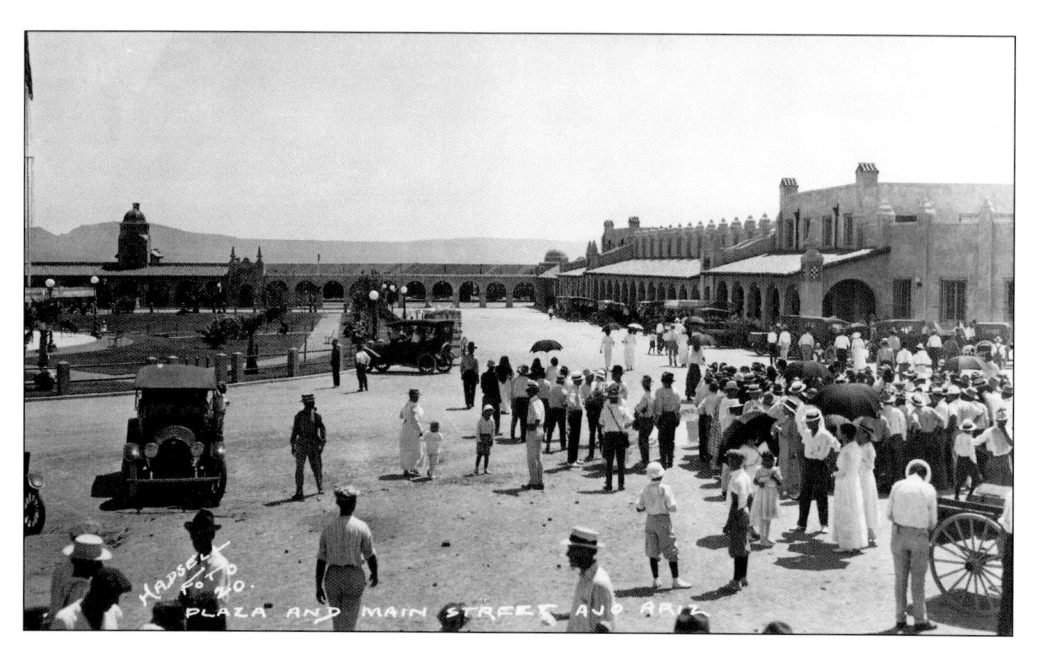

In 1918, the community of Ajo gathered in the town's new plaza for a Fourth of July celebration. Wearing white and carrying umbrellas to protect themselves from the hot July sun, the crowds gathered in the street for the festivities. The Spanish Colonial–style plaza, pictured above, had been completed the year before under the direction of Isabella Greenway, who went on to become the first congresswoman from Arizona. Below, seven young participants in the pie-eating contest pose with their faces and shirts displaying the remains of the pies. Walter P. Hadsell, a graduate of the University of Arizona Mining Department, caught the day's activities on camera. (Above, AHS PC55f5_64020B; below, AHS 64184.)

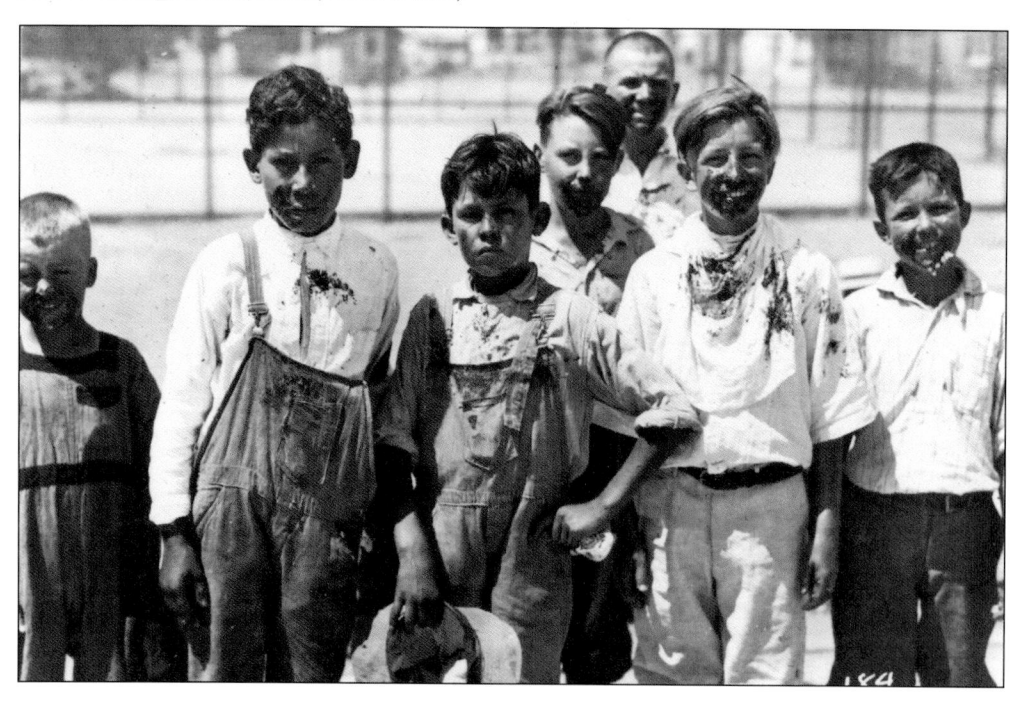

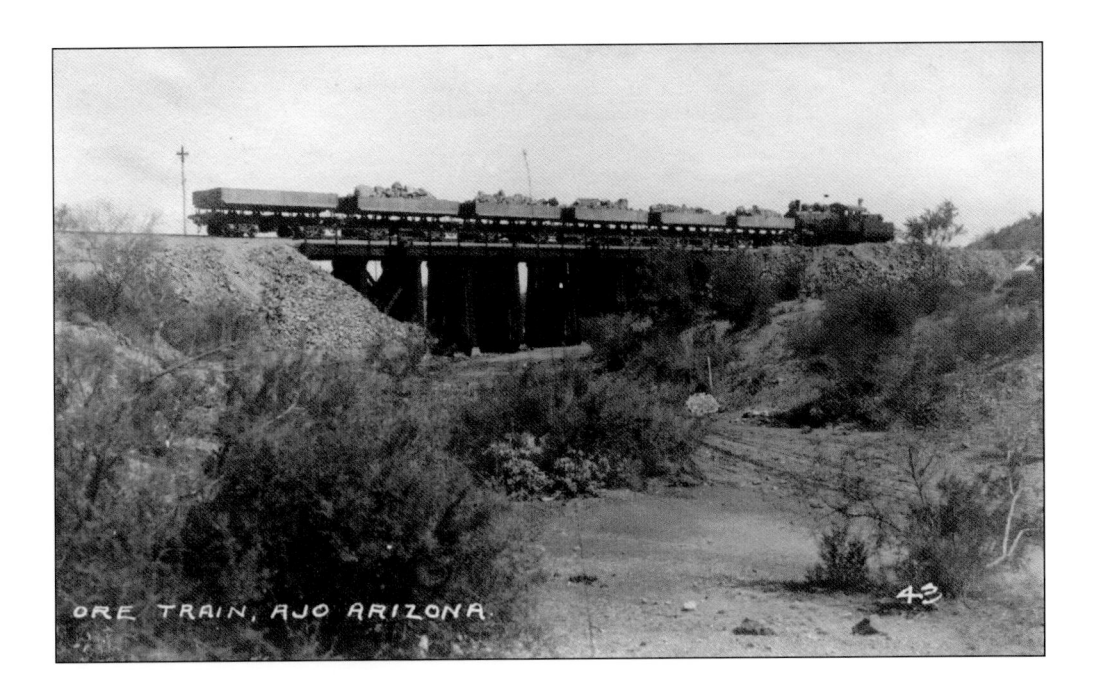

Ajo, a town west of Tucson and about 40 miles north of the Mexican border, can credit copper mining for much of its growth. The origins of Ajo's name vary by source. Some claim that Ajo comes from the Spanish word for garlic, which grows wild in the area. Others credit the Tohono O'odham name for the area, *au'auho*, meaning red paint, referring to the pigment obtained from the ore-rich rock found around Ajo. Above, an ore train travels the Tucson, Cornelia & Gila Bend Railroad, which links Ajo with Gila Bend. Below, the train station, built in 1916, sits adjacent to the town's plaza. (Above, AHS PC134v; below, AHS PC134cl.)

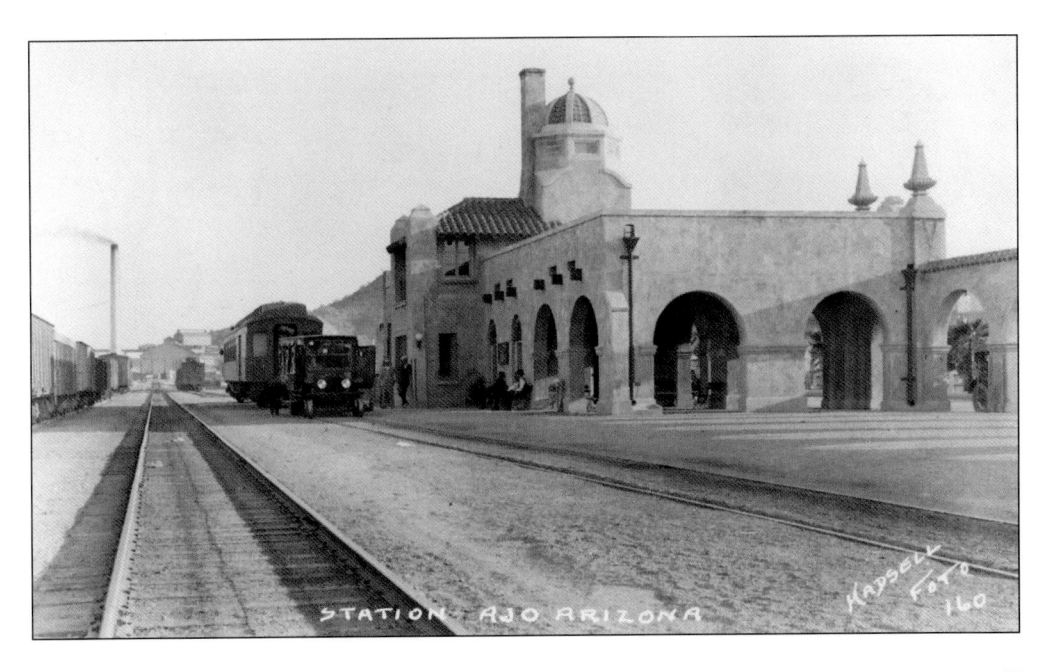

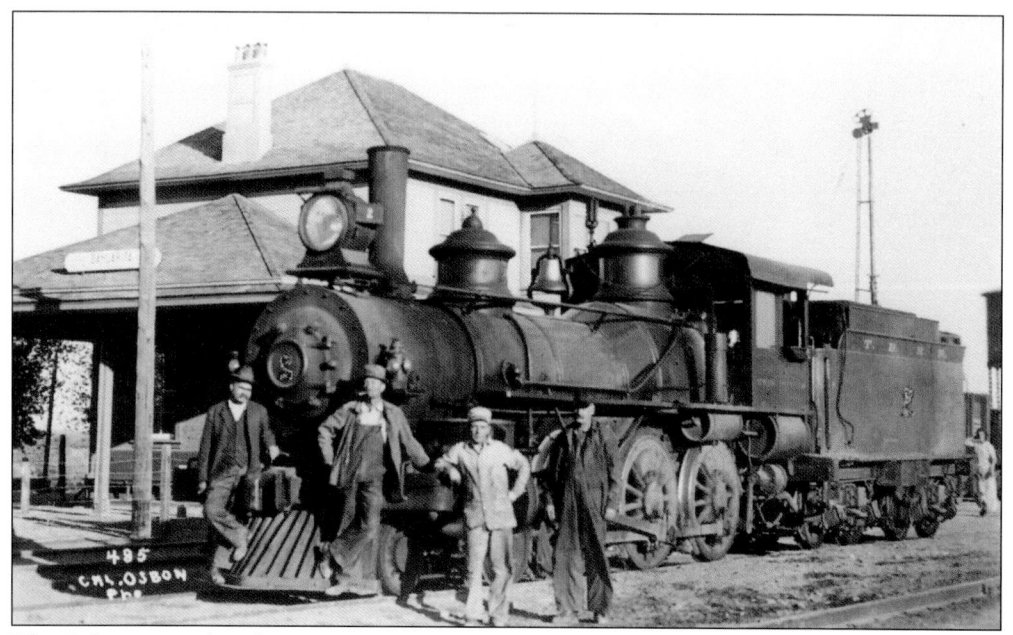

The Sahuarita railroad station was part of the Southern Pacific Railway that ran through Pima County. The area was first developed in the late 1870s as the Sahuarita Ranch and was originally owned by one-time Pima County sheriff James Kilroy Brown. Prior to the arrival of the railroad, the ranch area was used as a stage stop between Tucson, Arivaca, and Quijotoa. (AHS PC98_6866.)

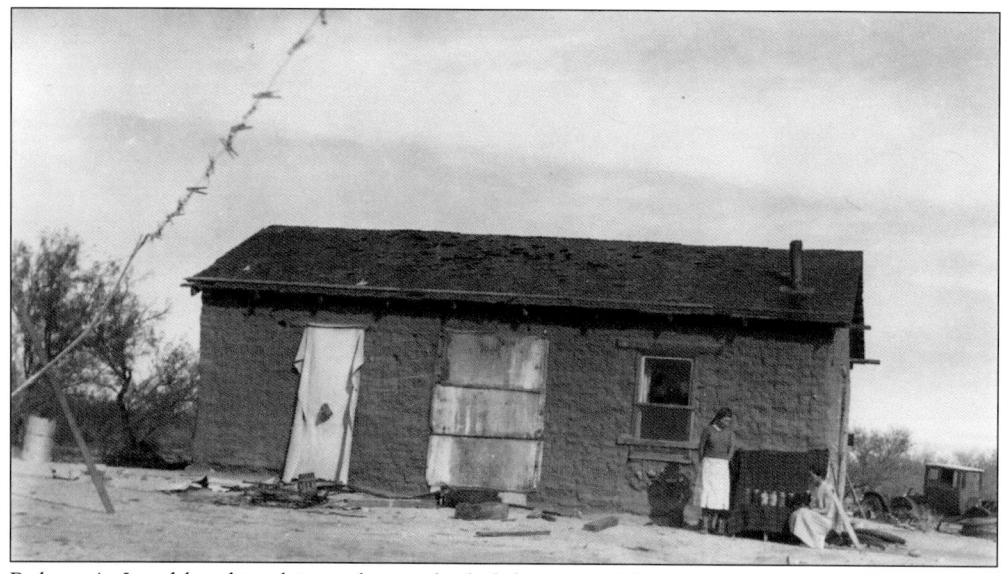

Robert A. Land lived in this modest makeshift home in Sahuarita with his wife, Fannie, and three children, Robert, Elbert, and Mable. Born in Texas, Land had moved to New Mexico before arriving in Arizona, where he worked as a truck driver. In 1934, Fannie won second place in the Arizona State Canning Contest. Her hard work is proudly displayed in the lower right corner of the photograph. (UA Photograph Files.)

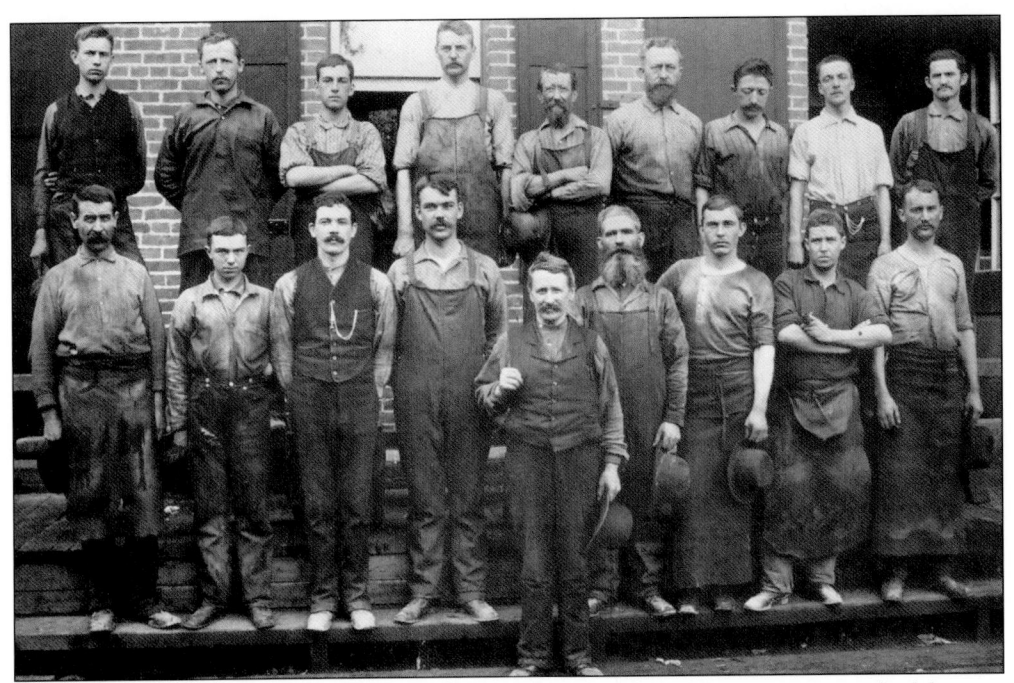

The arrival of the Southern Pacific Railroad in Tucson was met with excitement and celebration on March 20, 1880. The local paper reported that thousands of citizens assembled to watch as the first iron horse arrived and a "grand soiree" was held at Park Hall to celebrate. Making shipment of both people and goods relatively easy for the first time, the railroad permanently changed the lives of those living in Pima County. Pictured above, the mechanics for the Southern Pacific Railroad Shops were photographed in Tucson in 1889. Below, the Western Ways Features Company took this snapshot of the Southern Pacific Depot in the mid-20th century. (Above, AHS BN39443; below, AHS MS1255f.135.)

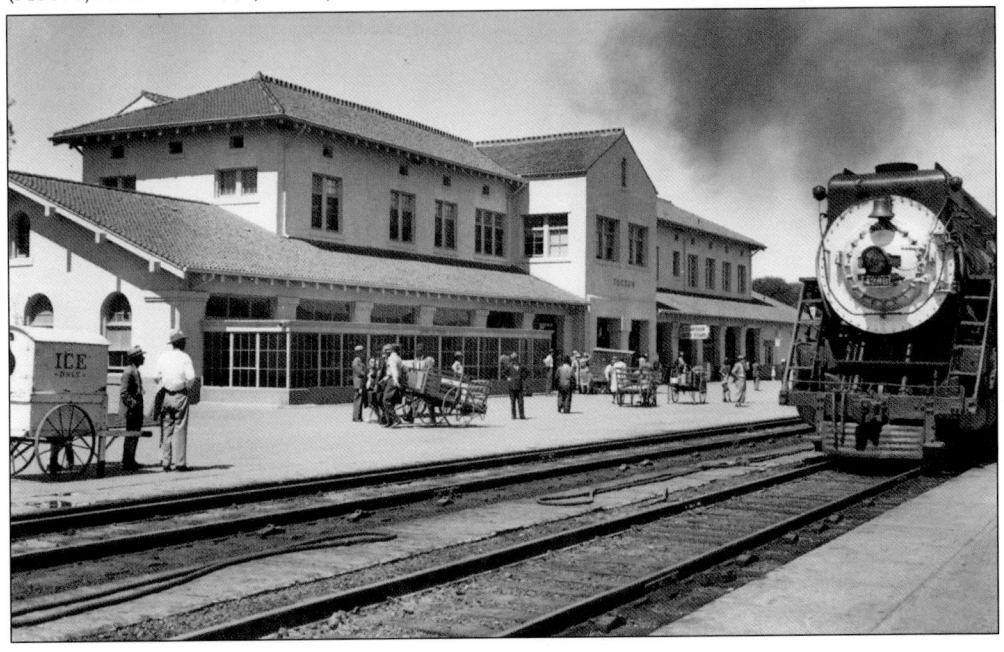

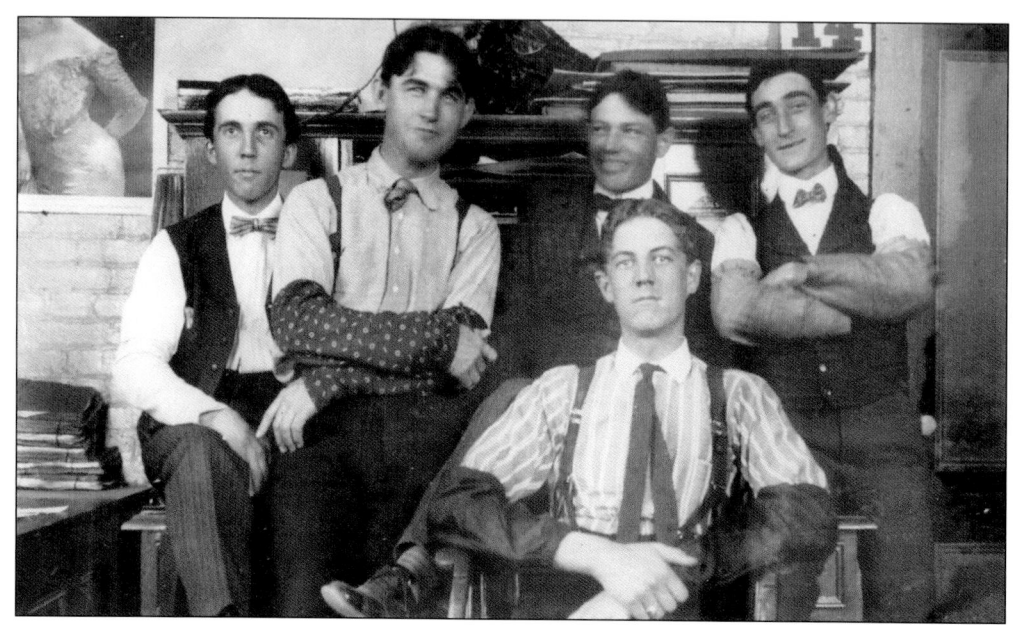

As Pima County's population grew, jobs outside mining, ranching, and farming became more readily available. One of the largest employers from the 1880s to the 1950s was the Southern Pacific Railroad. Above, five Southern Pacific Company Store employees take a break from work around 1904. Below, the staff of the Washington Meat Market on North Sixth Avenue in Tucson poses for a photograph around 1912. The market was owned by J.B. Simpson and advertised itself as a wholesale and retail butcher. Front right stands Francisco "Frank" Fimbres, a driver for the market. (Above, AHS 62328; below, AHS 64329.)

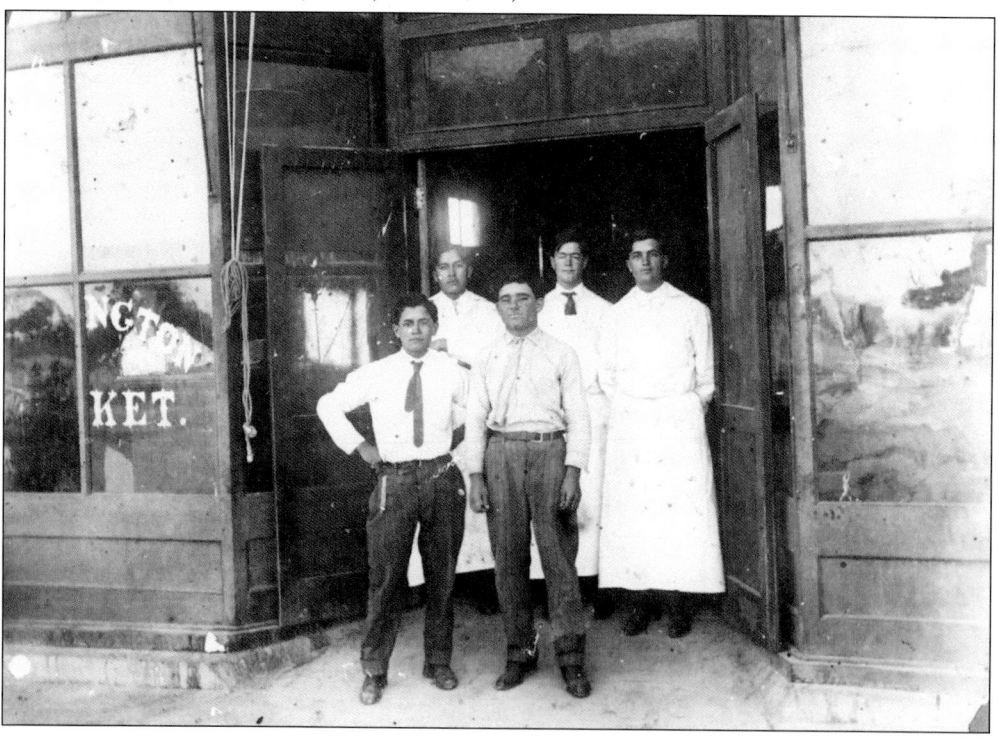

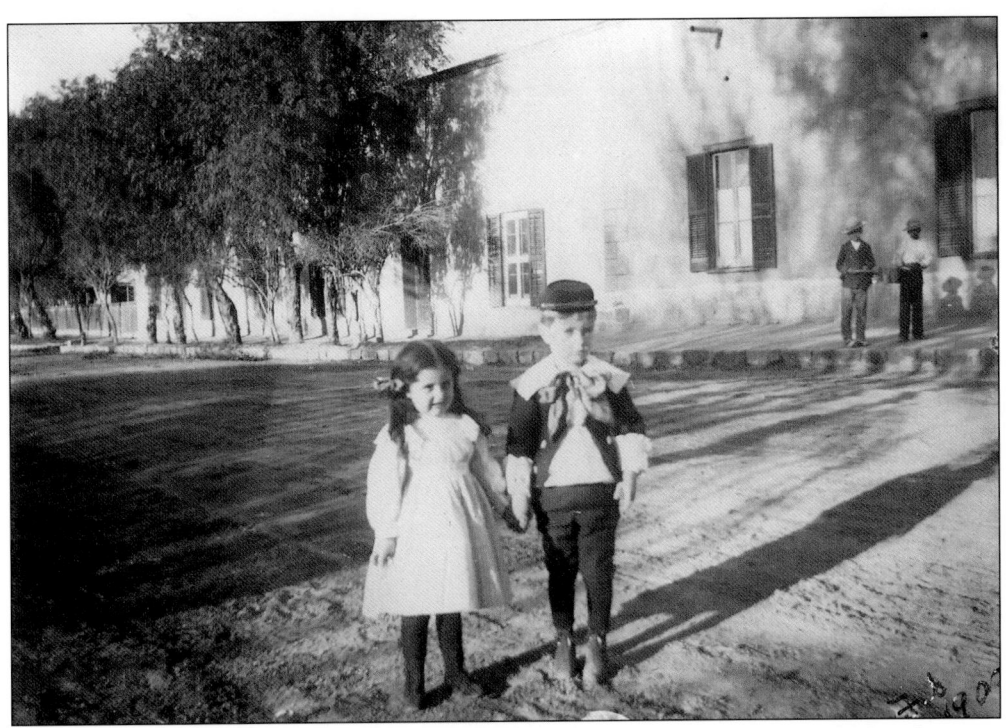

Lola Estberg and Henry Bennett take a moment from play to pose for a picture on Main Street in Tucson in February 1900. Behind them stands the house of Edward Nye Fish. Today, this portion of Main Street is preserved as part of the Tucson Museum of Art Historic Block. Lola went on to marry and settle on the East Coast. Henry fought in World War I and lived in Prescott, Arizona. (AHS PC 111 95648.)

Clara Fish snapped this photograph of her father, Edward Nye Fish, as he was preparing for bed in the summer of 1900. Dressed in a nightgown and cap, Fish's summer bedroom was in the backyard of his adobe home on Main Street in Tucson. Prior to the arrival of air-conditioning, the extreme summer heat led many in Pima County to sleep outside in search of cool air. Today, the Fish home is preserved as part of the Tucson Museum of Art Historic Block. (AHS PC111.)

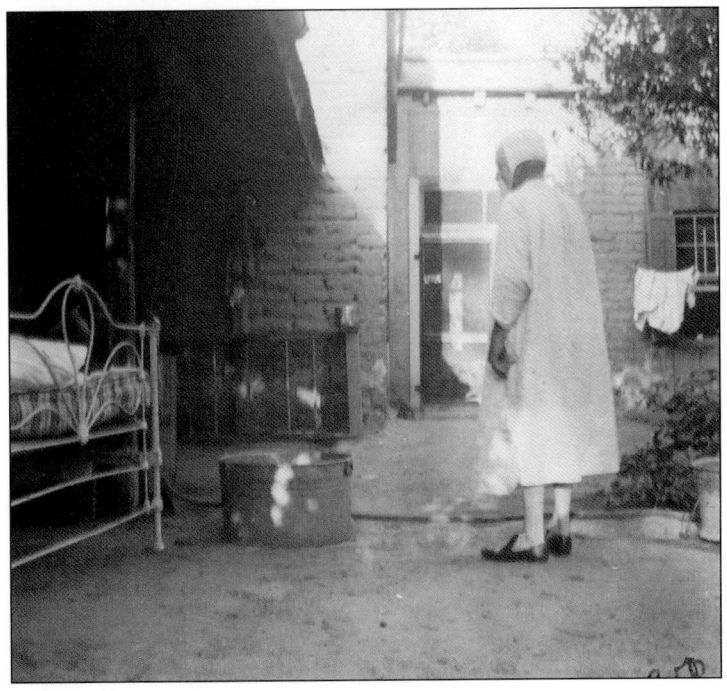

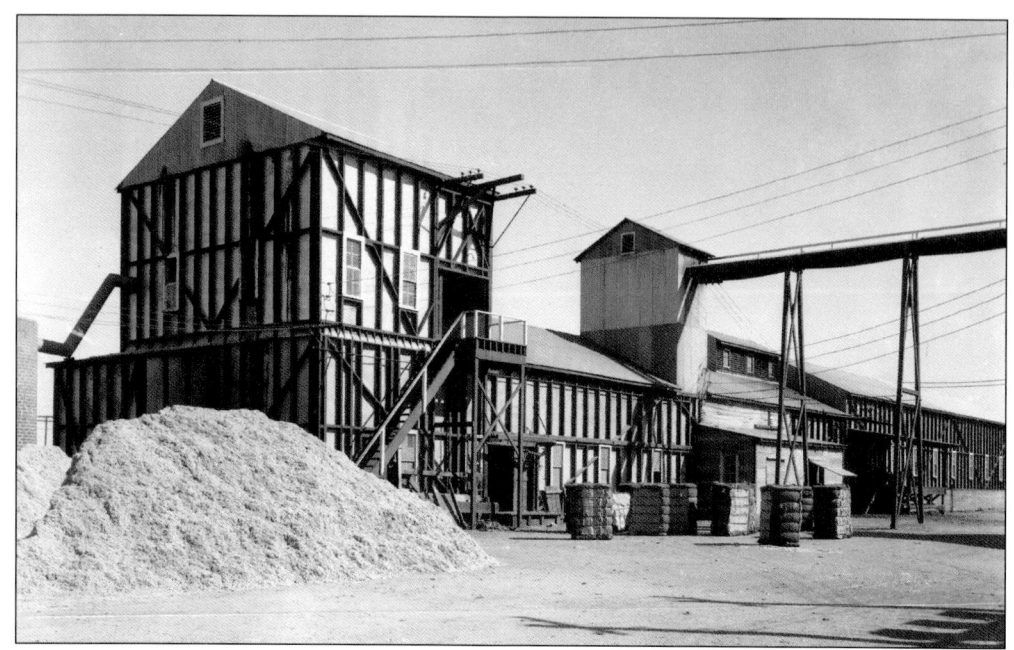

Cotton, one of the "Five Cs" of Arizona (climate, citrus, cattle, and copper are the others), has been grown in Pima County for decades. Above, a 1928 picture of a cotton gin in Marana calls back to a time when cotton was a major part of Pima County's economy. At one point, Pima County farmers grew as much as 50,000 acres of cotton. Much of the cotton was produced in the northwestern part of the county, in and around Marana. Below, a 1979 photograph taken in a cotton field in Marana shows the advancing technology used for agriculture in the county. (Above, AHS 10514; below, AHS 61620.)

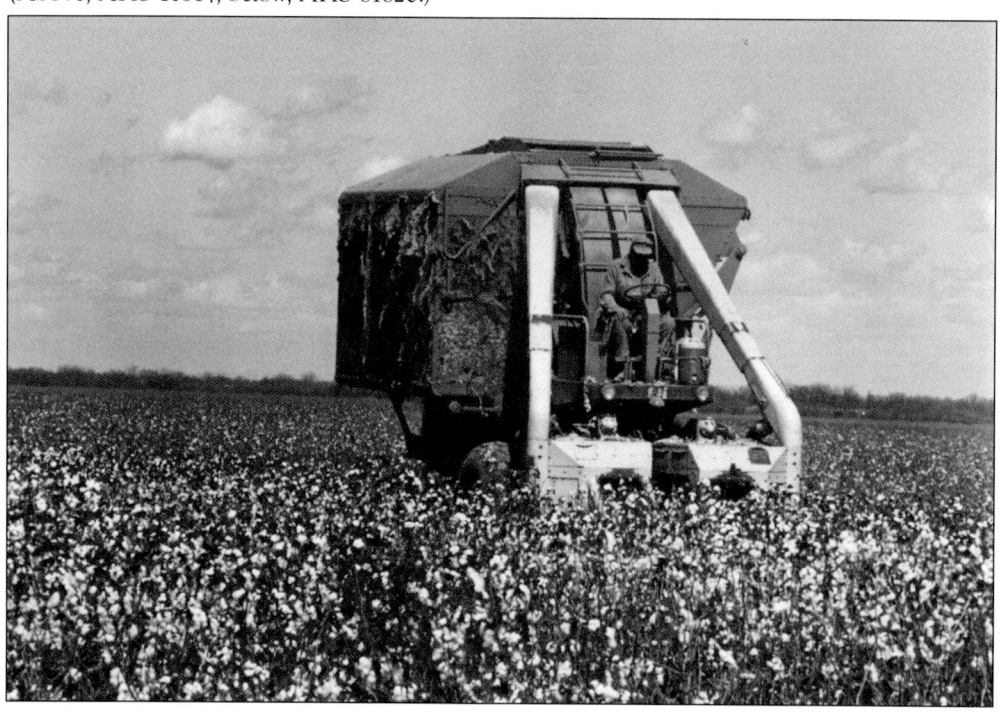

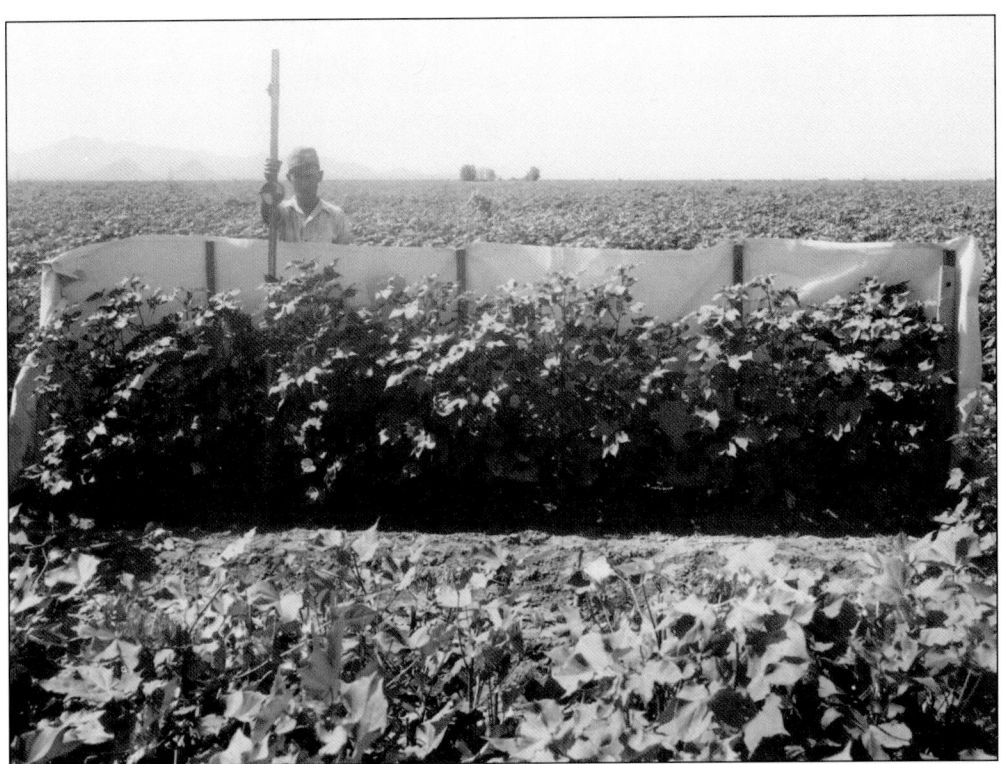

A farmer stands next to cotton plants in Cortaro, Arizona, with a ruler, measuring the height of the crop. Cortaro, located northwest of Tucson, got its name from the Spanish word *cortar* (meaning "to cut") because of the large amounts of mesquite and ironwood that came from the area for firewood. Starting in the 1920s, portions of Cortaro, Rillito, and Marana were owned by the Pima Farms Company and supported alfalfa, cotton, cattle, and poultry. (AHS BN205878.)

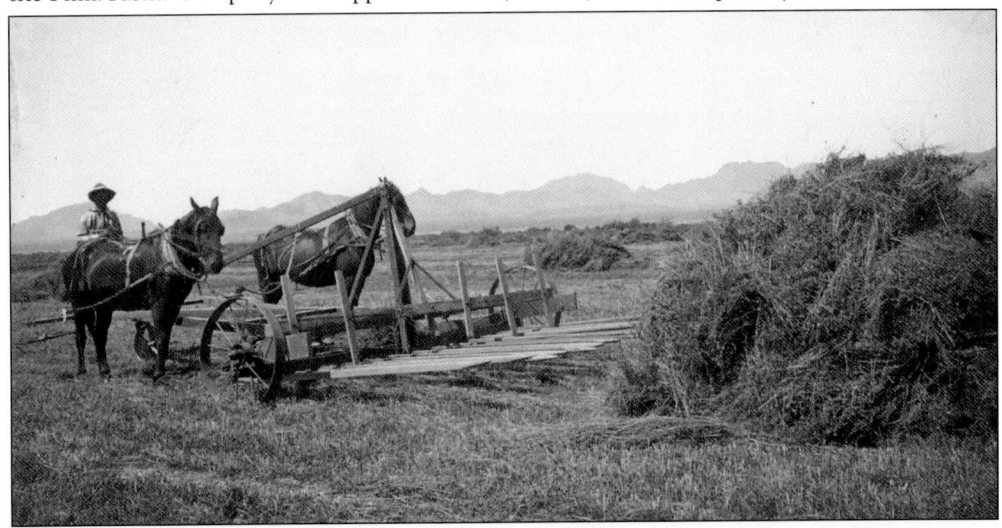

Agriculture was at the heart of the growth of Flowing Wells, an area northwest of Tucson. This photograph, taken around 1895, shows the harvesting of hay at Flowing Wells Ranch, owned by the Allison family. Warren Allison was a Tucson merchant who developed the farming area so that he could provide his customers with fresher grains and fruit. (AHS 43864.)

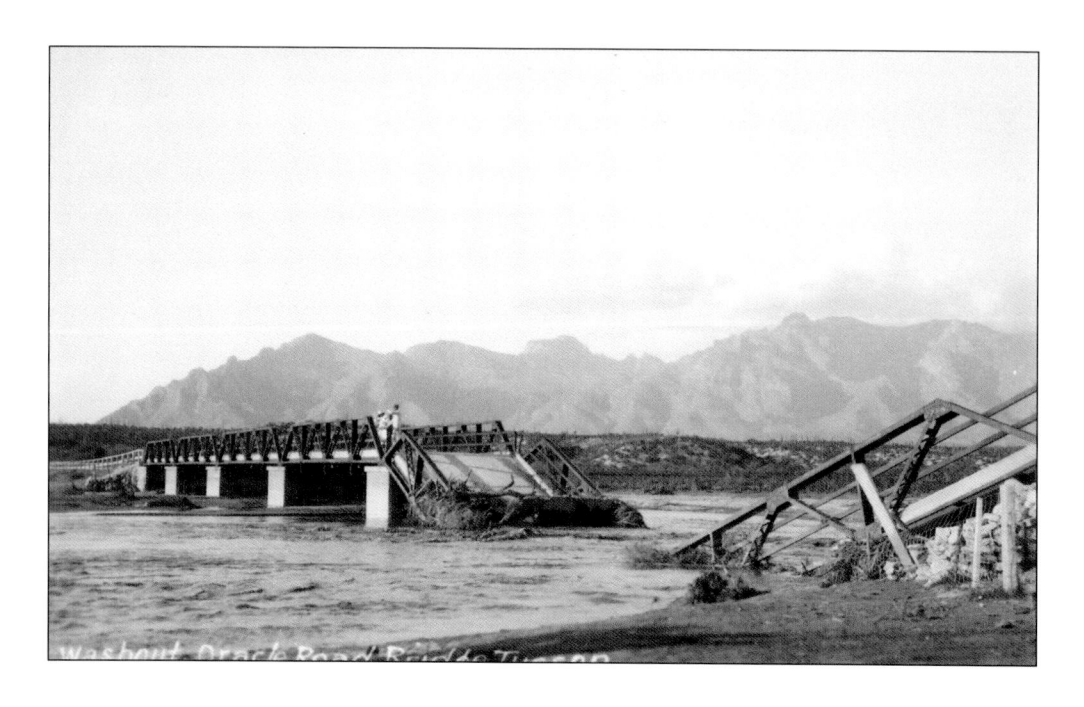

Although Pima County is often hot with its rivers dry, heavy rains occasionally cause flooding. The view above, looking north toward the Santa Catalina Mountains, shows extensive damage to the Oracle Road Bridge caused by Rillito River floodwaters. Below, a woman is pulled across the flooded Rillito River on an aerial rope-way in order to return to Tucson from Mount Lemmon. Stranded motorists had to temporarily abandon their cars and belongings on the north side of the river in order to safely cross the raging waters. Both photographs may depict the flood of 1915. The two-lane bridge was replaced by four lanes in 1970. (Above, AHS BN203267; below, AHS PC180f.262a.)

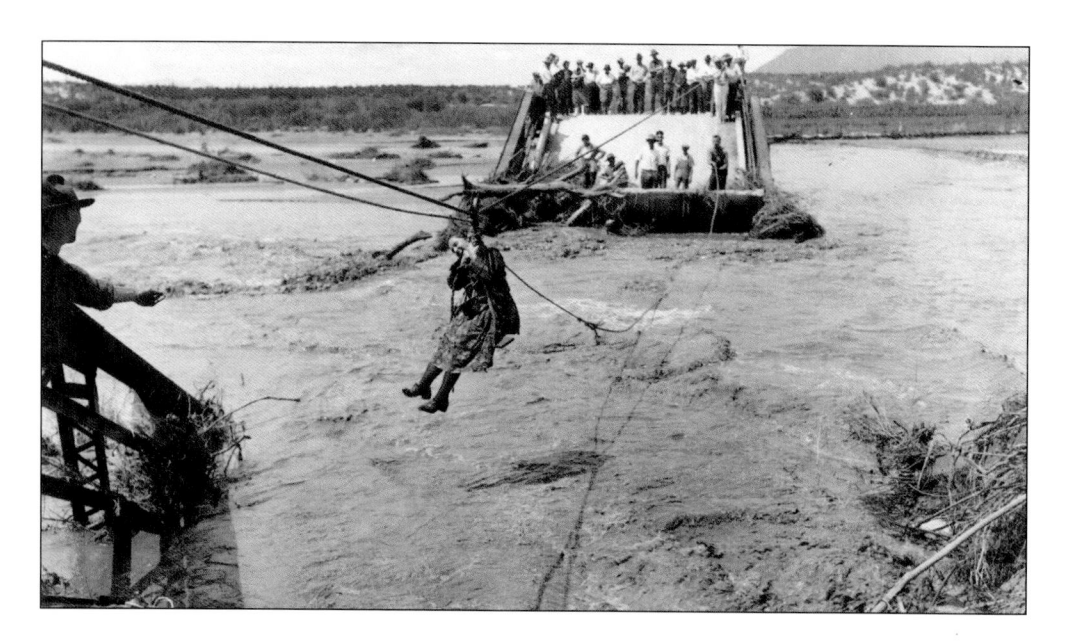

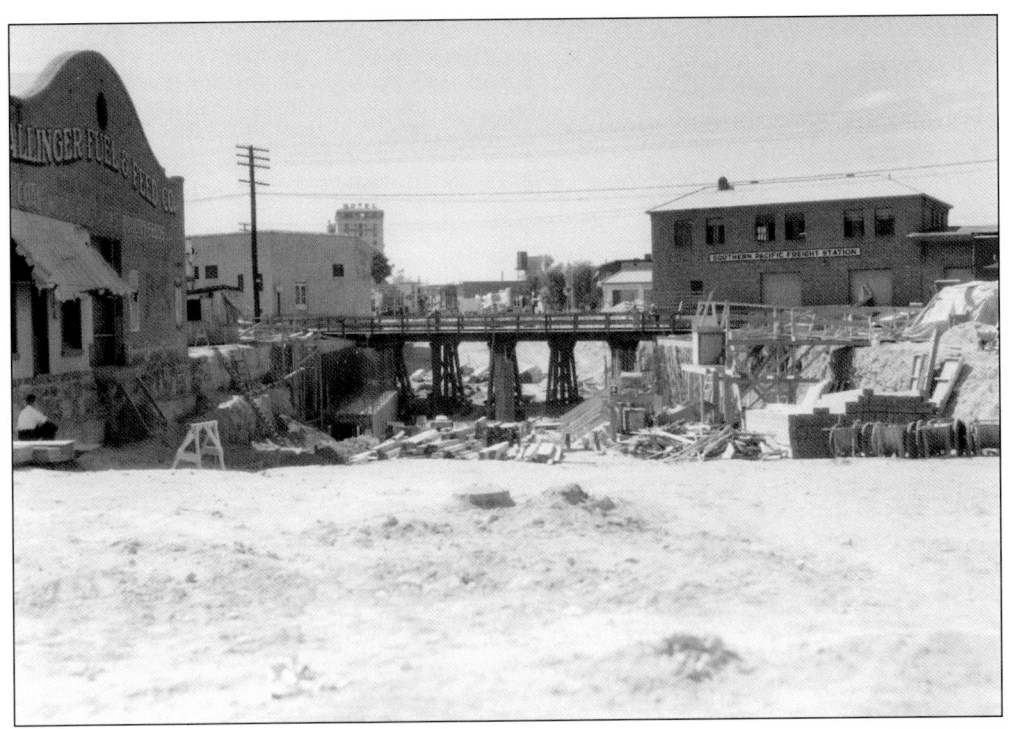

In 1934, about 10,000 cars used Stone Avenue in Tucson every 24 hours, many of them delayed by passing trains. To alleviate the problem, the "ultra-modern vehicular and pedestrian subway," pictured above, was completed the following year thanks to funding from a federal grant procured by Monte Mansfield. Those in town quickly found that the new subway flooded easily, and on October 5, 1945, photographer Jack Scheaffer snapped a photograph of one unlucky driver caught in the water, pictured at right. A water gauge was installed in 1971 to help prevent motorists from entering the underpass when flooded, a simple tool that is still in use today. (Above, AHS PC180,1875; right, UA MS435.)

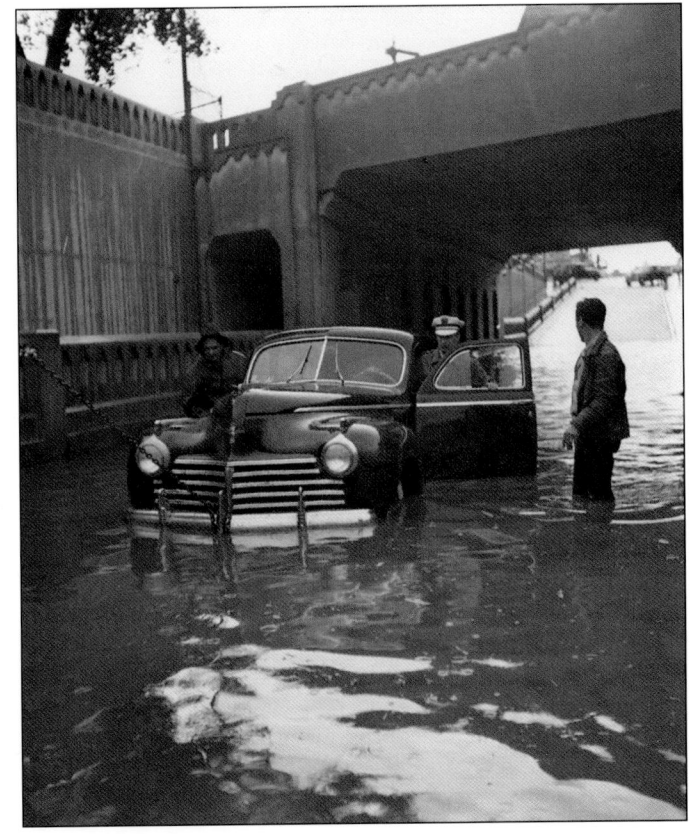

The last of the Mule Trolley Tucson 6/06

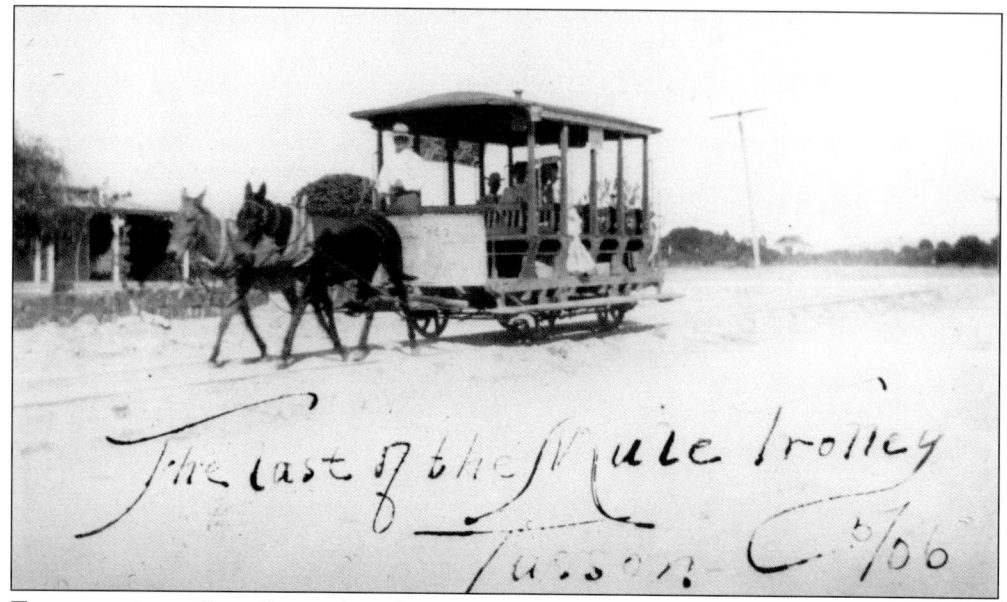

Transportation in Pima County has changed significantly throughout its history. In 1906, it was announced that the mule trolley system that had been servicing the streets of Tucson for almost 20 years would be ending. Knowing that a moment in Tucson's transportation history was coming to a close, Gauis Upham grabbed his camera and took the above picture of the trolley at work. On June 1, 1906, a crowd gathered to celebrate the initial run of the city's new mode of public transit—the electric streetcar. Below, a wagon fords the Santa Cruz River near Tucson about 1910. (Above, AHS PC142B1f3; below, AHS PC85_61742.)

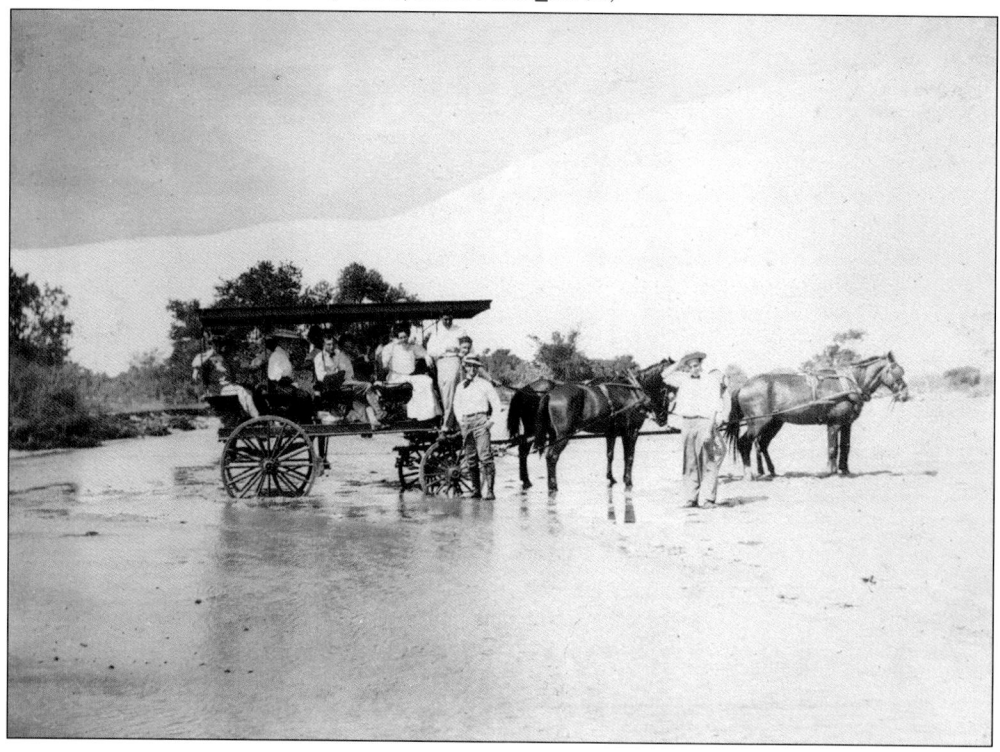

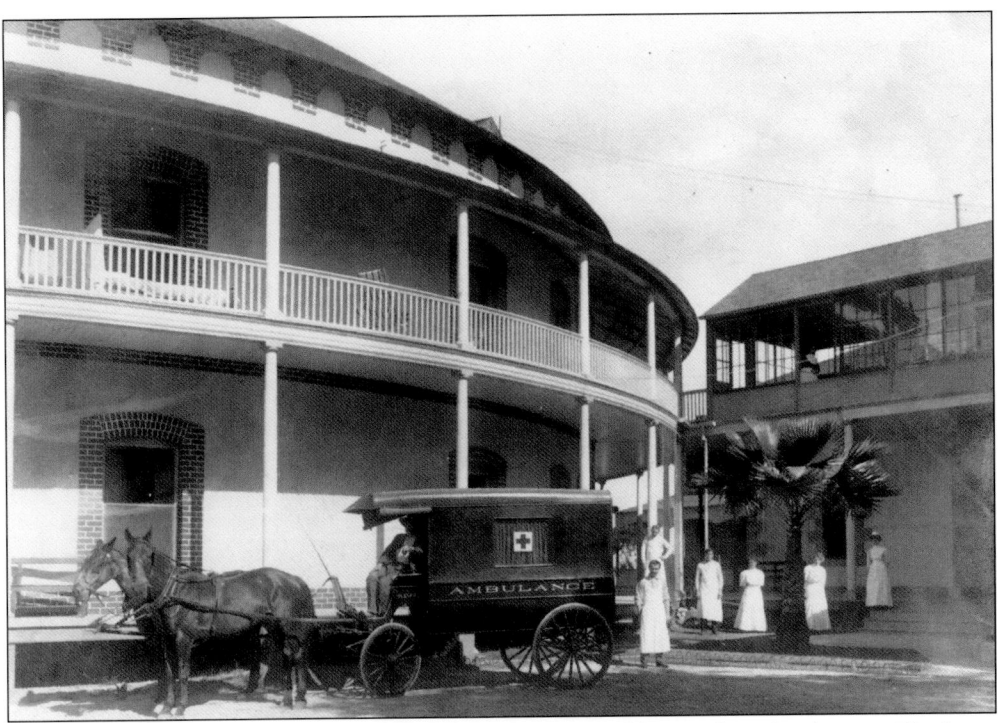

Founded in 1880, St. Mary's Hospital was the first general hospital in the Arizona Territory. Originally a two-room adobe structure, the hospital grew quickly in size and added additional buildings. The hospital's sanatorium was built in 1900 and is shown here with a horse-driven ambulance and members of the hospital staff. The sanatorium's round shape was intended to provide a maximum amount of sunlight and fresh air for tuberculosis patients. (AHS 62510.)

Children from underprivileged homes or suffering from tuberculosis spent summers at the Pima County Preventorium in the Catalina foothills near Oracle. Under the supervision of Supt. Kitty McKay and a staff of about 22, the Preventorium oversaw approximately 130 children. The children's amount of rest, food intake, and recreation were closely monitored. This photograph, taken in June 1940, shows one of the dormitories where the children slept. (AHS 7929.)

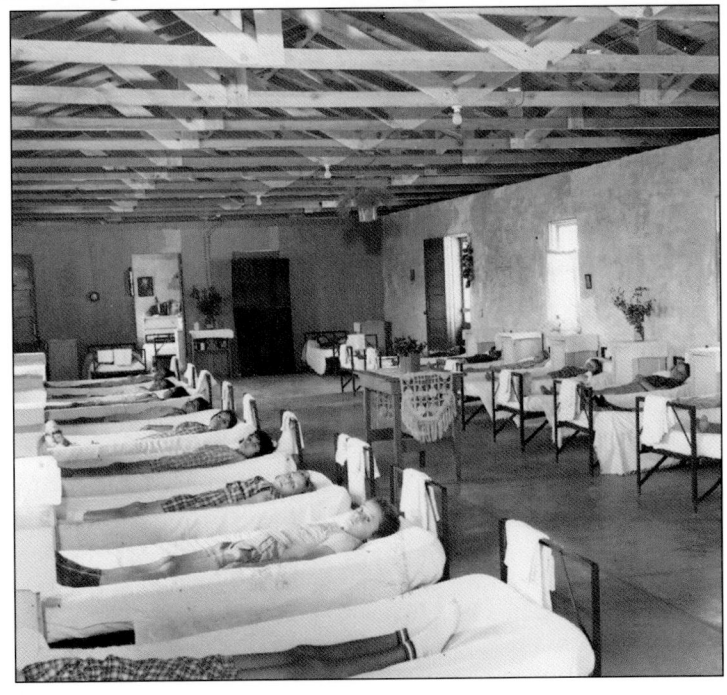

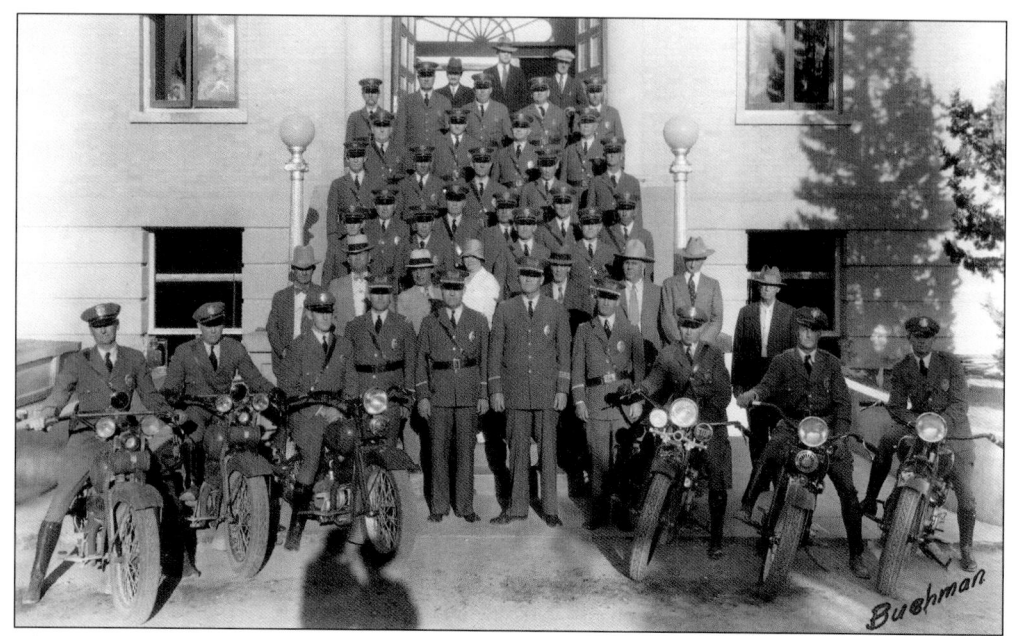

The 1930s saw a complete reorganization of the Tucson police force. During the decade, new regulations went into effect that restricted smoking, drinking, and loafing while on duty and required policemen to learn all city laws and locations of city buildings. Along with the new rules came new uniforms, shown here in a picture taken at 109 North Meyer Street. (AHS 10465.)

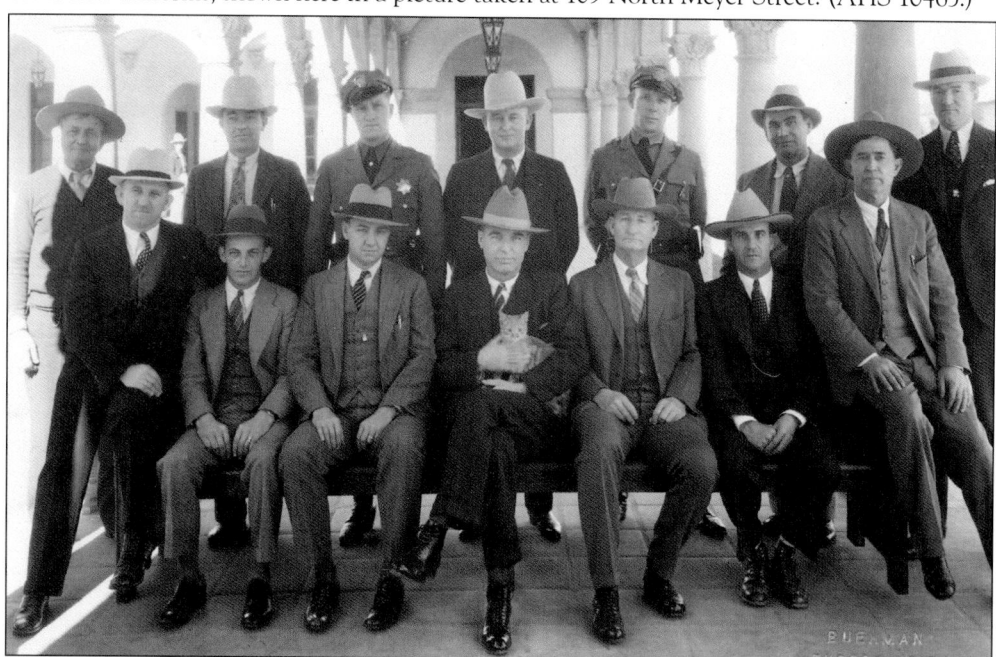

The 1931 Pima County Sheriff's Force poses for a picture at the Pima County Courthouse building in Tucson. Pima County sheriff Walter W. Bailey sits in the middle of the first row holding a cat named Pretty. Bailey, a native of Florence, Arizona, ran for sheriff several times and held the position off and on in the 1920s and early 1930s. He later worked at the federal prison camp in the Santa Catalina Mountains, known today as the Gordon Hirabayashi Recreation Site. (AHS 10472.)

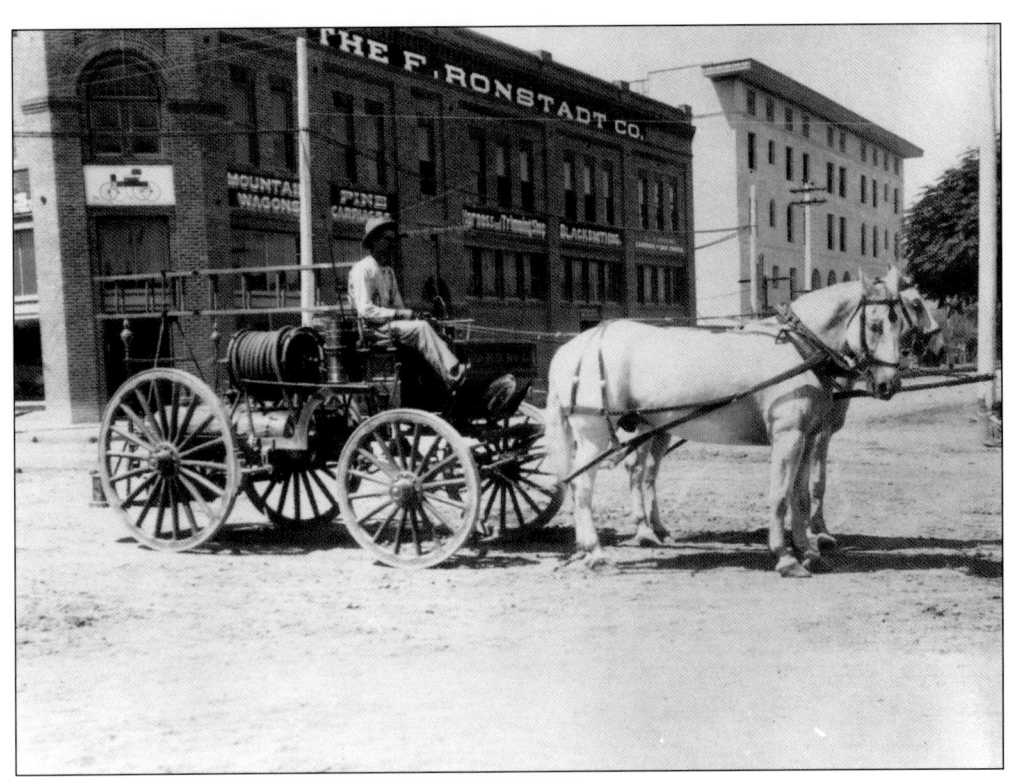

When the Tucson Fire Department was founded in 1881, a total of 20 unpaid volunteers used an inventory of six axes, six picks, two chemical extinguishers, and twenty-two rubber buckets to fight fires. The department relied heavily on horses for transportation, as seen above, until the steam engine replaced horsepower in 1908. It was not until 1913 that the Tucson Fire Department used a mechanical fire truck in its efforts to keep Tucsonans safe. In the right photograph, taken long after the early modest years, firefighters train in one of the many exercises that hone their skills. (Above, AHS BN205197; right, AHS 72574.)

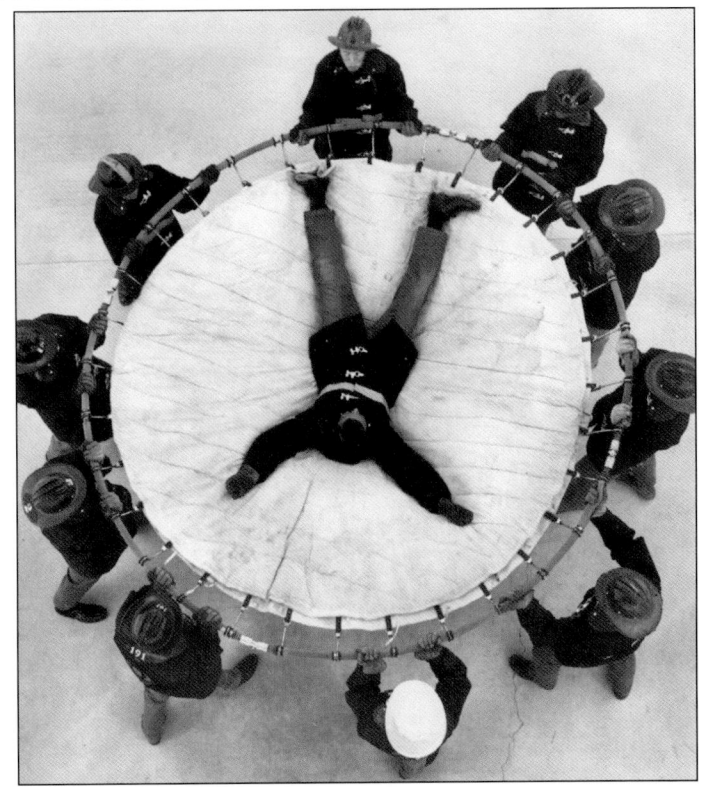

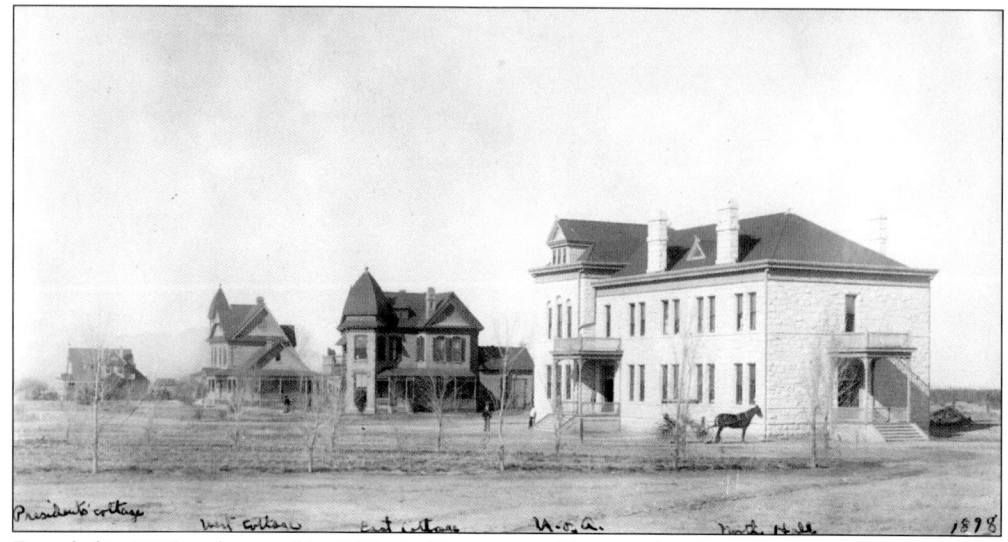

Founded in 1885 and opened in 1891, the University of Arizona has been a significant part of Pima County's growth and history. With only six individuals in the school's inaugural freshman class, it now serves almost 40,000 students. Above, Clara Fish Roberts captured this early photograph of the University of Arizona in 1898. Roberts was the University of Arizona's first student, having signed the enrollment book in 1891 when she was only 14 years old. Pictured are, from left to right, President's Cottage, West Cottage, East Cottage, and North Hall. Below, students enjoy the landscape of the university. Covering 387 acres, the university claims to be the oldest continually maintained green space in Arizona. (Above, AHS PC111 95616; below, AHS MS1255f.524c.)

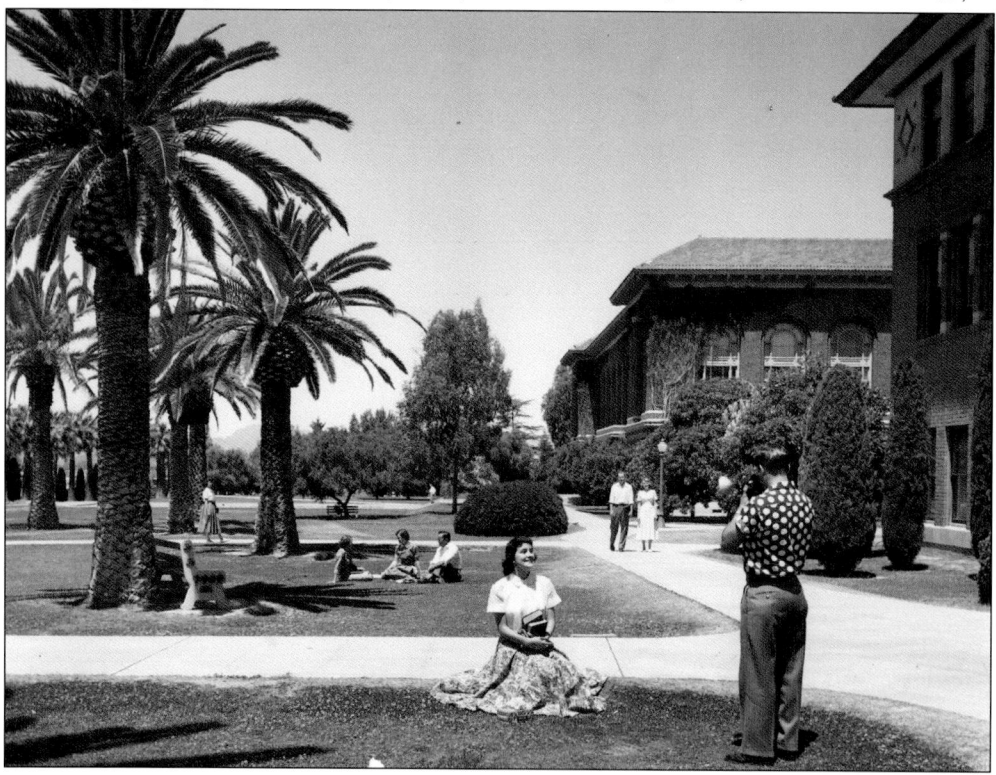

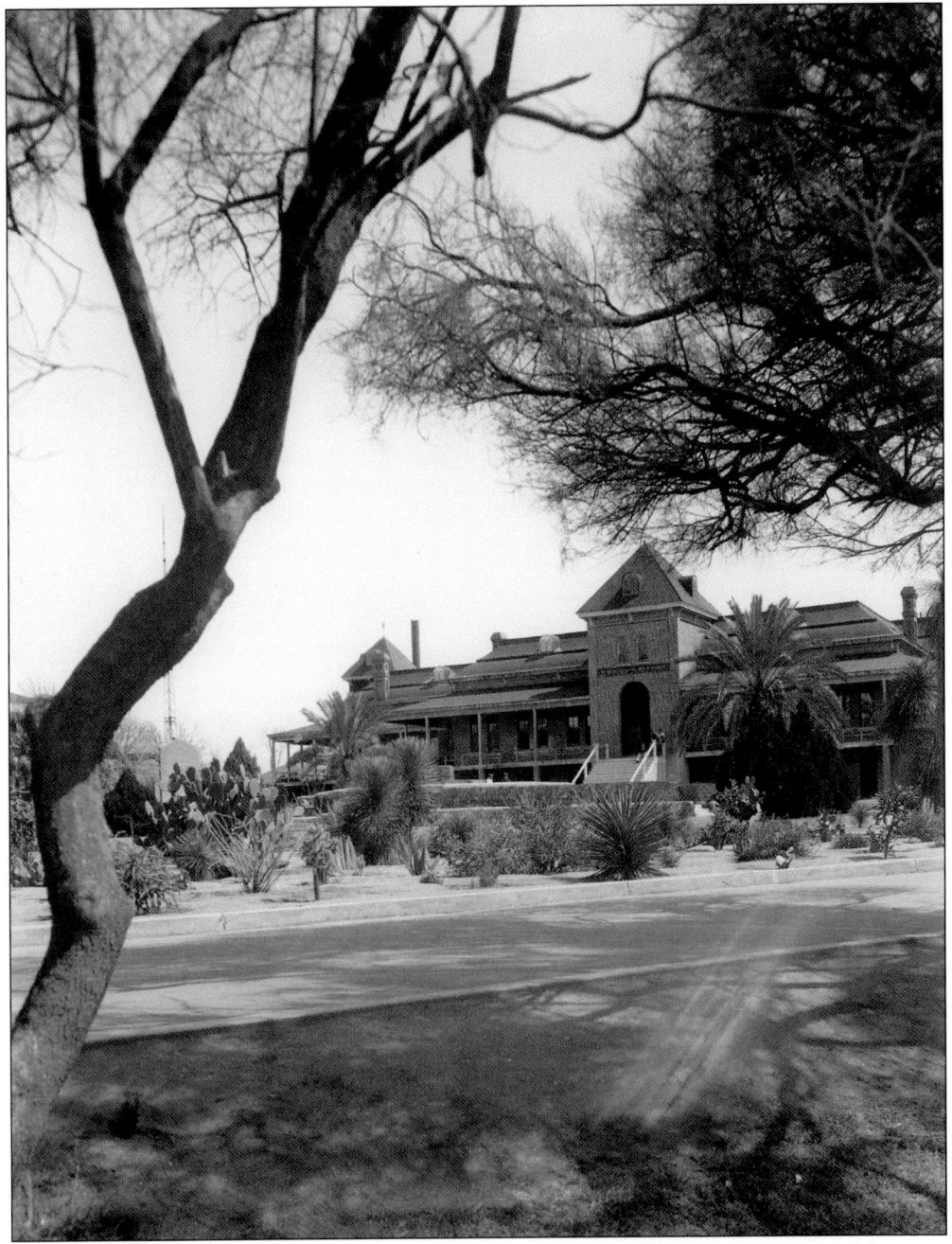

Constructed in 1891, Old Main was the first building constructed for the University of Arizona. When the university started classes the same year, the building housed classrooms, laboratories, a mess hall, and even temporary sleeping quarters. The building continues as a historic landmark and is used for administrative purposes to this day. (AHS BN26531.)

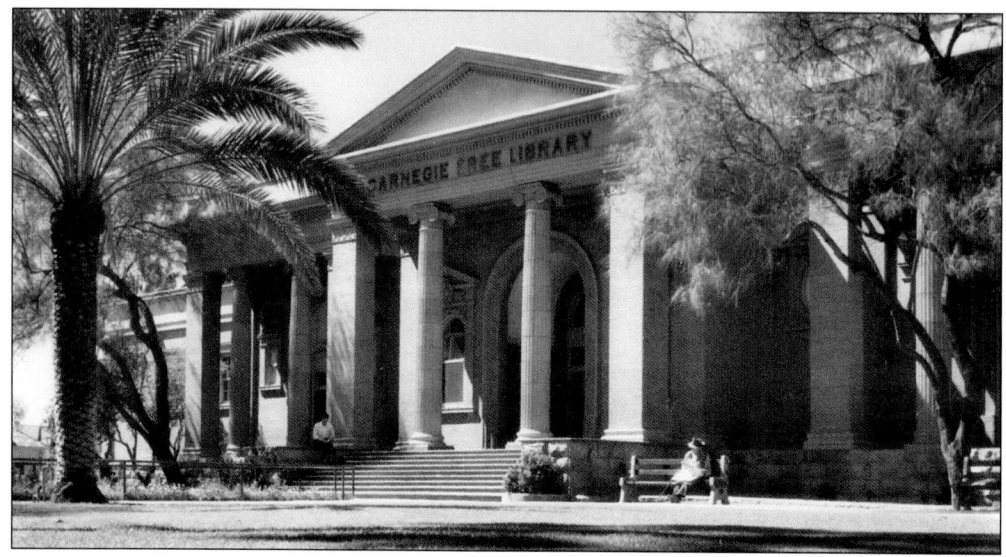

Tucson's Carnegie Library on South Sixth Avenue opened its doors in 1901 with a modest collection of 450 books. Made possible with a $25,000 grant, it was one of over 1,500 libraries funded by the steel baron Andrew Carnegie. For the first 23 years of the library's existence, patrons under the age of 16 were not allowed inside. In 1990, a new library was built, and the Carnegie Library closed its doors. Today, the building houses the Tucson Children's Museum and welcomes all ages. (AHS MS1255f135q.)

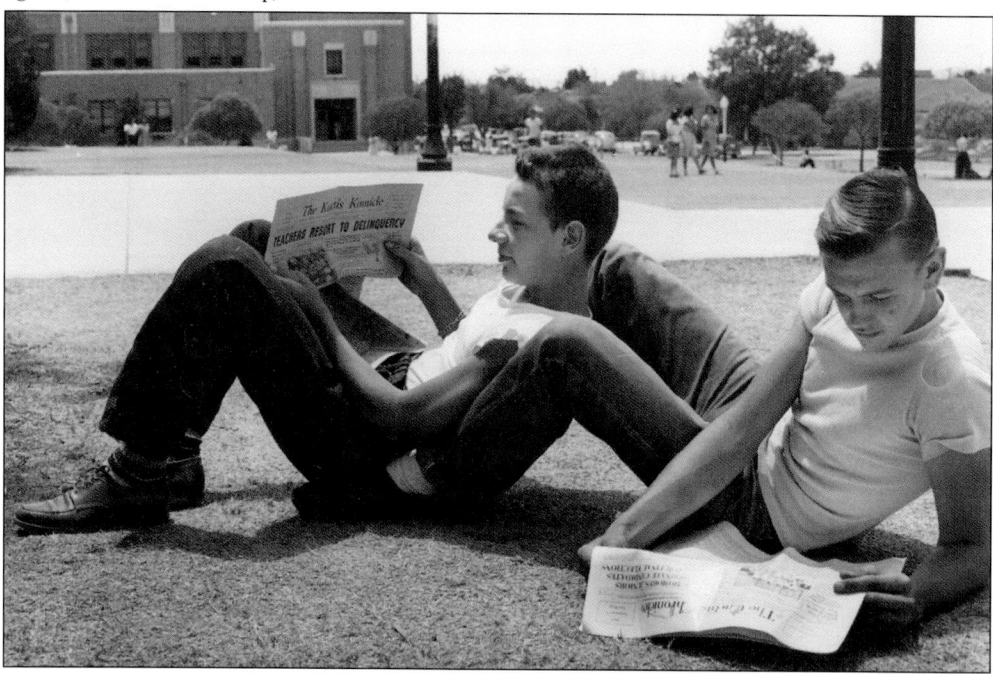

Established in 1906, Tucson High School had already been a part of the community for half a century when the Western Ways Feature Service took this photograph in the 1950s. Pictured here, two students read different versions of their school's paper. One reads the *Cactus Chronicle*, while the other reads a spoof on the original, the *Kactis Komicle*. The day's headline of the comical spoof is "Teachers Resort to Delinquency." (AHS PC151 56396.)

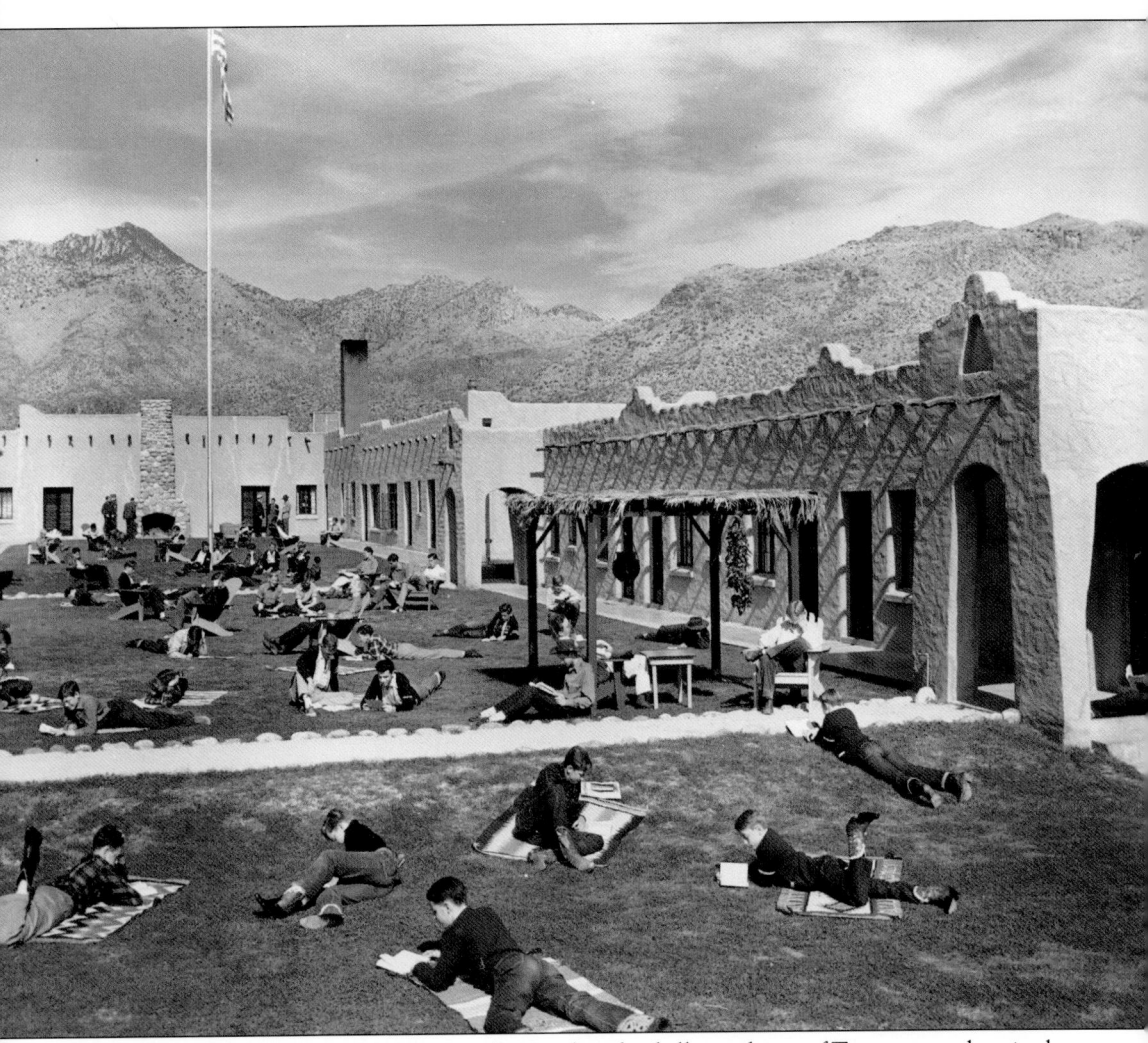

The Southern Arizona School for Boys in the Catalina foothills northeast of Tucson was advertised as a place where boys could "grow strong and robust through outdoor life in the glorious sunshine and pure, dry air of the great Southwest." While preparing educationally for college, the boys also participated in outdoor activities such as horseback riding, polo, tennis, and volleyball. The school ran until 1974, when the Fenster School acquired it. Pictured here, the students are given time to read outside the school's walls. (AHS MS1255f.522c.)

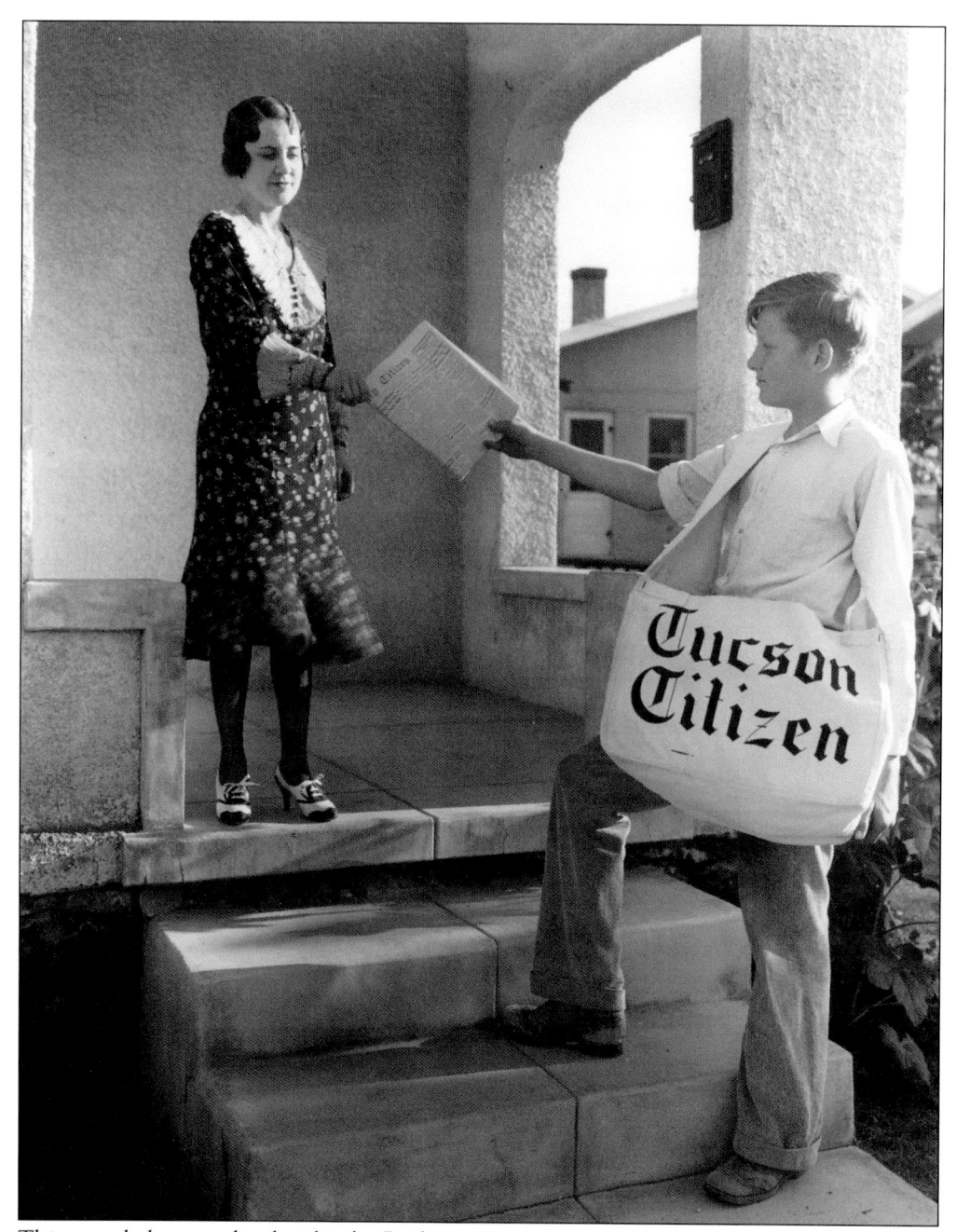

This staged photograph taken by the Buehman Studios in the 1930s shows a common sight in Pima County for generations, the delivery of the *Tucson Citizen*. The first issue of the *Citizen* was published on October 15, 1870, and the paper ran continuously until a difficult economy, declining circulation, and lower advertisement sales caused the state's longest running paper to close in 2009. (AHS BN20584.)

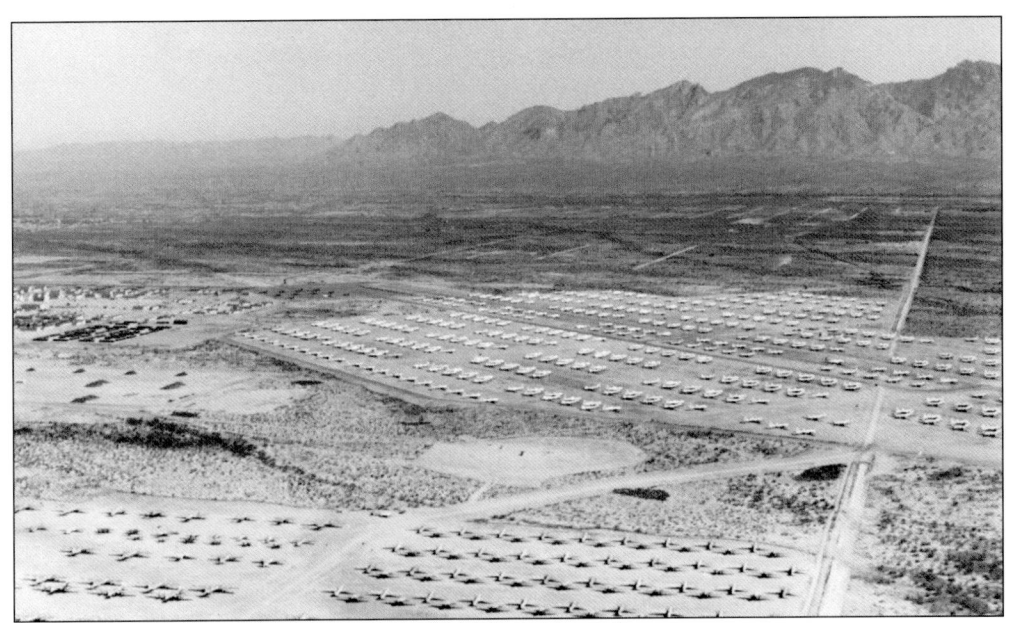

Davis-Monthan Air Force Base in Tucson is named in honor of two Air Force officers who lost their lives in airplane crashes, Lt. Samuel H. Davis and Lt. Oscar Monthan. The above image shows the facility adjacent to Davis-Monthan, the Aerospace Maintenance and Regeneration Center (AMARC), which is frequently referred to as the "boneyard." Storing thousands of planes, the facility provides long-term storage for military aircraft. Many of the planes are put through the "cocooning process." They are covered in plastic sheeting to help preserve and protect aircraft from the elements. Below, a B-29 airplane at Davis-Monthan Air Force Base is "de-cocooned." (Above, AHS 52298; below, AHS PC151_56328.)

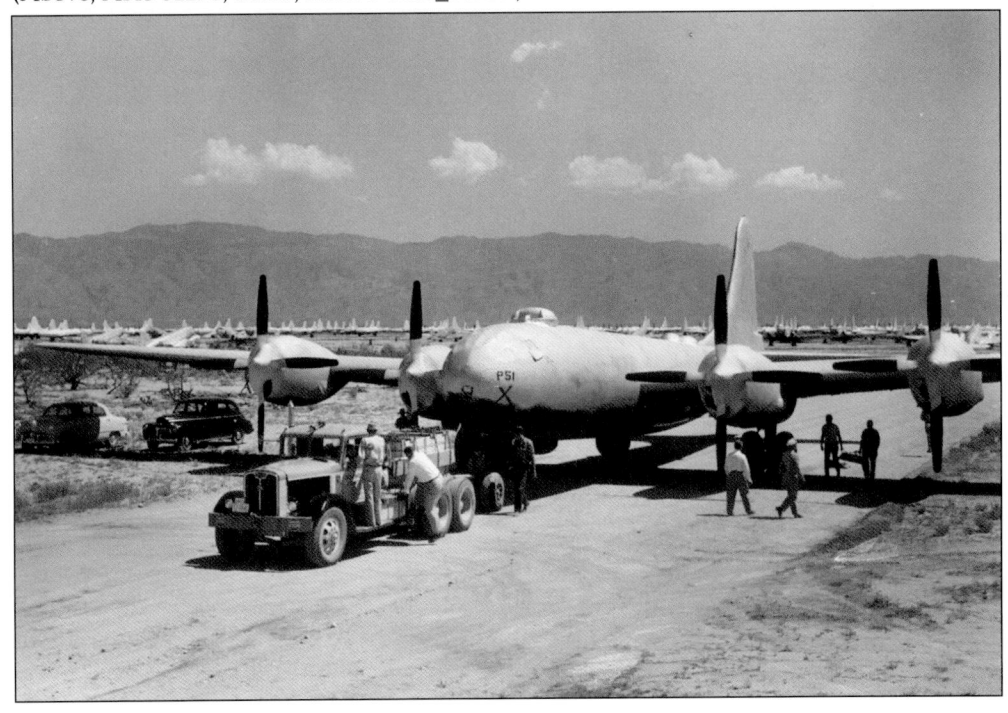

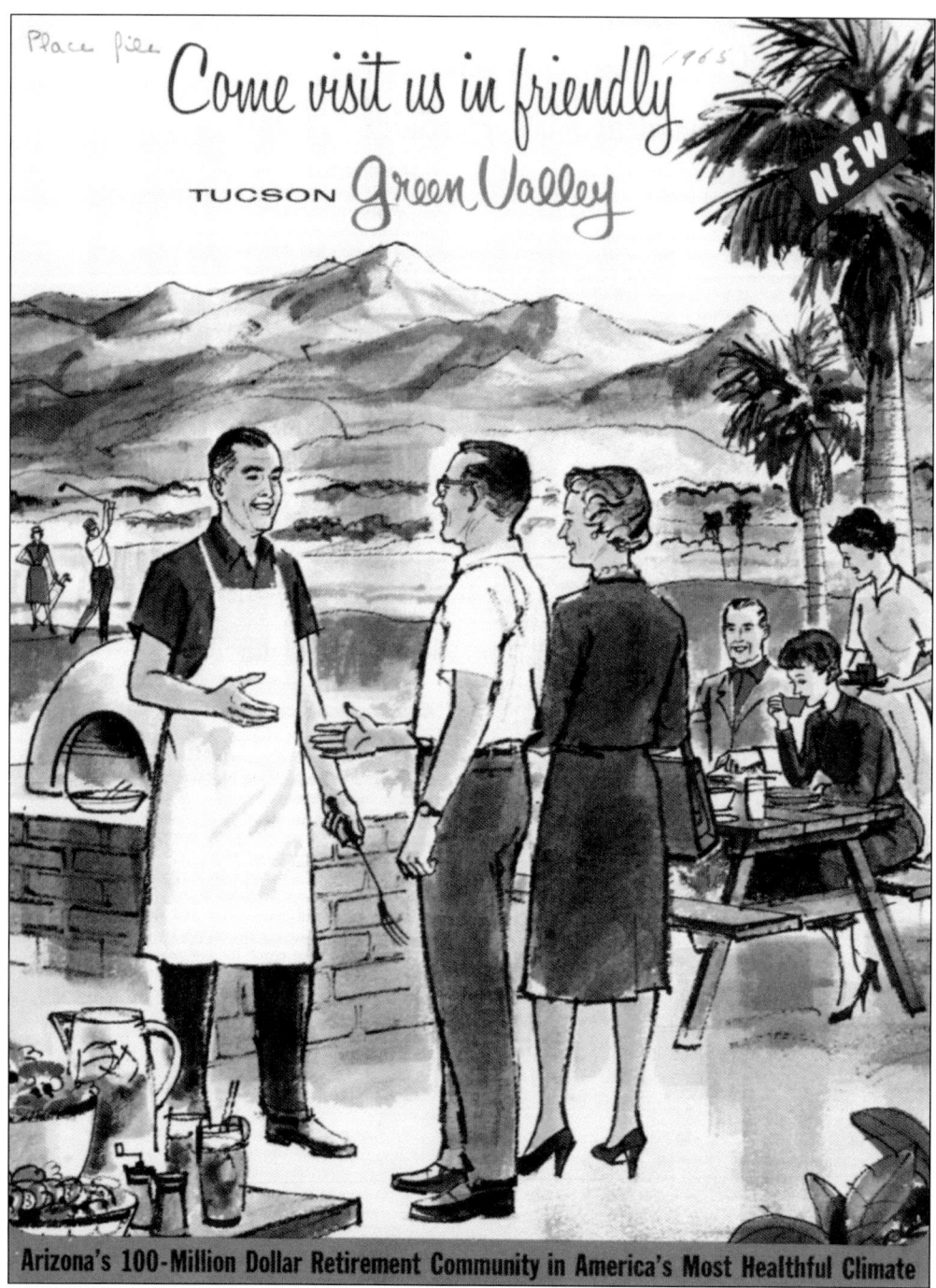

The cover of this 1965 brochure hoped to attract thousands to the newly developed retirement community of Green Valley. Showing a barbecue and an invitation to "come visit us in friendly Green Valley," the brochure was meant to be a welcoming advertisement for those seeking a new location for retirement. In January 1964, the first 107 people had moved to the area. Within 25 years, the community grew to a population of 16,500, composed almost entirely of individuals over the age of 55. (AHS Ephemera.)

Four

ATTRACTIONS AND TOURISM

The soaring mountain ranges that punctuate the vast desert landscapes of the Greater Southwest are sometimes referred to as "sky islands" due to their stark changes in elevation and environment. An irresistible attraction for visitors and residents of Pima County for centuries, both the Santa Rita Mountains (at nearly 9,500 feet) and the Santa Catalina Mountains (over 9,000 feet) form a spectacular backdrop to the Santa Cruz Valley and are home to a remarkable diversity for animals, birds, and plant life. Sabino Canyon is a ruggedly beautiful place to hike, and in winter, snow covers Mount Lemmon, the southernmost ski area in the United States. In the summer, these mountains are a cool respite from the heat of the desert floor below.

One of the earliest draws for visitors to the Southwest was its climate with its abundant warmth and blue skies. The "Tucson Sunshine Climate Club," established in 1922, promoted the area for these very qualities and sparked new accommodations, like the El Conquistador Hotel, guest ranches, and small inns marketed to tourists. This was truly the guest ranch capital of the world in the 1930s, with over 115 dude ranches welcoming guests to experience "cowboy life" and the romance of the Old West.

Today, visitors can find health spas, golf resorts, dude ranches, hotels, movie studios, birding and hiking areas, astronomical observatories like Kitt Peak, museums, ghost towns, historic sites like San Xavier Mission and Fort Lowell, Colossal Cave Mountain Park, the Titan Missile Museum, Pima Air and Space Museum, Agua Caliente Park, and the Arizona Sonora Desert Museum.

Living traditions from the region's diverse heritage provide an exceptional vitality to the region. Annual rodeos, music and food festivals, the county fair, Indian art fairs, art galleries and museums, and special observances like Dia de los Muertos on All Souls' Day, the Pascua Yaqui Easter ceremonies, and Las Posadas at Christmas are all inspired by the county's cultures and traditions. A sense of history is retained through preserved landscapes, neighborhoods, buildings, and a host of specialty museums, all of which provide the visitor with an insight into the county's rich past and its future.

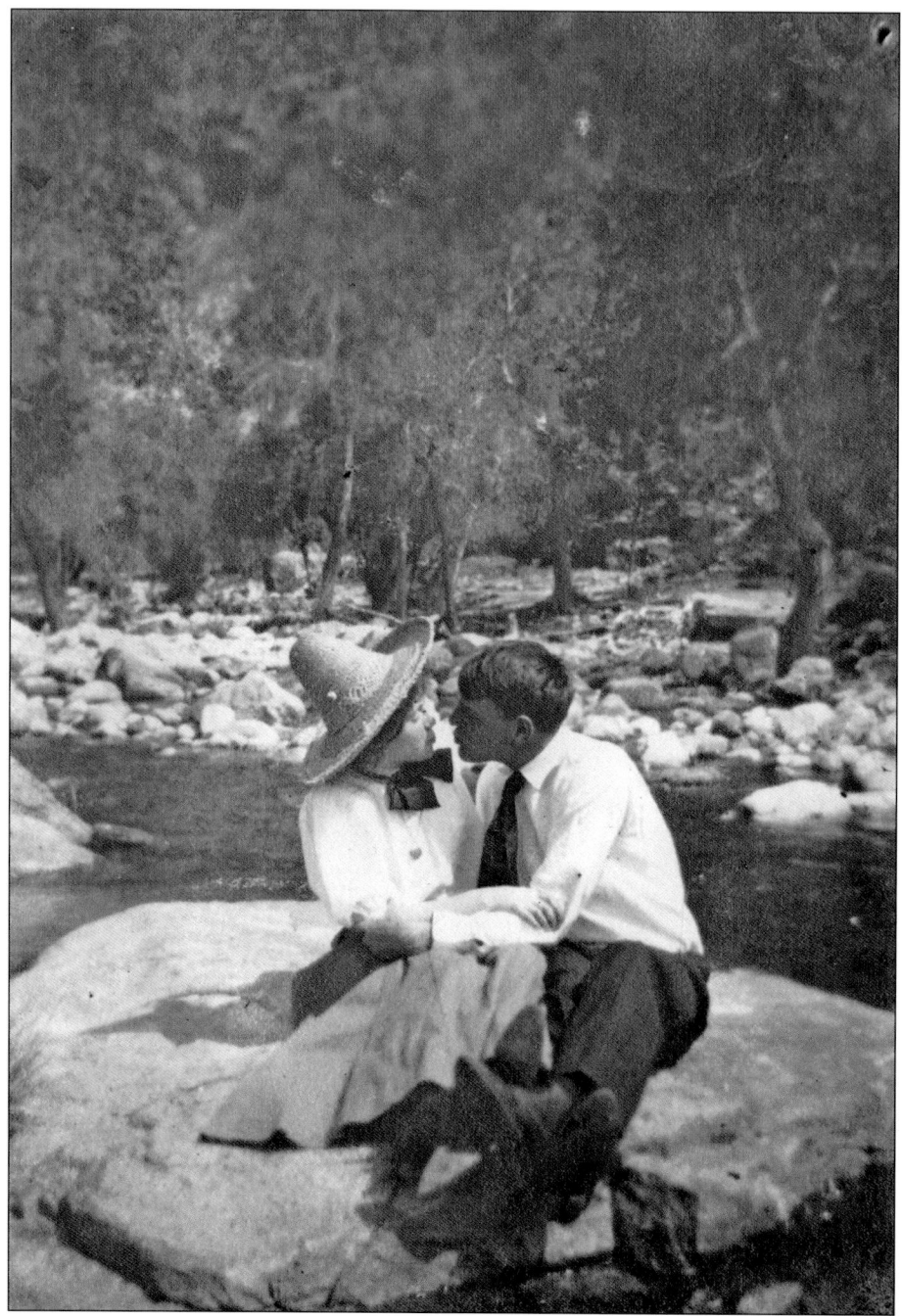

Pima County youths have visited Sabino Canyon for well over a century. Pictured here, Samuel B. Jones and a young woman kiss on a rock in Sabino Canyon around 1915. The young woman may have been Samuel's future wife, Gladys, whom he married around 1918. At the time of the photograph, Samuel was working as a bookkeeper at a general store in Tucson; he later moved to California to continue his work as an accountant. The couple spent the day at Sabino Canyon with Samuel's sister Mary Virginia Jones, who went on to work for Pima County government for over 20 years. (AHS PC86.)

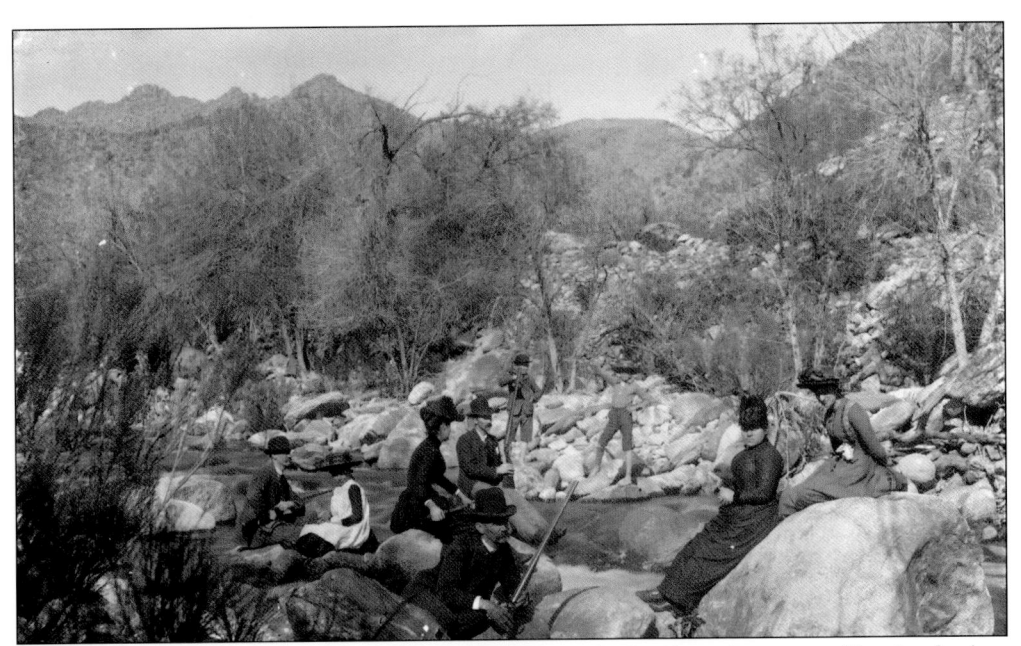

For decades, Sabino Canyon has been a popular spot for locals and tourists alike. In the late 19th and early 20th centuries, it was a common get-away spot for picnics, hiking, and relaxing, shown above around 1890. In 1902, Pres. Theodore Roosevelt declared Sabino Canyon part of a protected forest reserve. Thirty years later, the Civilian Conservation Corps and Works Progress Administration made the area more accessible by building bridges, picnic tables, and campgrounds. In 1981, the canyon was closed to private vehicles, and a shuttle bus was put into operation. Below, the Upham family photographed the saguaro-studded area just outside Sabino Canyon in February 1904. (Above, AHS B68670; below, AHS PC142 92916.)

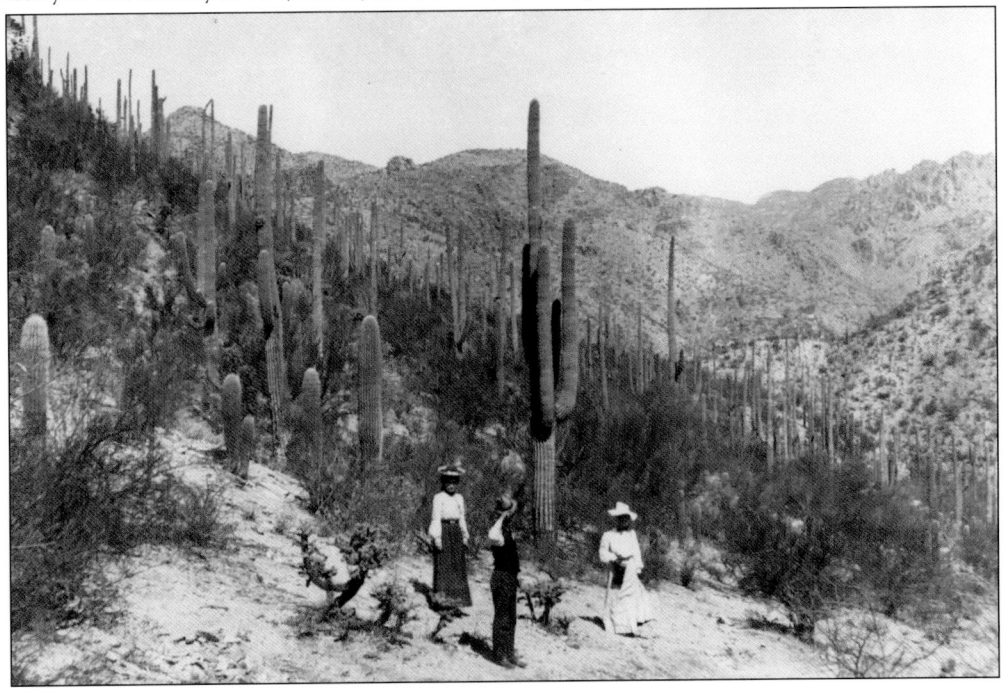

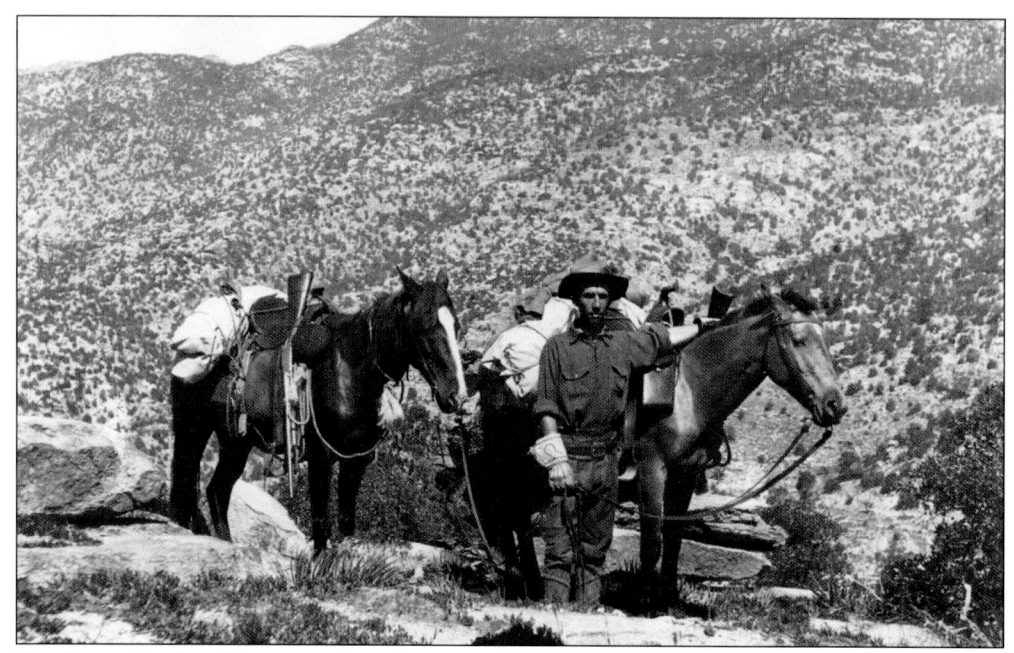

The Santa Catalina Mountains have been an area of exploration for mining, hunting, study, and amusement. Above, George Upham is pictured during a trip into the mountains on September 11, 1913. Two horses carry his extensive equipment as he returns down the mountain. Below, the Estill Cabin was used for lodging during trips into the Santa Catalinas. Richard Lusk (second from left) was a teacher for Pima County schools and was known to take trips with his studens into the mountains for the study of fauna and flora. Also pictured are Alice Estill (far left), Mr. Winters (middle), and Howard Estill (far right). The woman standing next to Howard Estill is unidentified. (Above, AHS PC142_92944; below, AHS PC27_446.)

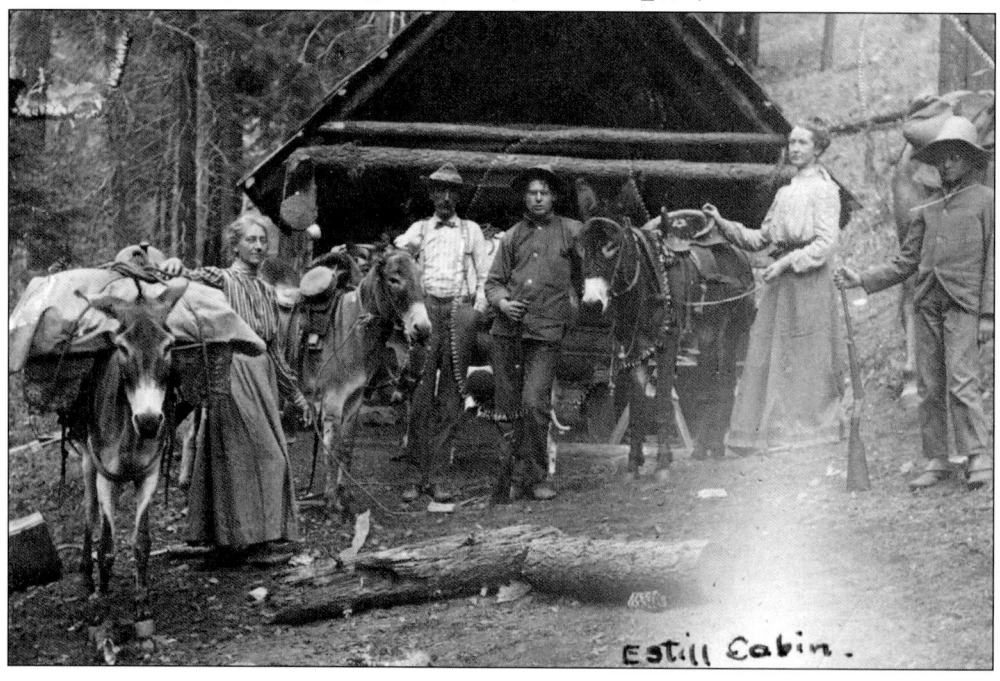

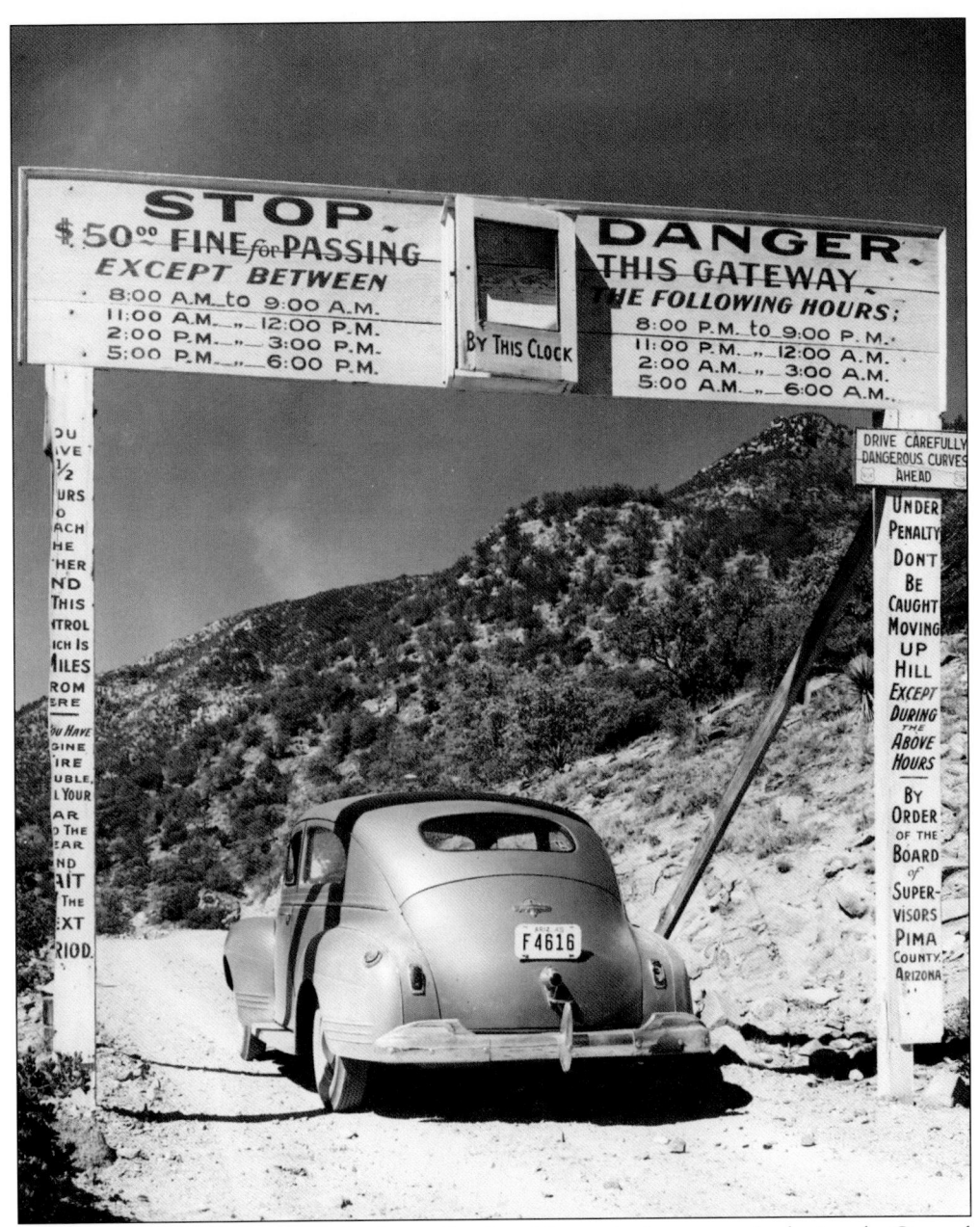

For many years, the only way up the Santa Catalina Mountains by car required using the Control Road. Part of the road had only one lane, so the road had to be "controlled" to keep cars from meeting head on while going both directions at the same time. To manage the flow of traffic, a sign and clock determined the times that drivers could go up or down the road. Pictured here in 1945, the entrance stated that cars could go uphill at eight different times of the day. Driving at any other time meant one risked a $50 fine. (AHS MS1255f.452v.)

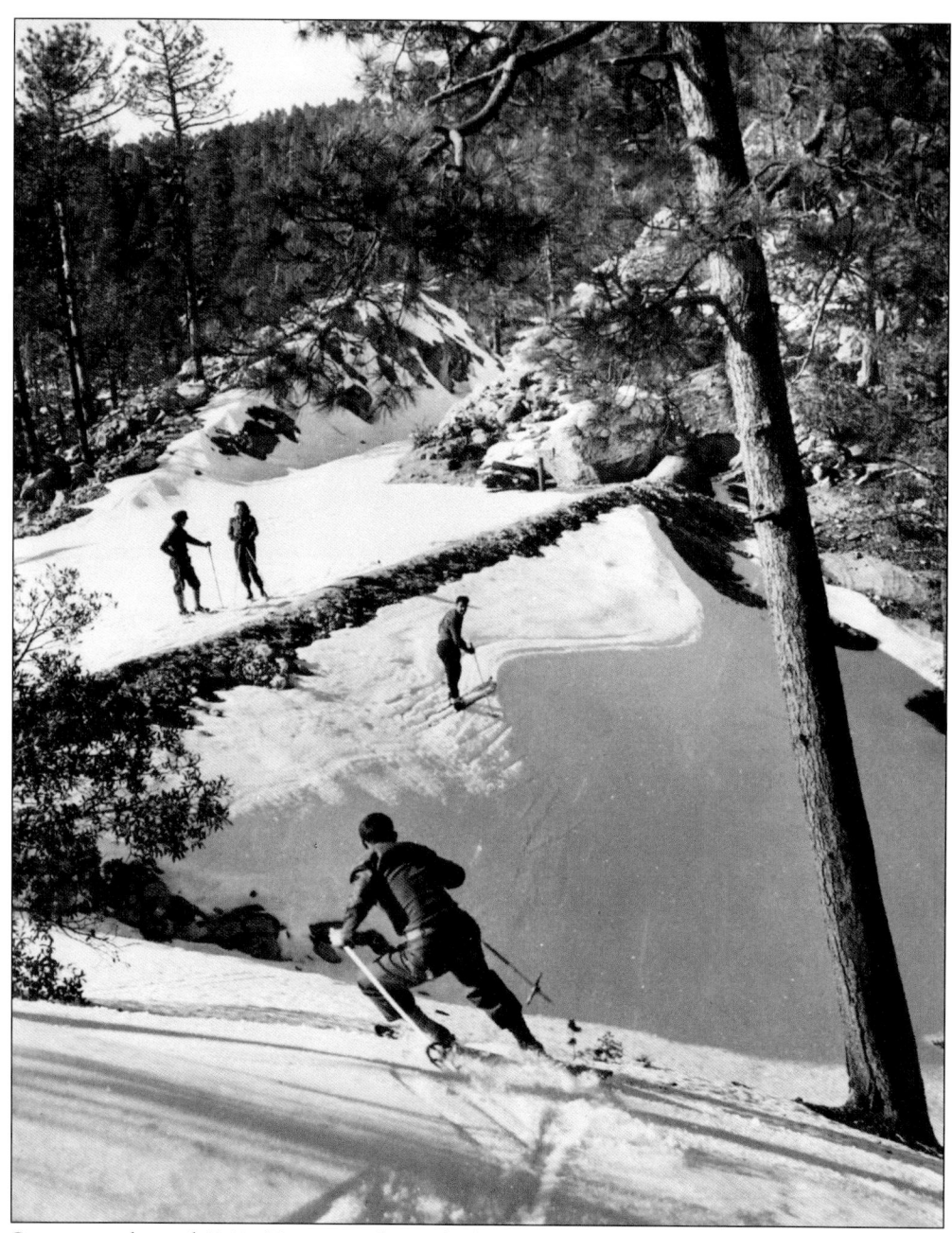

Starting in the mid-1940s, Tucsonans began looking to the Santa Catalina Mountains for skiing opportunities. During the earliest years, there were no designated skiing areas available, and adventurous skiers had to seek out suitable locations. With the help of the Sahuaro Ski Club and local enthusiasm, interest in skiing grew, and in 1963, a 2,800-foot-long lift was installed on Mount Lemmon. By 1965, a local newspaper was describing skiing on Mount Lemmon as "big business." The same article stated that more than 100,000 people had used the ski run that winter alone. (AHS MS1255f.452_AK.)

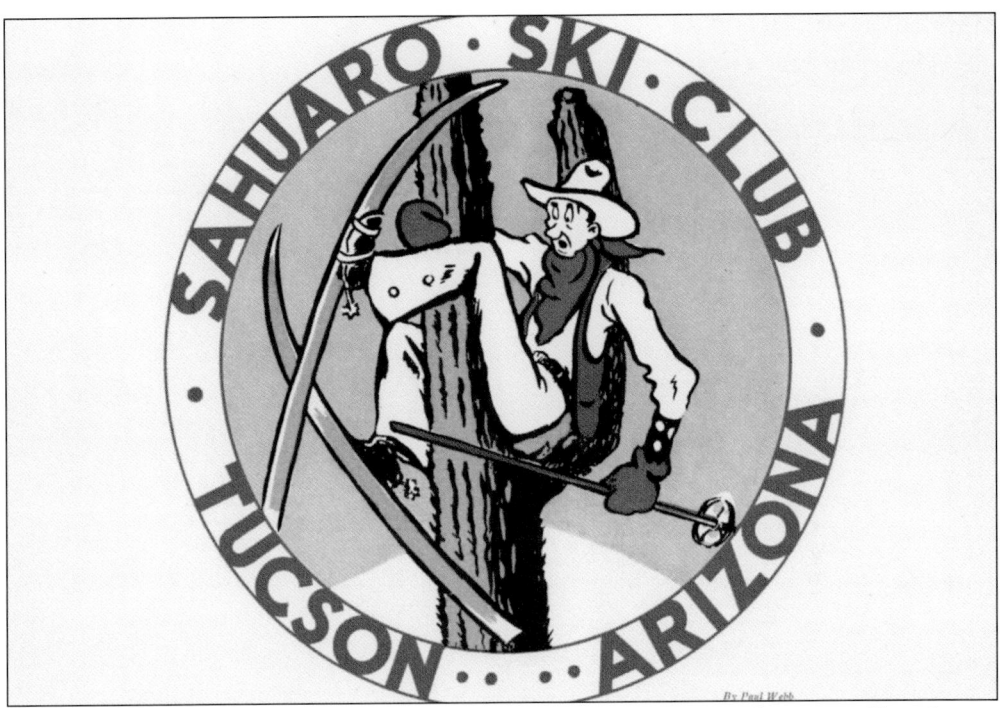

The Sahuaro Ski Club's origins are attributed to Lowell Thomas, a noted writer and broadcaster who visited Tucson to see his son at Davis-Monthan Air Force Base in the 1940s. During his flight to Tucson, Thomas noticed snow on the Santa Catalina Mountains, a sight he had not expected to find in Arizona. Driving up the Control Road on the north side of the mountains, Lowell successfully found a place to ski, and soon, the club was formed. The group continued to grow and boasted around 120 members in the late 1960s. Above, Sahuaro Ski Club member Paul Webb designed a humorous logo for the club, complete with a skier stuck in a saguaro cactus. Below, the club poses for a photograph in the desert before heading into the snow. (Above, AHS Ephemera; below, AHS MS1255f452_M.)

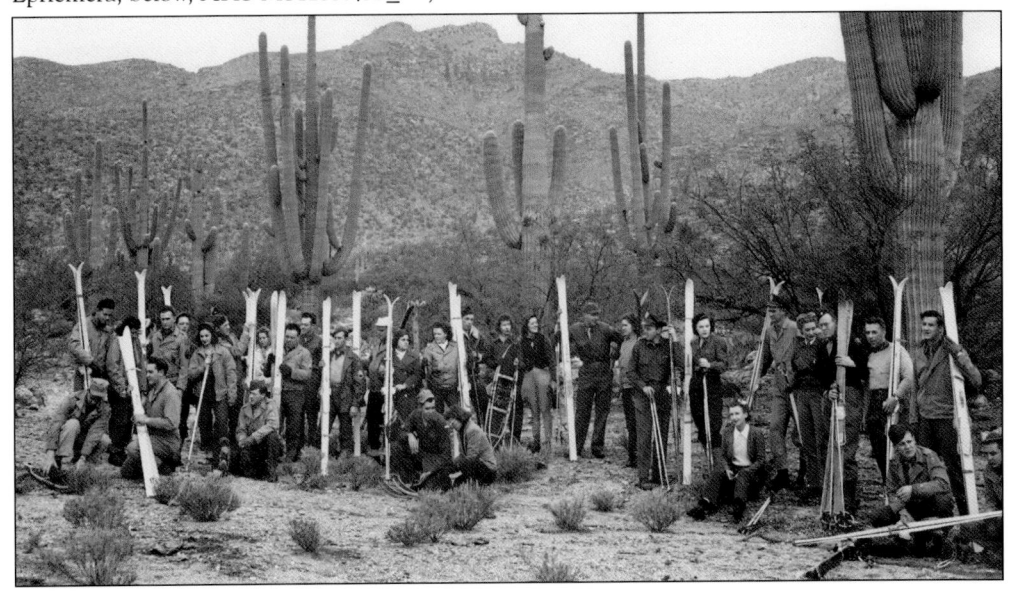

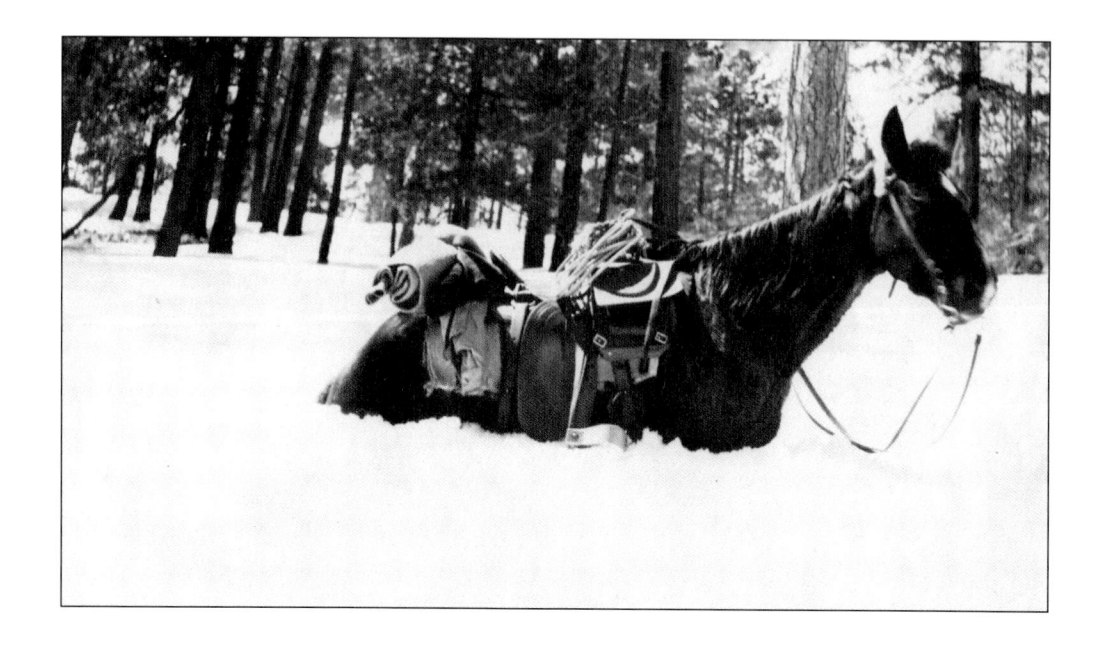

Although Pima County is better known for its extreme heat rather than large amounts of snowfall, the Santa Catalina Mountains receive a fair share of winter weather. On March 26, 1917, a late snowfall brought a ranger's horse to a standstill, with snow reaching the top of the horse's legs. Below, a group of men and women stop for a meal break during a trip into the Santa Catalina Mountains. With a small pine tree attached to the driver's side of the car, the group may have been venturing out to find a Christmas tree. (Above, AHS PC27 445; below, UA Photograph Files.)

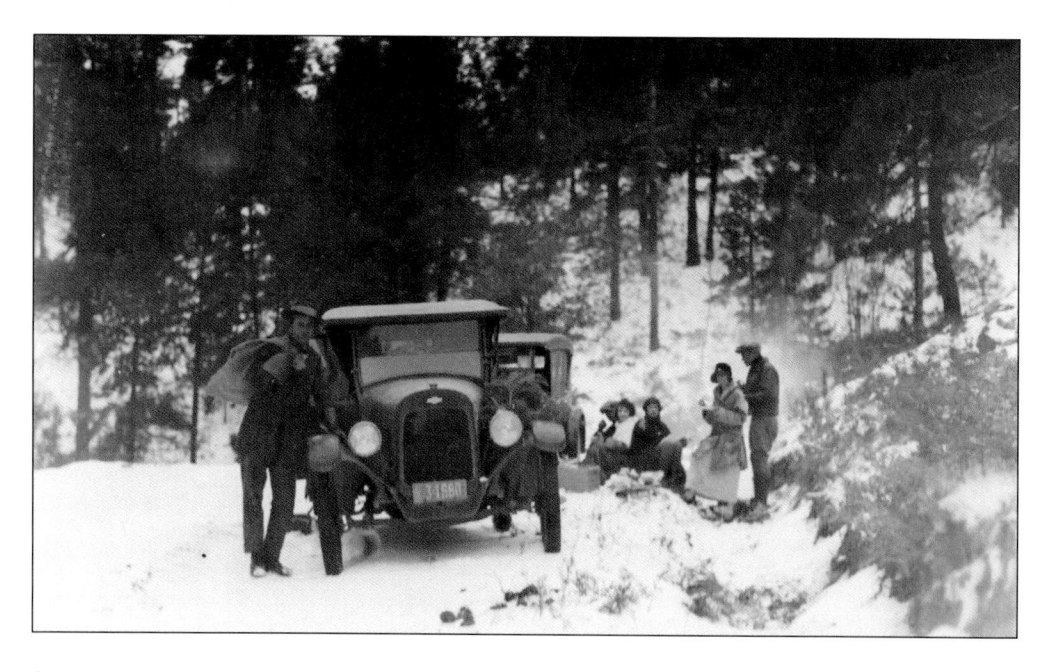

Helen and Murial Upham, ages five and three, were all smiles from the rare sight of snowfall in Tucson. Bundled in their winter coats, with gloves and hats, they were likely photographed during the February 1909 storm that brought four inches of snow to the Old Pueblo. (AHS PC142 92807.)

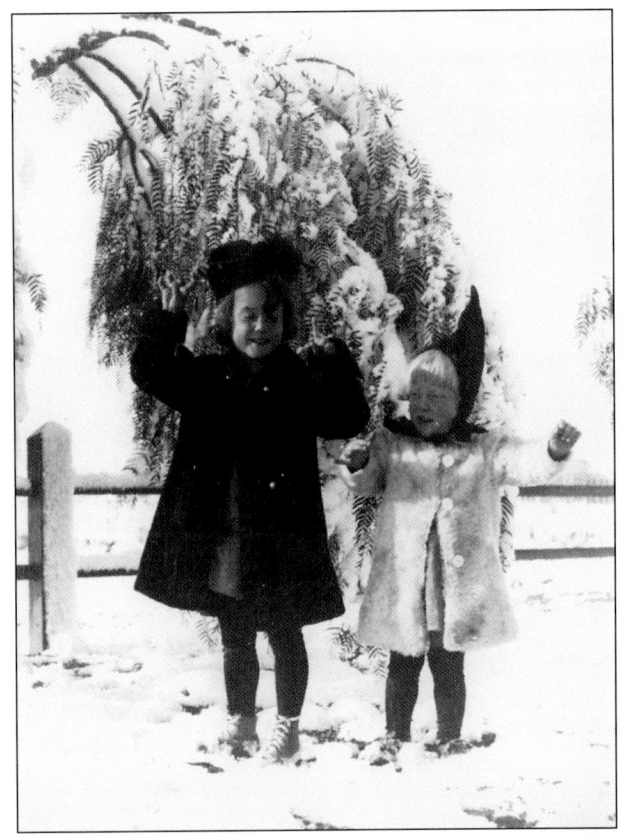

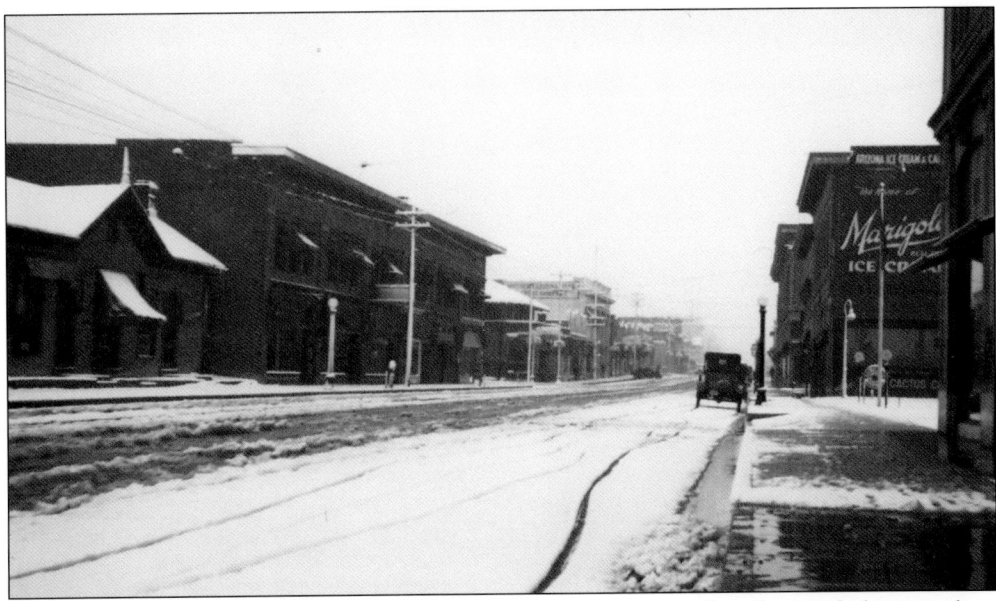

The occasional snow in Pima County prompted many amateur and professional photographers to pull out their cameras. This snow scene on Stone Avenue in Tucson was likely photographed during a March 1922 storm that left six inches of snow. The largest snowfall ever recorded in Tucson took place on December 8, 1971, when 6.8 inches fell on the city. (AHS PC142f.6 62901.)

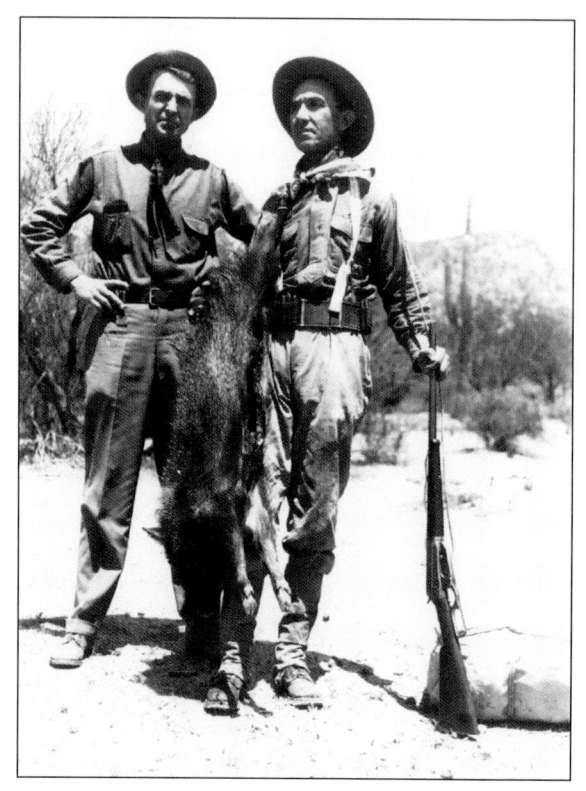

Hunting and exploring were popular pastimes for many Pima County residents. At left, a javelina was the prize of a hunting trip to the Tortilita Mountains in April 1918. The Tortilitas (meaning "little turtle doves" in Spanish) straddle northern Pima County and southern Pinal County. At one time called the Bloodsucker Mountains, the name was changed in recognition of the large number of doves found there. Below, the same man from the right side of the left image poses for the camera before taking his first trip into Stratton Camp on the road to Mount Lemmon in 1916. (Left, AHS PC142_ 92949; below, AHS 92945.)

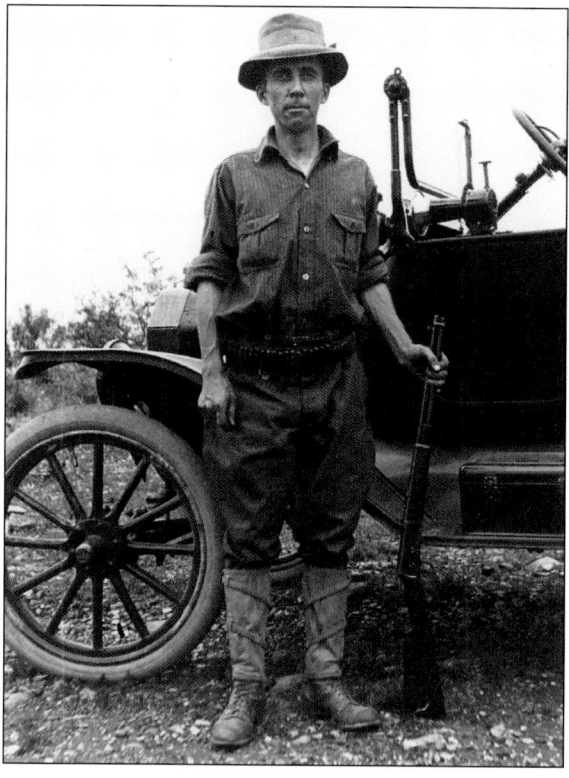

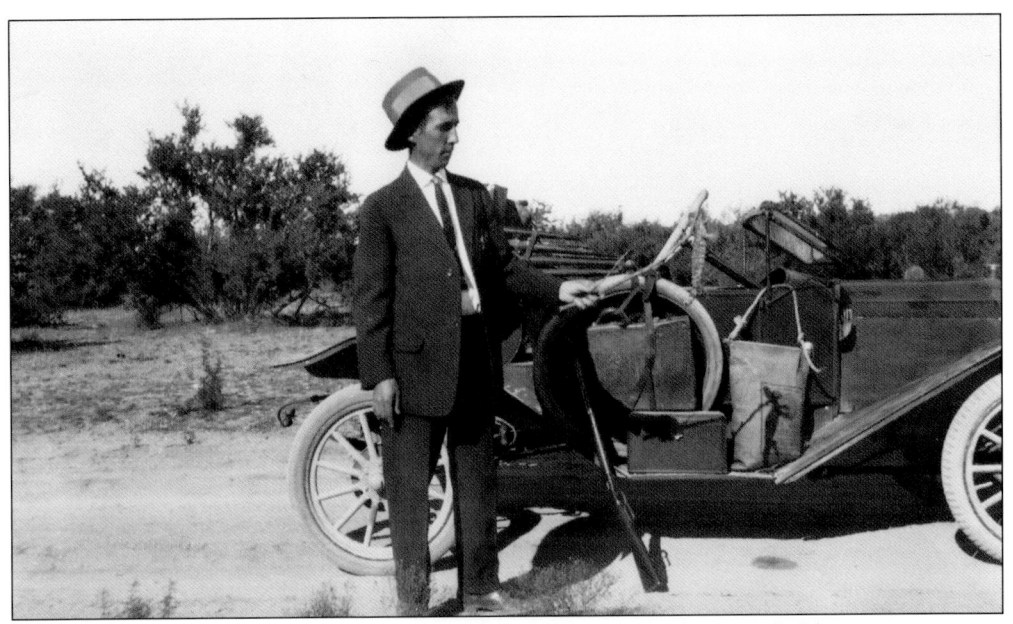

Stopped on a trip between Oracle and Tucson on June 12, 1915, a man holds out a venomous Gila monster at the end of a stick. Almost 40 years later, in 1952, the Gila monster became protected under Arizona state law, making it illegal to collect, kill, or sell them in the state. The Gila monster was the first venomous reptile to fall under legal protection in the United States. (AHS PC142f.9 62943.)

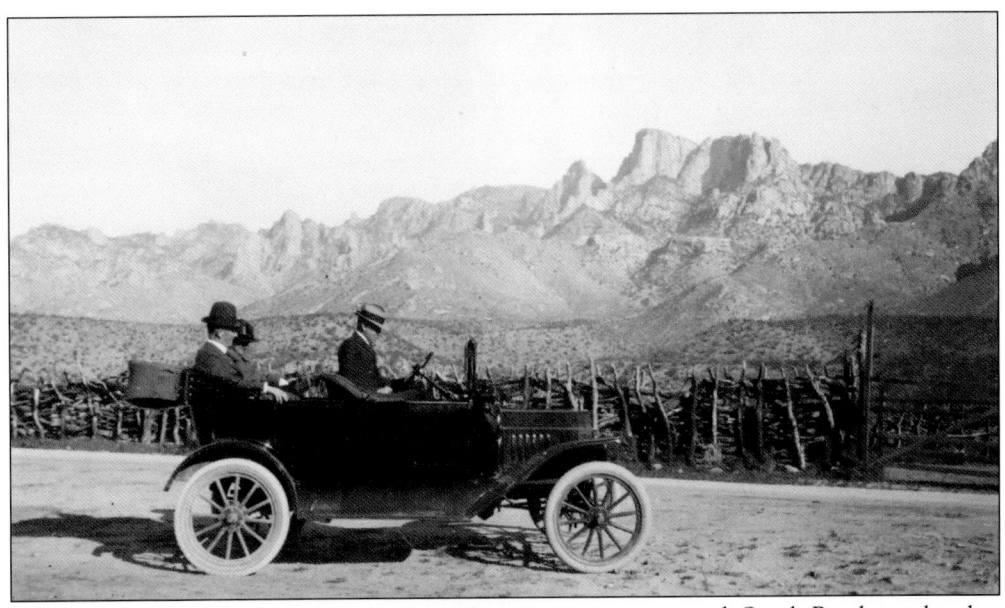

Long before Oro Valley was founded or Pima County streets were paved, Oracle Road was already a thoroughfare for tourists and travelers. This photograph shows the Upham family taking a break near the Steam Pump Ranch off Oracle Road about 1915. Automobiles like this Ford Model T allowed those living in Tucson easier access to more parts of Pima County. (AHS PC142f.9 62944.)

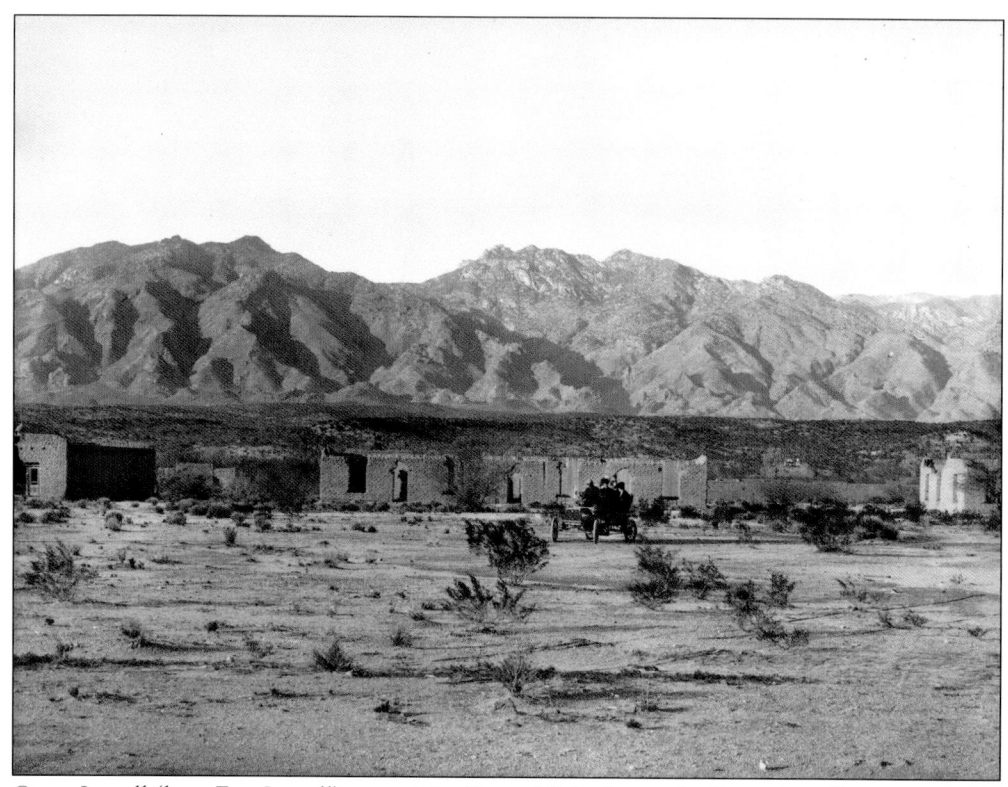

Camp Lowell (later Fort Lowell) was originally established near the Santa Cruz River at present-day Scott Avenue and Fourteenth Street. In 1873, low water supply prompted the move northeast, near the Rillito River. Soldiers stationed here protected settlers and property and also fought in the Geronimo campaigns. The fort was abandoned in 1891. The community left behind eventually merged with Tucson as the city expanded. By the time the photograph below was taken in 1904, the adobe buildings had already gone into ruin. Above, motor tourists visit the fort well past its prime. (Above, AHS PC142 62347; below, AHS B113637.)

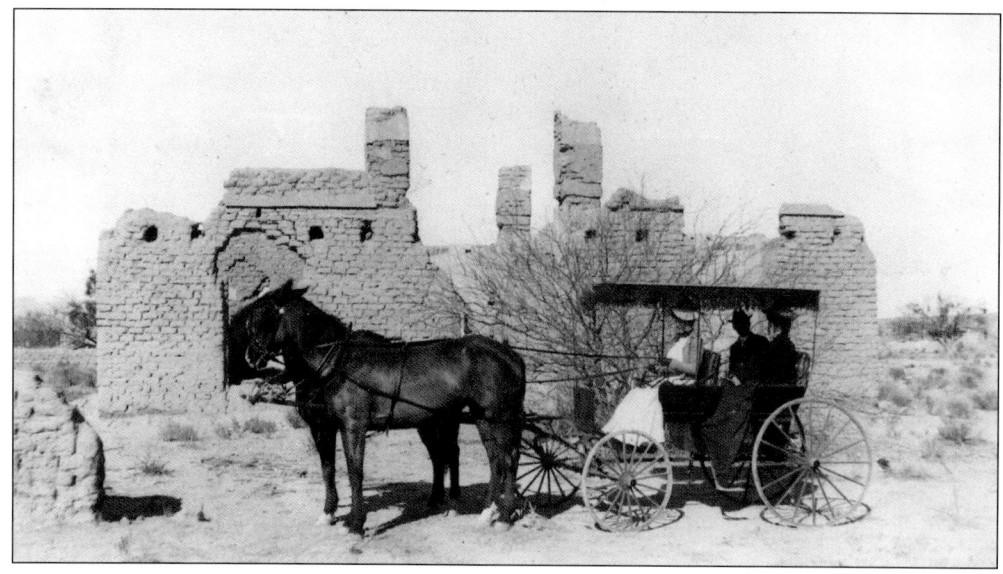

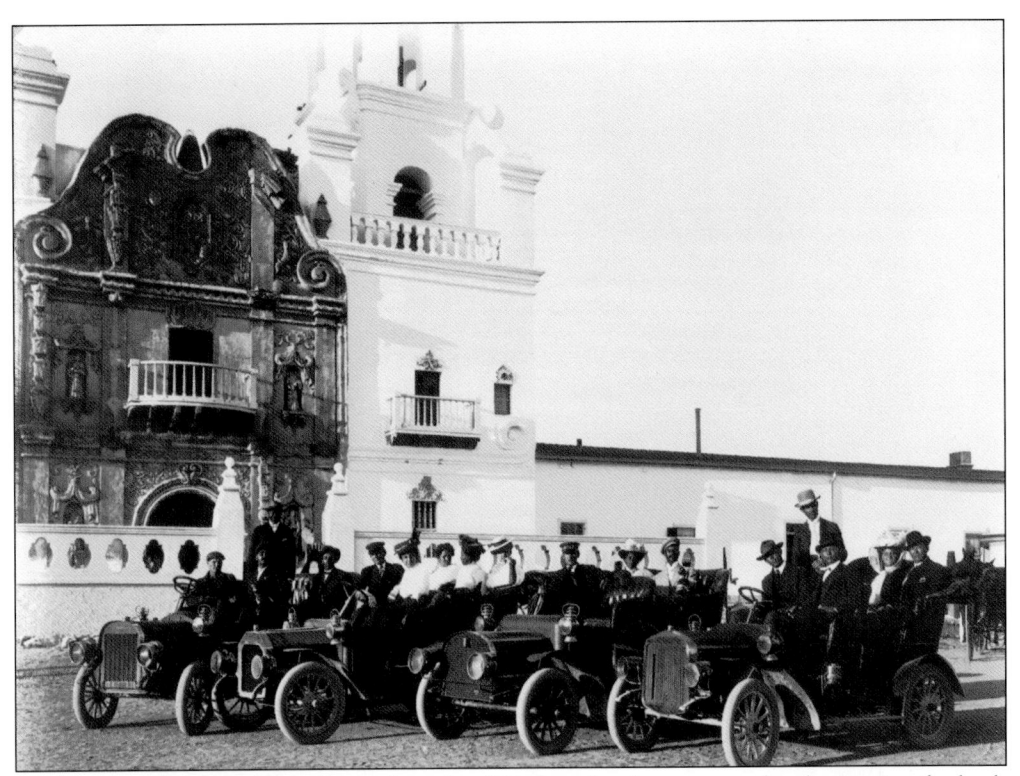

Mission San Xavier del Bac, located south of Tucson, has been a popular destination for both tourists visiting Pima County and local citizens. In the image above, a group of African Americans pose during an automobile excursion to the mission. The hill to the east of Mission San Xavier del Bac, known as Grotto Hill, has also been a frequent stop. On February 22, 1911, three women and three young girls found themselves fighting the winds on the top of the hill, pictured below. Posing for the photograph, they held on tight to the hats that were fashionable for the time. (Above, AHS B89407; below, AHS PC142b.4_92922.)

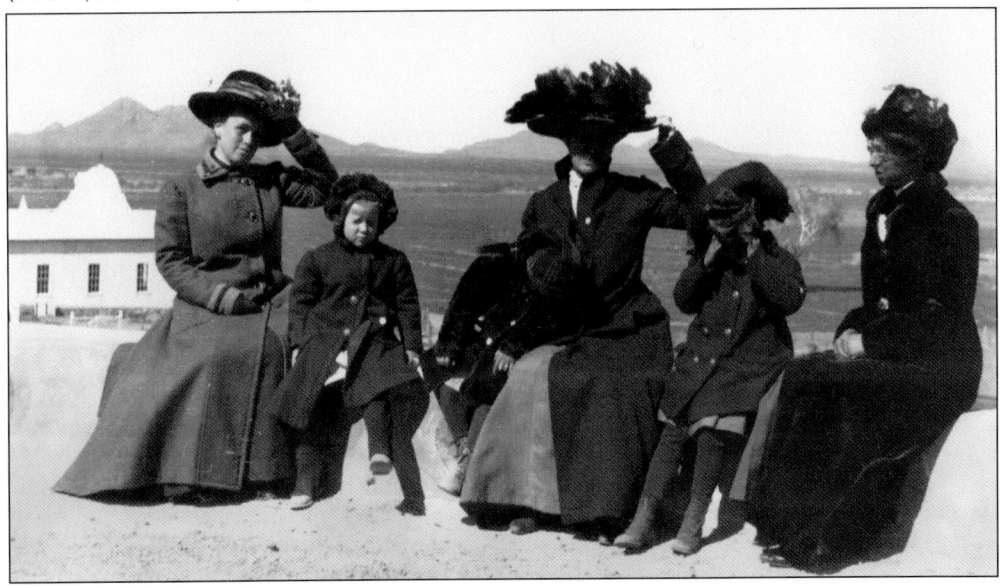

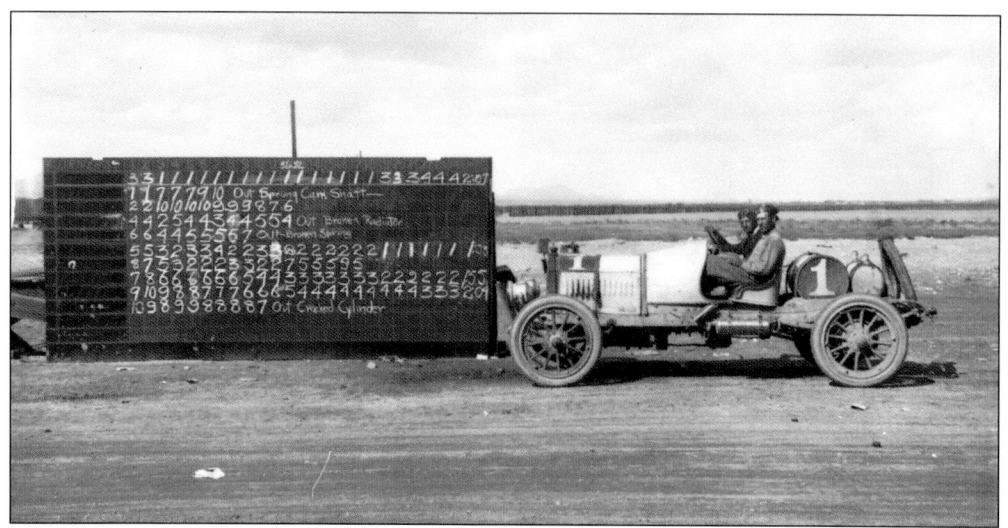

Pima County had an early love for automobile racing. The Tucson Automobile Club was formed in 1910, and the American Automobile Association sanctioned races in Tucson as early as 1911. The results of a November 1915 race at the Southern Arizona Fair (today called the Pima County Fair) show the stats from the 24-lap, 100-mile race. The winning time was one hour and 53 minutes. (AHS BN38471.)

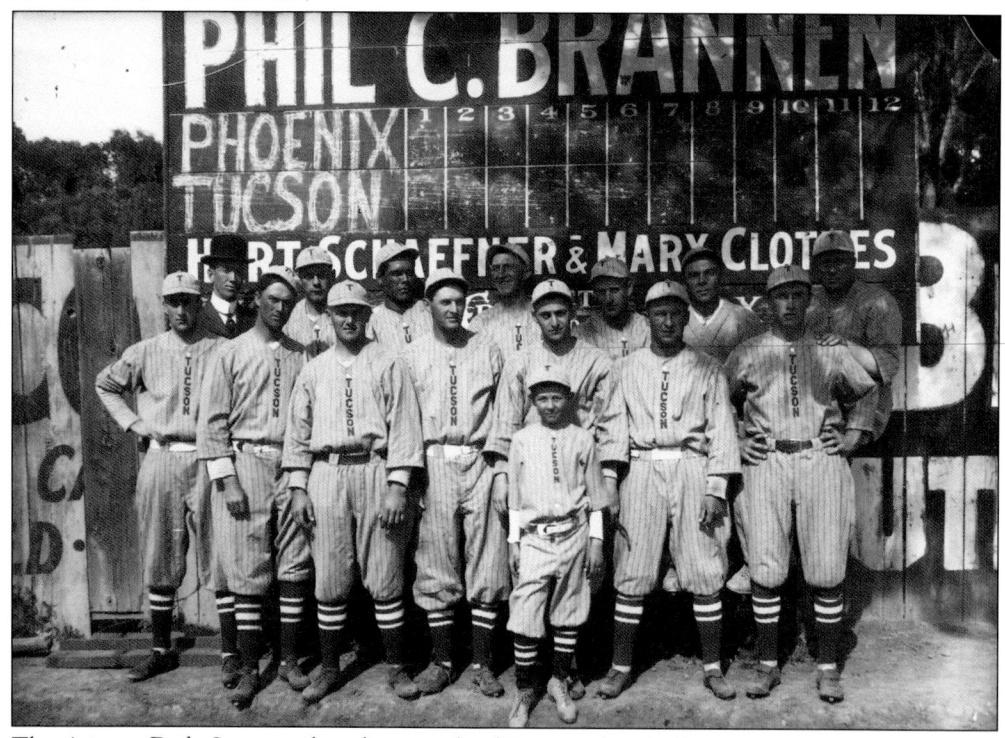

The *Arizona Daily Star* ran this photograph of Tucson's baseball team after a game against El Paso in 1915; the newspaper cropped out the scoreboard showing a game against Phoenix. The most memorable part of the game was an El Paso player's hit to right field that struck and killed a sparrow. Tucson fans unsuccessfully tried to get the El Paso player called "out" for hitting the bird. (AHS B32856.)

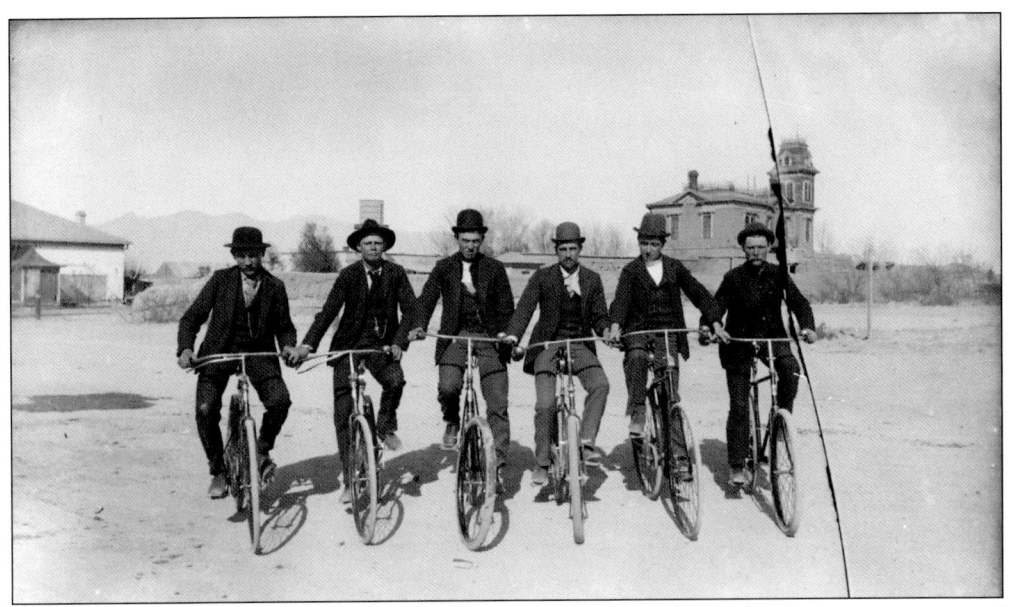

In the late 1800s, Tucson saw a rise in the popularity of bicycles for both transportation and amusement. The interest in bicycling was so high that in 1892 the Tucson Cycling Club was formed, and in 1894, cyclists raced between Nogales and Tucson in the Great Territorial Long-Distance Bicycle Race. Pictured here is a good-humored group of bicyclists in front of the large home of Wheeler Washington Williams in Tucson. (AHS PC107_25264.)

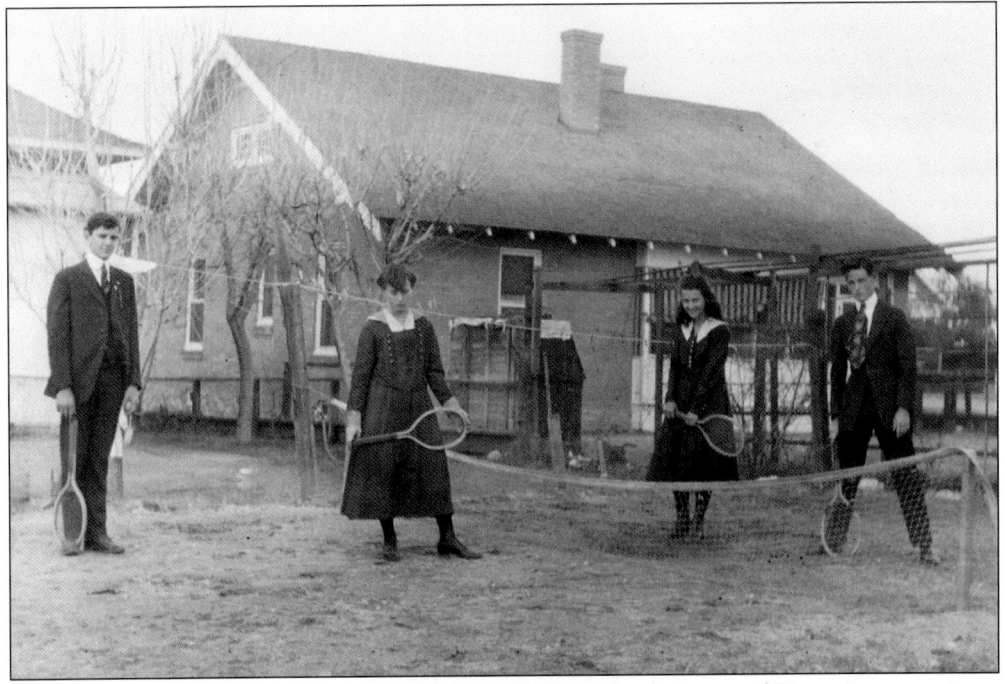

On January 28, 1918, a group of young tennis players took advantage of Tucson's warm winter climate to play a game. Dressed in suits and dresses, the group was likely at the Upham family home on Fourth Avenue in Tucson. From left to right are Chestor Mathews, Harriet Kellond, Helen Upham, and Oswald Kellond. (AHS PC142f.4 92887.)

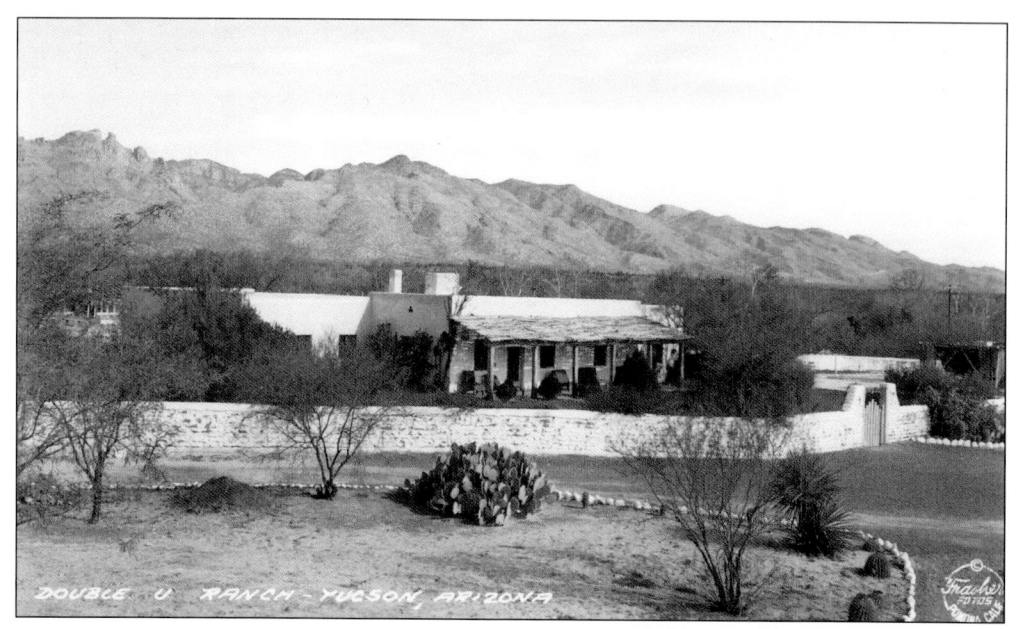

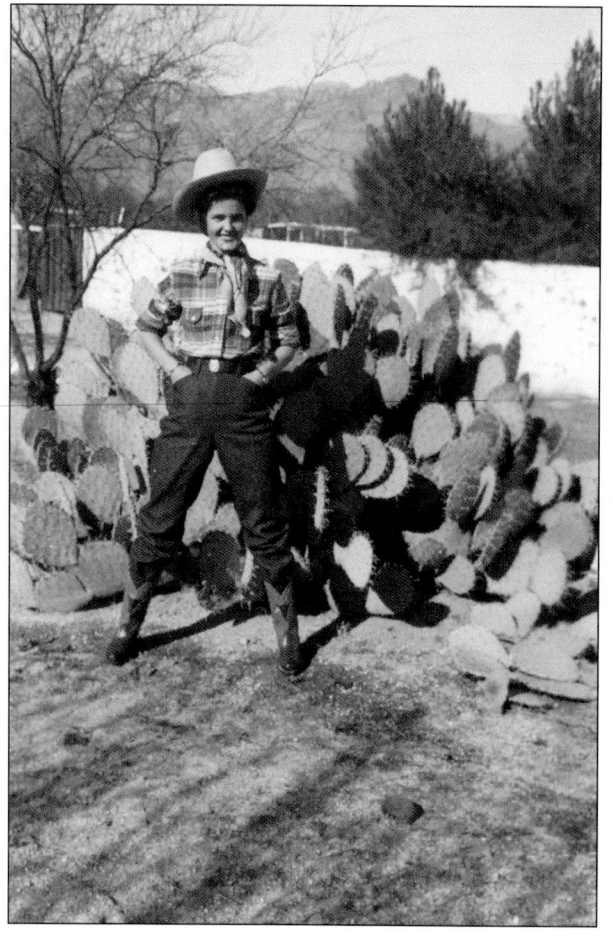

A 28-year-old Bella Tyktin Stern picked up the above postcard of the Double U Ranch during her stay in Pima County in 1942. The ranch was located about 15 miles outside of Tucson in the foothills of the Santa Catalina Mountains. The ranch was used for scenes in the 1940 Columbia Pictures movie *Arizona* and advertised itself as a "gem of the desert." With accommodations for 38 guests, recreational opportunities included horseback riding, hunting, badminton, and archery. Additionally, trips to "Old Mexico" could be arranged. Like many ranches in southern Arizona, the Double U Ranch was open during the peak of tourist season, from October to May. At left, Bella Stern poses in Western clothing at the Double U Ranch. (Both, UA Photograph Files.)

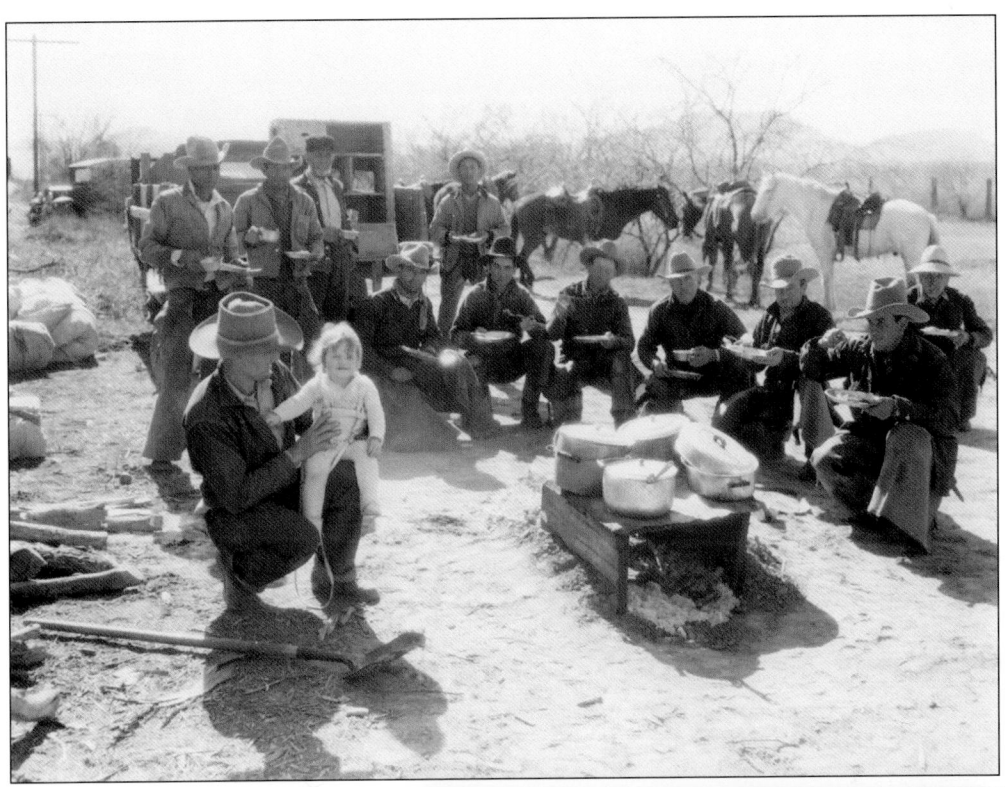

Chuck wagons were originally mobile kitchens used to feed cowhands who traveled for miles to transport cattle overland. The cook, sometimes known as "Cookie," prepared food that did not easily spoil, such as jerky, beans, coffee, and biscuits. In this photograph, a group of working cowboys and a small child enjoy an old-fashioned chuck wagon meal at one of the Gill family ranches in Pima County. (AHS BN205497.)

For decades, the Wild Horse Guest Ranch was a popular location for parties, including Christmas celebrations such as this one. A bonfire accompanied Santa Claus, gifts, and a holiday-themed saguaro. Howard W. Miller purchased the guest ranch, located off of Ina Road near Saguaro National Park West, in 1939. It stayed with the Miller family until it was sold in 1977. (AHS MS 1255f.343c.)

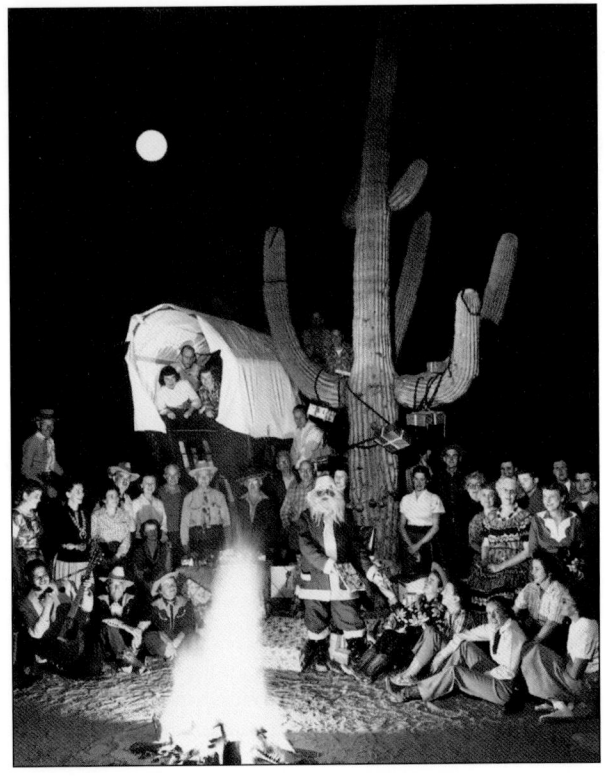

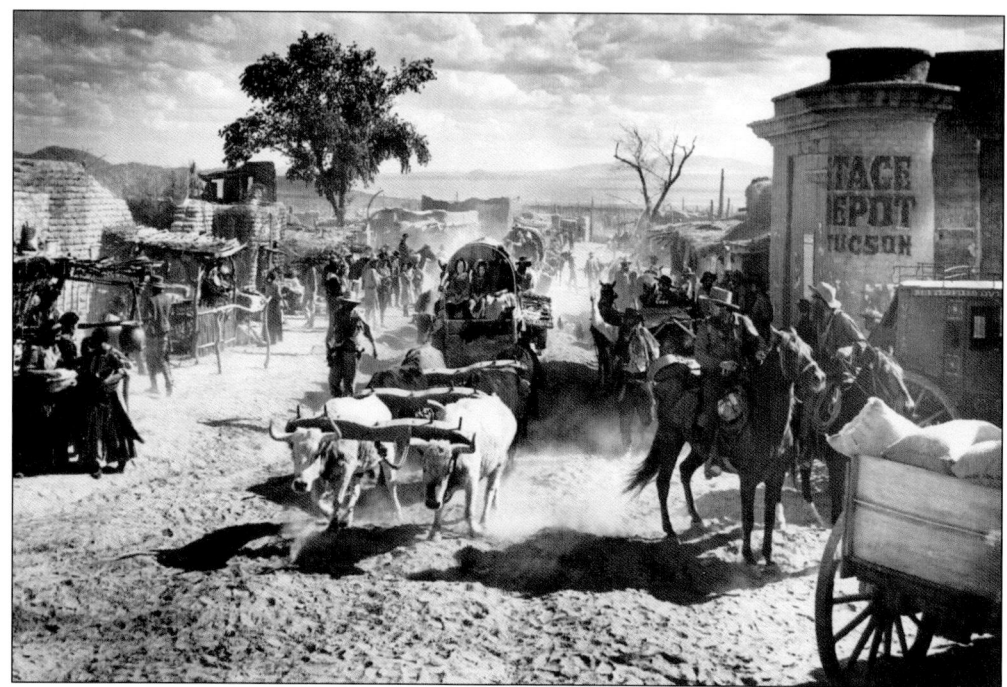

Old Tucson was created in 1940 as a set for the movie *Arizona*, starring Jean Arthur and William Holden. This photograph captures the filming of a scene from that movie, perhaps proving the film's poster's claim that *Arizona* was the "mightiest of all outdoor pictures." (AHS BN204563.)

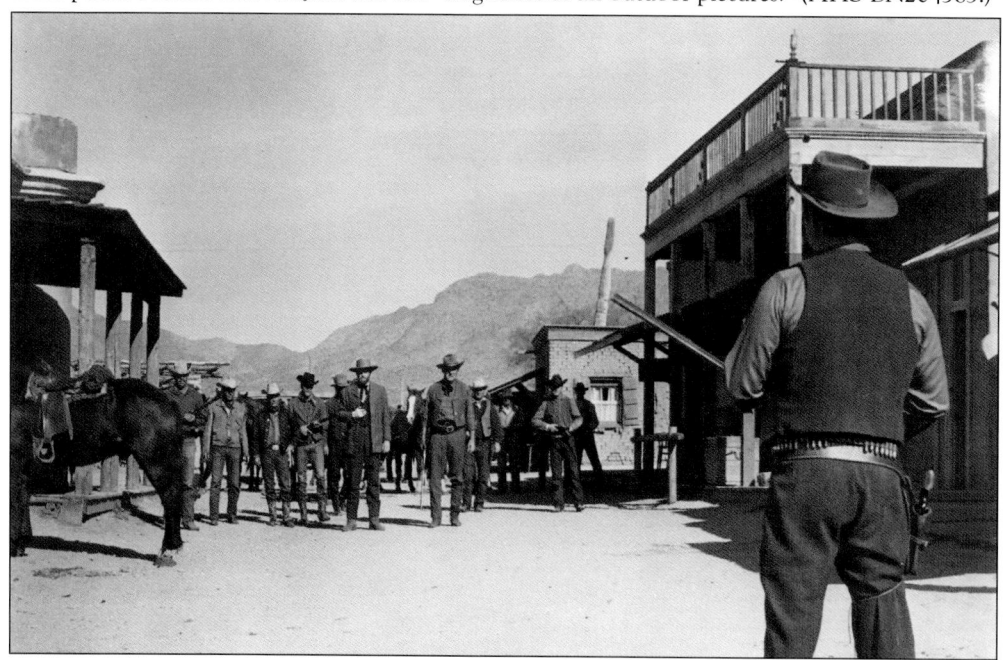

Old Tucson Studios provided the set for the 1958 picture *Gunsmoke in Tucson*. Old Tucson has long had a crucial role in the production of Western films. The sunny skies, cloud effects, and realistic 1860s Tucson backdrop have made Old Tucson an ideal locale for many years. (UA Photograph Files.)

The Rialto Theatre, shown here in 1928, underwent many changes in its nearly 100-year history in Tucson. Undergoing several name changes, it was also known as the Paramount and the Cine Plaza Theater. Today, the theater continues its legacy under the management of the Rialto Theatre Foundation, a nonprofit group dedicated to the continued stewardship of the historic theater. (AHS B39189.)

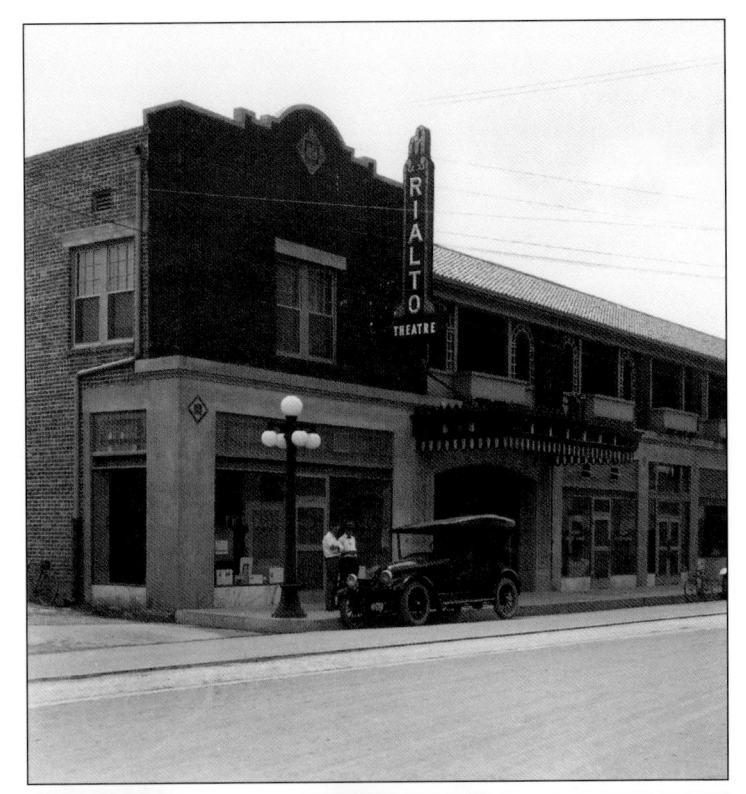

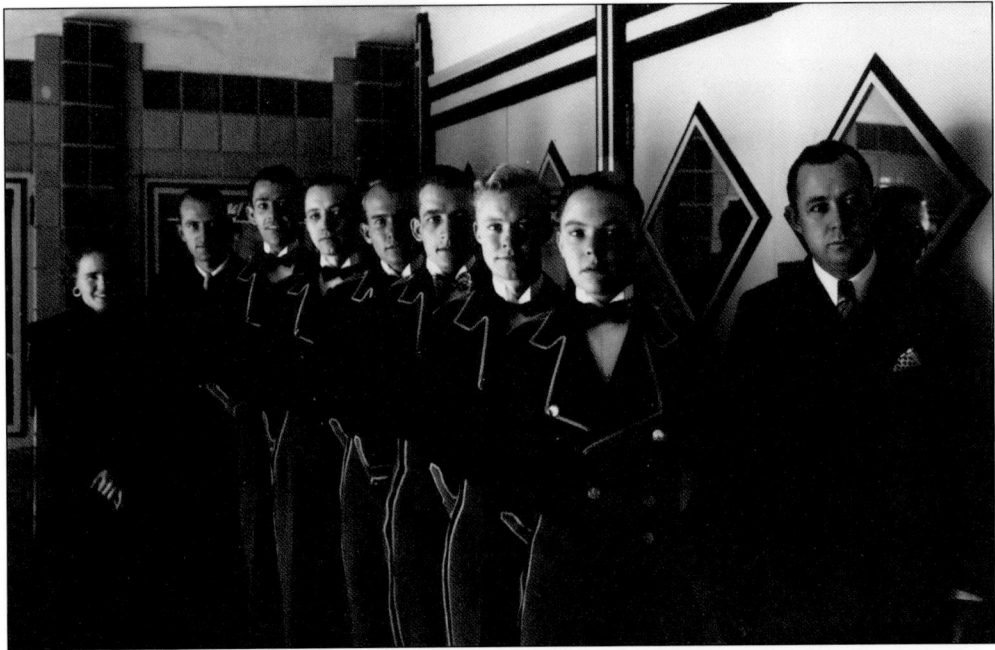

The Fox Theater in Tucson had its grand opening on April 11, 1930, and closed its doors 44 years later on June 18, 1974. Later designated a National Landmark by the National Register of Historical Places, the theater was renovated and reopened in the 2000s. A photograph of the sharply dressed staff around 1934 is shown here with Roy Drachman on the far right. (AHS PC173f.3B29264.)

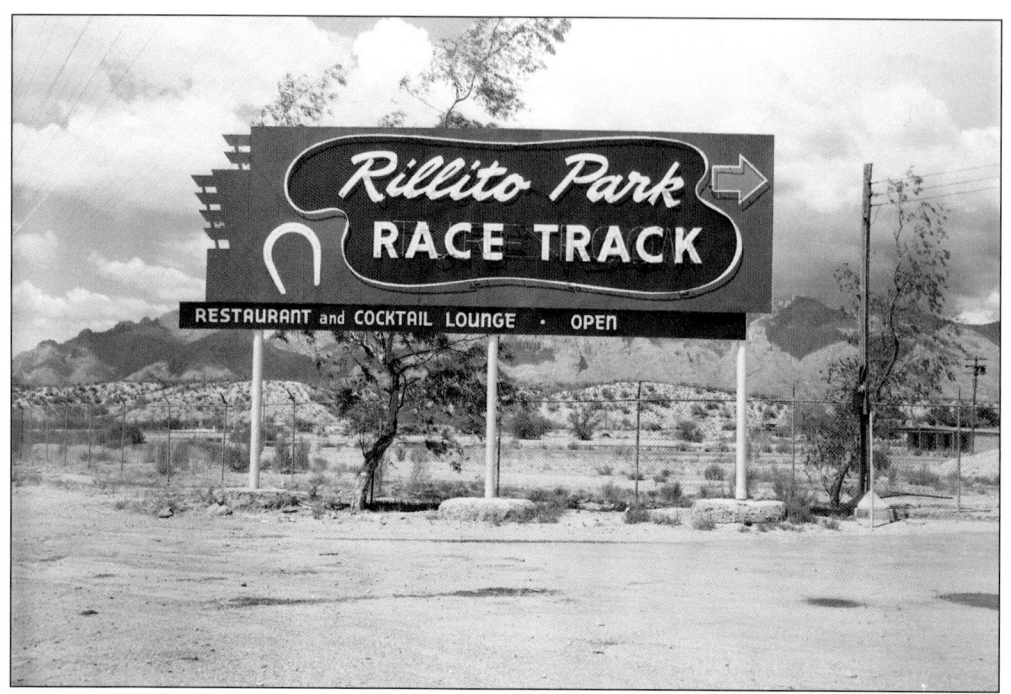

The Rillito Park Racetrack's humble beginnings trace back to two friends who bred quarter horses and needed a place to race them. The duo's hobby led to the track opening in 1943 and becoming the first regulated quarter horse facility in the United States. The track has been influential in setting standards in the racing industry and even claims to be the birthplace of photograph finishing. Scenes from the movie *Seabiscuit* were filmed there, and a portion of the park is in the National Register of Historic Places. Below, photographer Jack Shaeffer photographed crowds waiting for a race on February 14, 1955. (Above, UA 2160.2; below, UA 2937.2.)

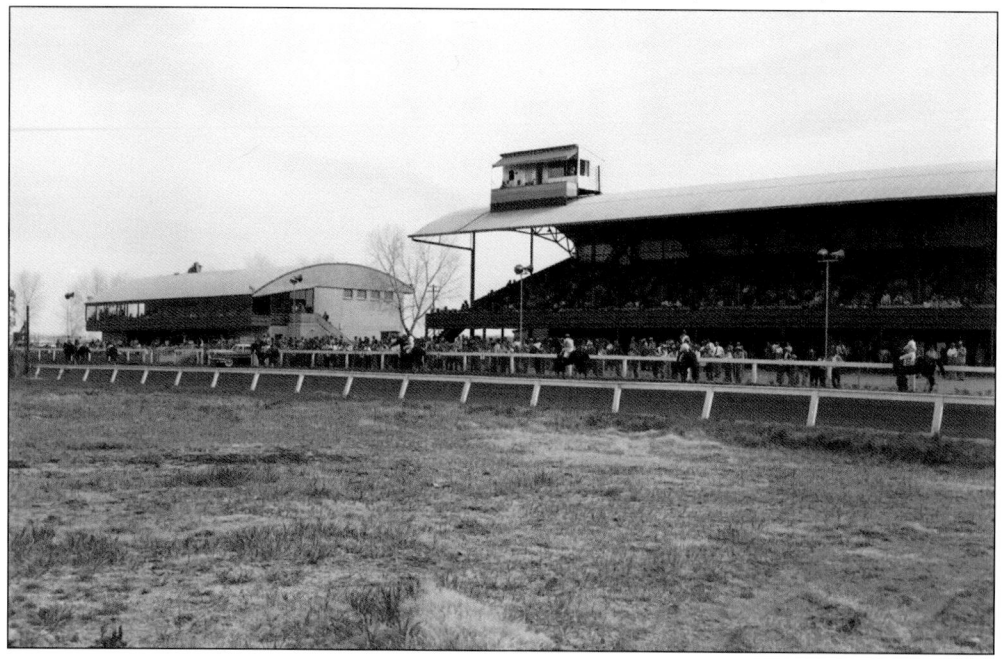

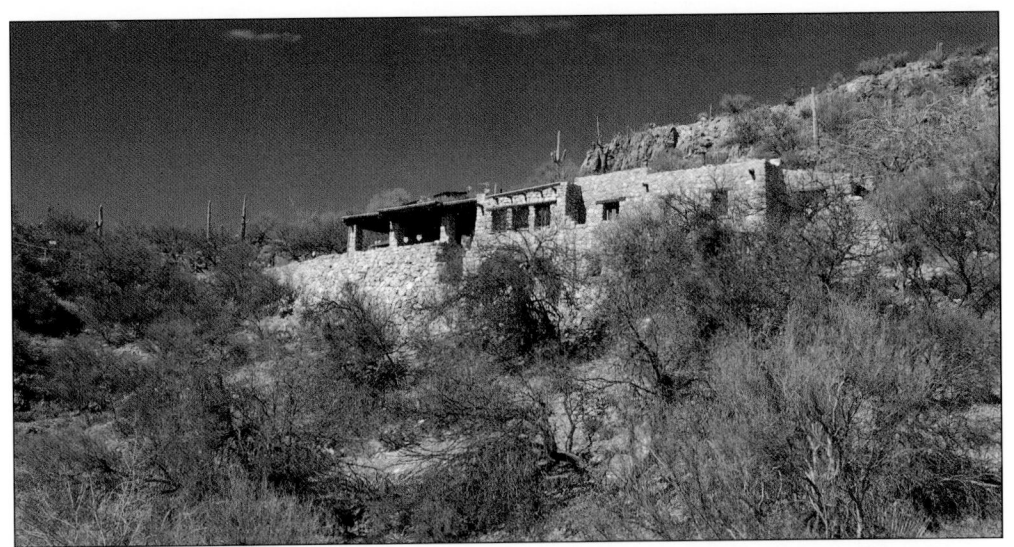

Once used by Native Americans, Colossal Cave has been a well-known site in Pima County for centuries. Believed to have been used by the Hohokam as early as 1,100 years ago, the cave was introduced to a larger audience when it was "discovered" by Solomon Lick in 1879. The first tours were given in 1917, and they started on a continuous basis in 1923. In the 1930s, the Civilian Conservation Corps made the cave more accessible by creating buildings, such as the Administration Building (above), and adding walkways and lighting. The dry cave, which is in the National Register of Historic Places, is no longer making formations and is considered dormant. (Above, photograph by Simon Herbert; below, AHS 44296.)

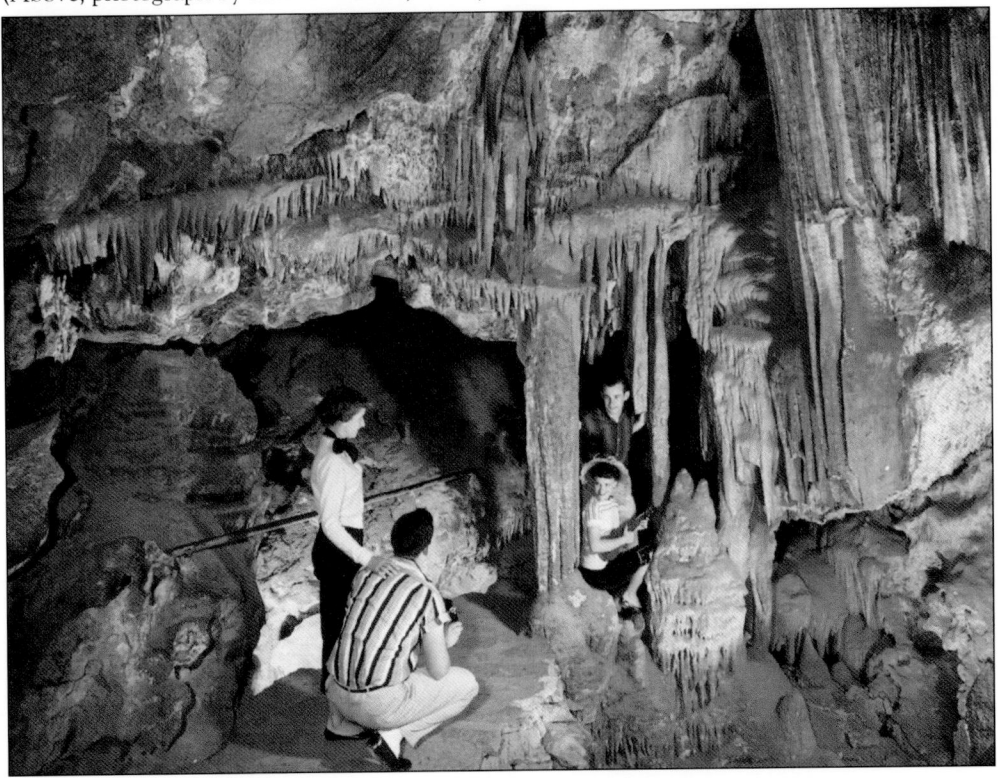

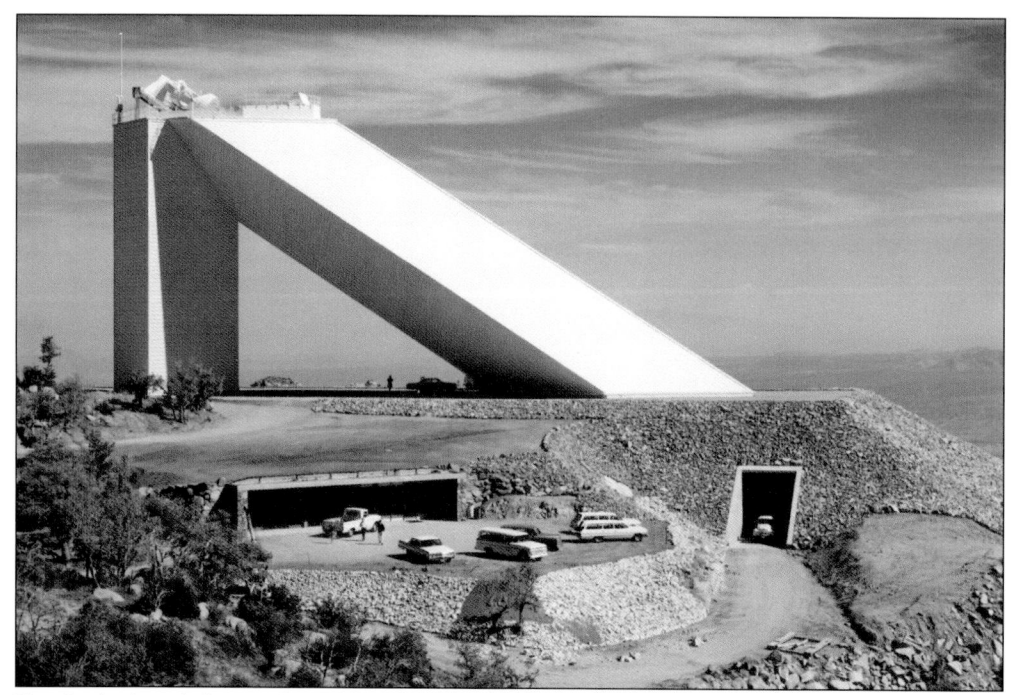

Kitt Peak, founded in 1958, maintains the world's largest collection of telescopes. Seen here is the McMath-Pierce Solar Telescope, dedicated in 1962. It is used to study sunspots and stands almost 100 feet tall. (AHS 44505.)

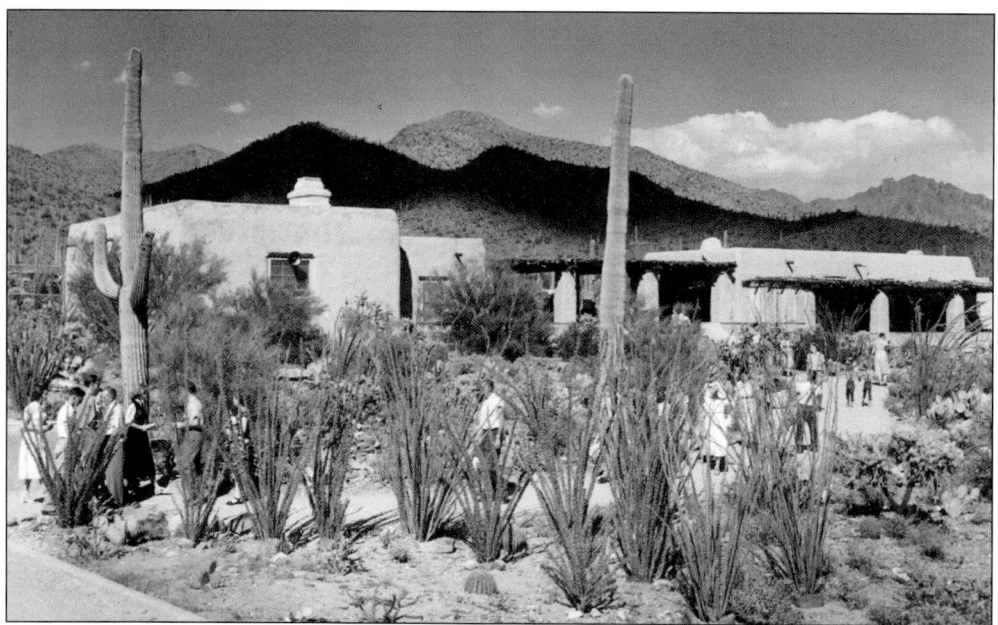

The Tucson Mountains provide a beautiful backdrop to the entrance of the Arizona-Sonora Desert Museum. The museum was founded in 1952 with a mission to "inspire people to live in harmony with the natural world by fostering love, appreciation, and understanding in the Sonoran Desert." The museum is a unique combination of zoo, natural history museum, and botanical garden. (AHS 55305.)

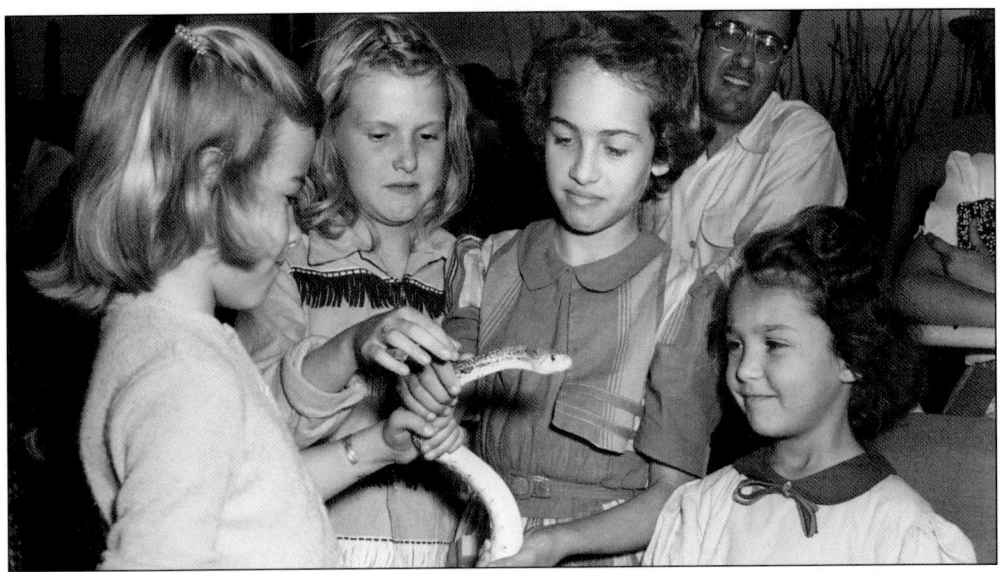

Allowing visitors to get "eye-to-eye" with desert wildlife is one of the attractions of the Arizona-Sonora Desert Museum. Here, four young girls bravely hold Charlie, one of the museum's bull snakes. (AHS 55315.)

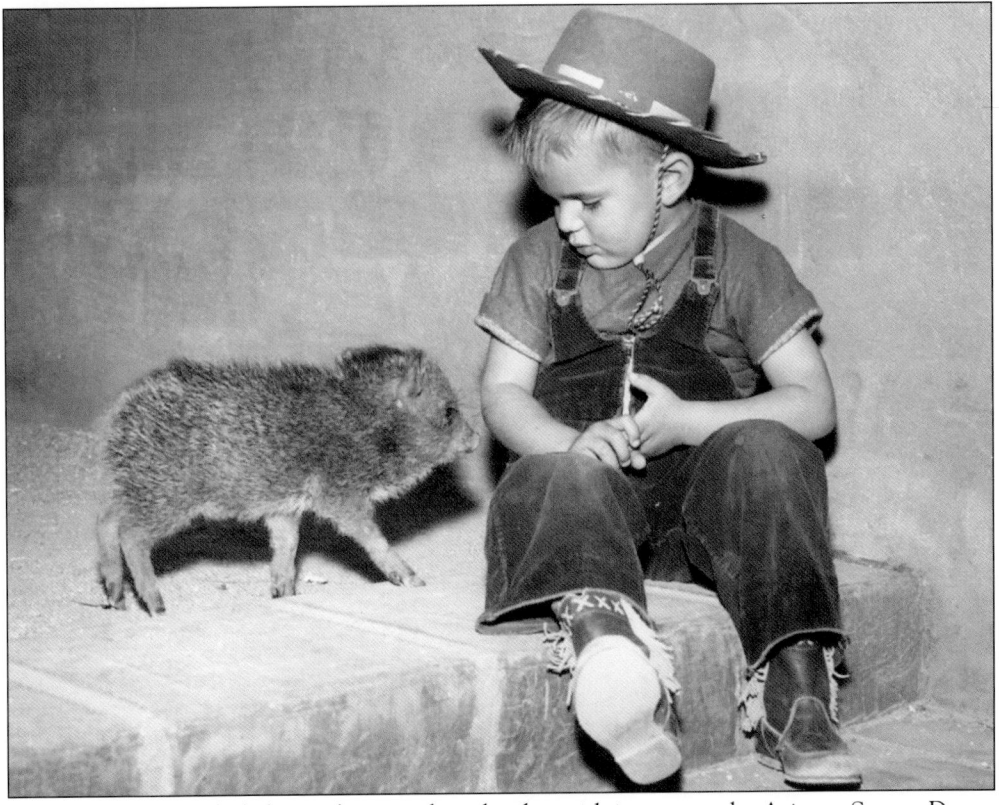

A young cowboy and a baby javelina watch each other with interest at the Arizona-Sonora Desert Museum. Javelinas, a member of the peccary family, live in the Sonoran Desert and are one of the many different types of wildlife on display at the museum. (AHS 55333.)

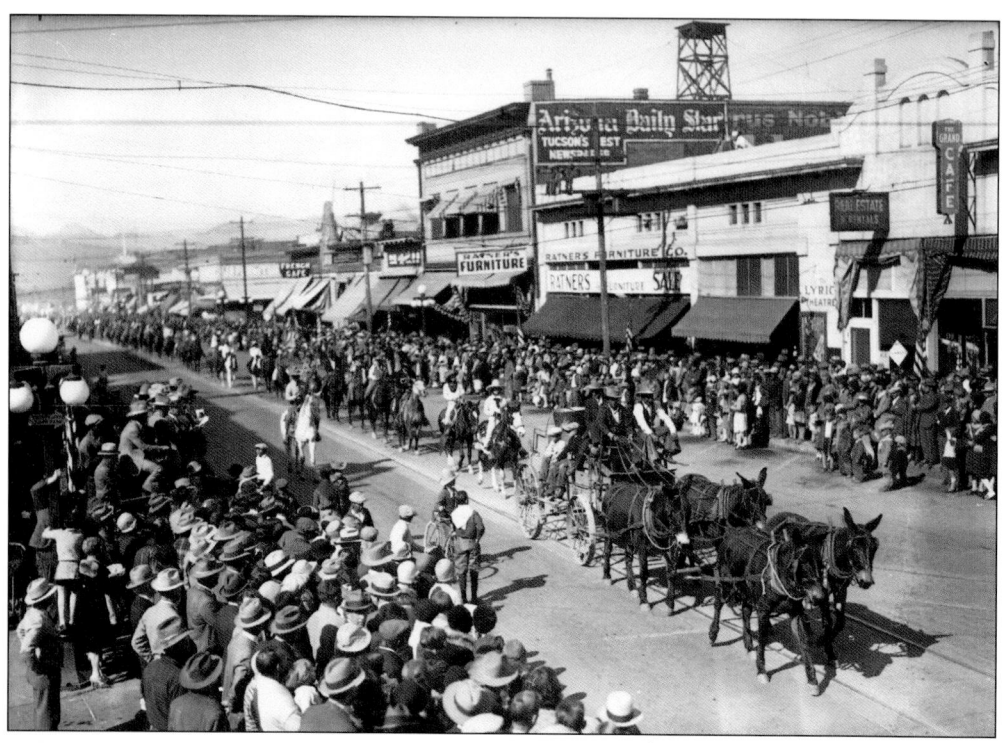

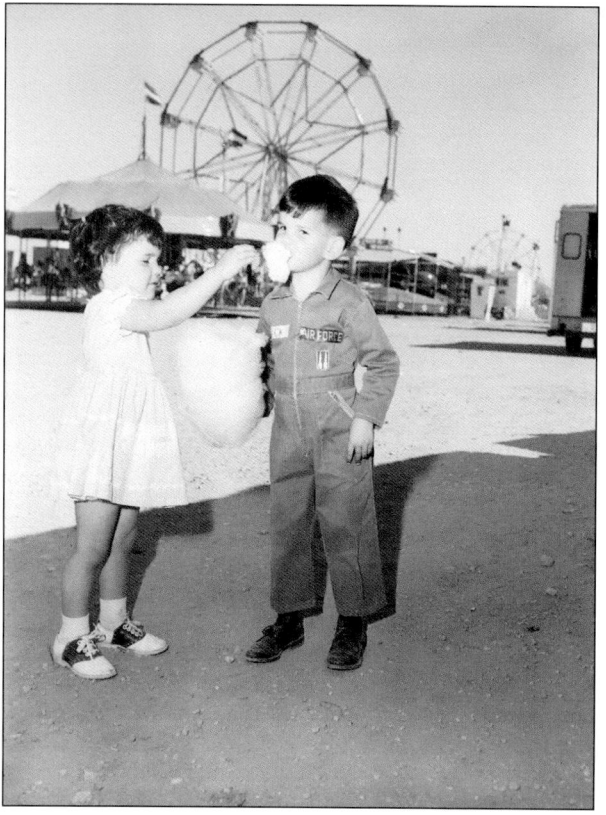

The Tucson Rodeo Parade's origins date back to the inaugural parade in 1925, when Leighton Kramer and the Arizona Polo Association created La Fiesta de los Vaqueros to draw visitors to Tucson. Rodeo participants were asked by Kramer to "parade through downtown to publicize the event." in 1929, Albert Buehman captured this procession on Congress Street. The official Tucson Rodeo Parade Committee was founded in 1932 by Pete Waggoner, Rodeo Parade chairman, with support from the Tucson Chamber of Commerce. (AHS B109965.)

On the first day of the Pima County Fair in March 1967, a young girl wearing a white dress and saddle shoes feeds cotton candy to a little boy dressed in an Air Force uniform. Three popular fair attractions—the Ferris wheel, carousel, and Tilt-A-Whirl—can be seen in the background. (UA MS435 32461.8.)

The Temple of Music and Art was the dream of Madeline Dreyfus Heineman Berger. After moving to Tucson from Los Angles, she started a group called the Saturday Morning Music Club, a group that organized concerts in Tucson. Her dedication and love for the arts led to the temple's ground-breaking ceremonies on November 11, 1926, with a total cost of $180,000. The building was renovated and rededicated in 1990 and is still used today. At right, Madeline Dreyfus Heineman Berger stands to the left of Amelita Galii-Curci of the Metropolitan Opera Company for the dedication. Pictured below is the entrance to the Temple of Music and Art. (Right, AHS 101662; below, AHS MS1255f.145a.)

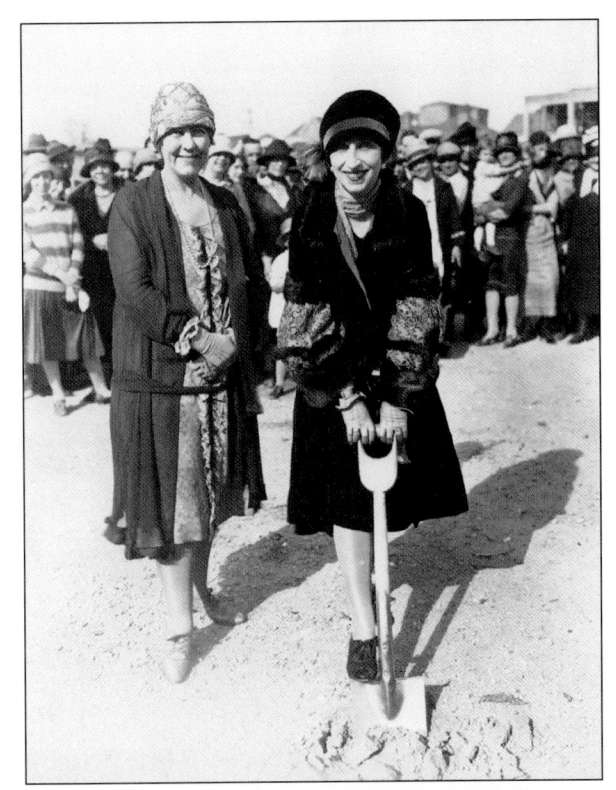

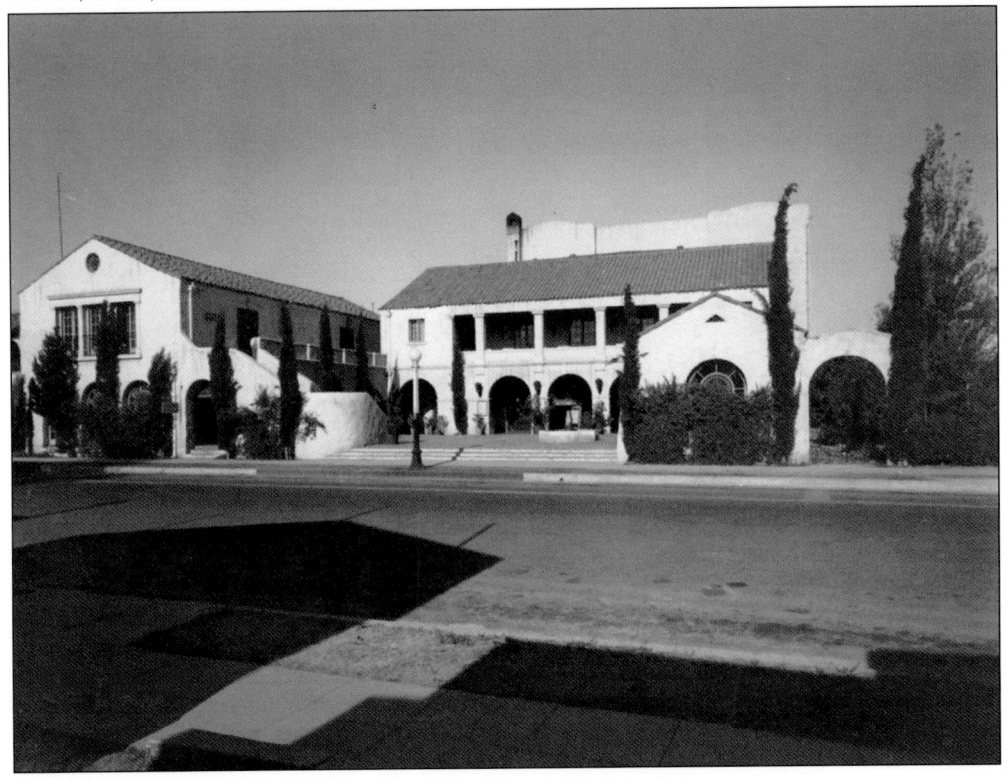

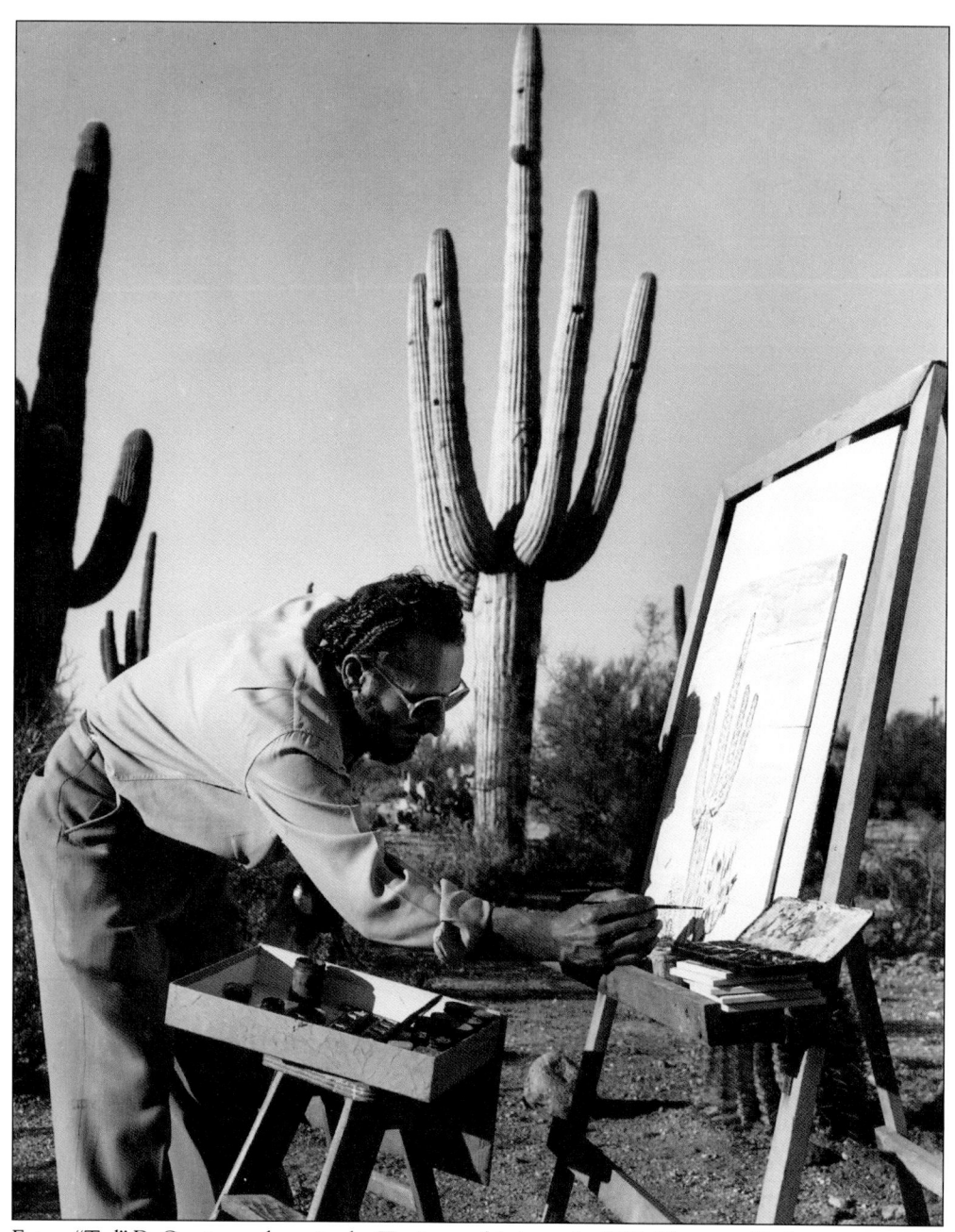

Ettore "Ted" DeGrazia was born in the Territory of Arizona in 1909. The son of Italian immigrants, Ted went on to become one of the best-known artists in the Southwest. His work included paintings and sculptures that were heavily influenced by Native American and Western scenes. DeGrazia passed away in 1982, but his well-known art studio, the Gallery of the Sun, is now a museum that showcases his work and continues to attract his fans to Pima County today. (AHS MS1255f.69e.)

Five

Building a Tradition of Conservation and a Sense of Place

Preserving and enhancing the natural and cultural environment is by no means a new concept for Pima County. As early as 1929, just 17 years after statehood, the county leased 29,988 acres of prime Sonoran Desert habitat, which was federal land at that time, to create Tucson Mountain Park. The creation of Tucson Mountain Park by Pima County was the first significant local expression of a land conservation ethic that was growing nationally.

The genesis of this ethic took root in the 19th century, when visionaries like Henry David Thoreau, John Muir, and Aldo Leopold advocated for the preservation of the nation's most extraordinary natural areas as national parks, including the preservation of cultural treasures and archaeological sites. In 1906, the landmark Antiquities Act allowed the president of the United States to proclaim historic landmarks and places of scientific interest to be set aside as national monuments. National preserves in Pima County today include Organ Pipe National Monument, Saguaro National Park, Las Cienegas National Conservation Area, Cabeza Prieta National Wildlife Refuge, Buenos Aires National Wildlife Refuge, and Ironwood Forest National Monument.

Unfortunately, by the 1960s, in cities across the nation, there was quite a different mind set. In Tucson, "urban renewal" claimed some 80 acres for redevelopment. Hundreds of adobe homes and buildings were demolished, displacing over 1,000 people from the city's oldest Mexican American neighborhood. Public outcry changed public policy toward historic preservation and social justice, and today, historic districts surround the lost city core.

By the 1990s, with a conservation ethic firmly in place and faced with immense development pressure, Pima County leaders sought an informed way to balance growth with conservation of those qualities that define the region—the historic places, working ranches, biodiversity, mountains, riparian areas, and sensitive habitat. The visionary Sonoran Desert Conservation Plan achieves all this and more; it protects the heritage, the land, and ultimately, the spirit and sense of place.

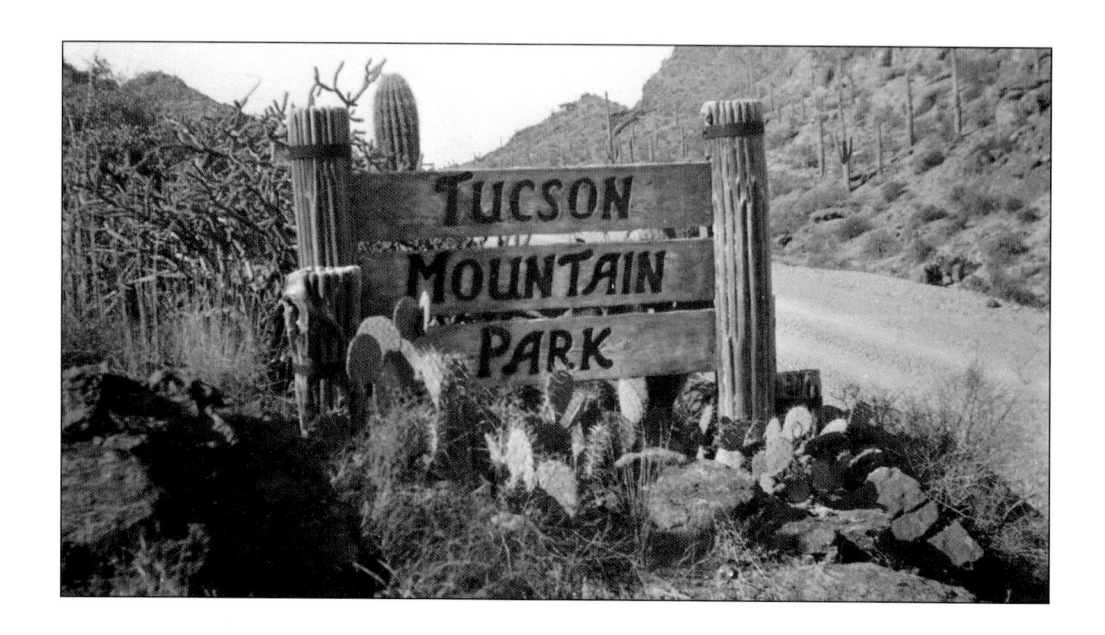

In 1929, most of the Tucson Mountains and their dense forest of saguaros came under protection as Pima County's first large conservation area, known as Tucson Mountain Park. C.B. Brown was among the first visionaries to see the value of protecting the Tucson Mountains and its exceptional Sonoran Desert environment from the threat of mining. With assistance from US senator Carl Hayden, nearly 30,000 acres were withdrawn from mining and homesteading and leased to Pima County, who by a vote of the board of supervisors established Tucson Mountain Park, then the largest county park in the United States. The National Park Service designed roads, trails, and amenities for Tucson Mountain Park that were built by the Civilian Conservation Corps in the 1930s. (Above, AHS 7138; below, AHS 7136.)

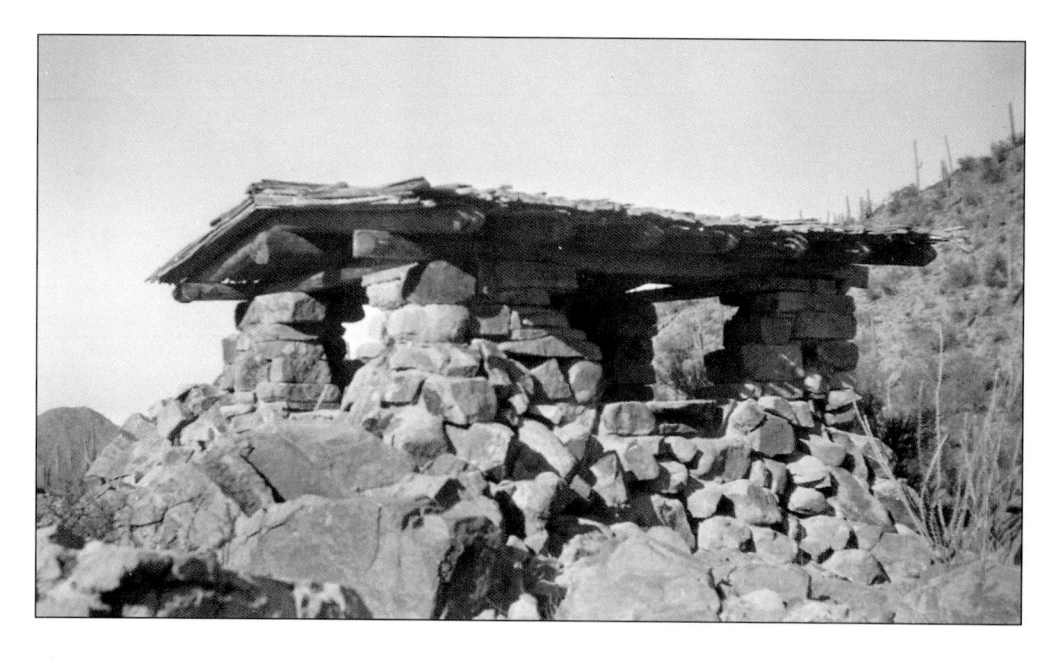

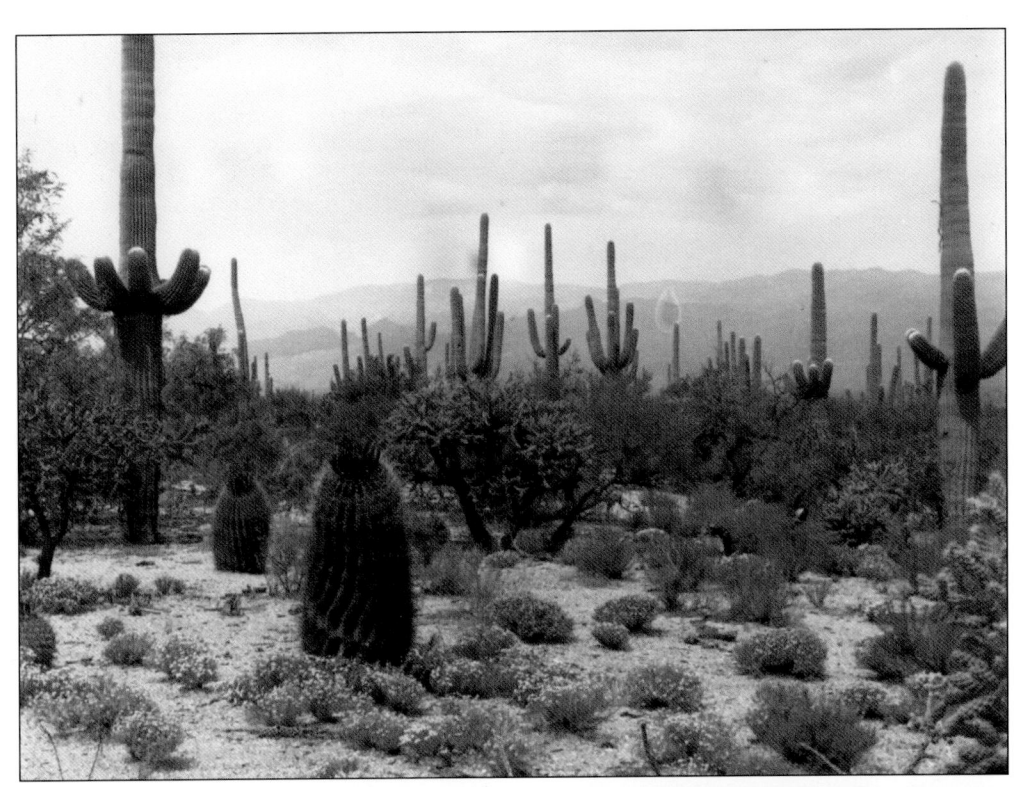

With support from botanists and leaders in the Tucson community to preserve the "Cactus Forest" east of Tucson, Pres. Herbert Hoover signed a proclamation establishing Saguaro National Monument on March 1, 1933. Pima County residents have often resisted threats to their natural environment, and when the US Department of the Interior threatened to open up part of the Tucson Mountain Park to mining in 1959, there was public outcry. Stewart K. Udall, at the time representing his hometown of Tucson in the US House of Representatives, asked President Kennedy to rescind the order. Udall's action led to more than 15,000 acres of Tucson Mountain Park being added to Saguaro National Monument in 1961. Soon afterwards, Kennedy appointed Udall as secretary of the interior. Both east and west units were designated Saguaro National Park in 1994. (Above, UA Photograph Files; right, AHS B204989.)

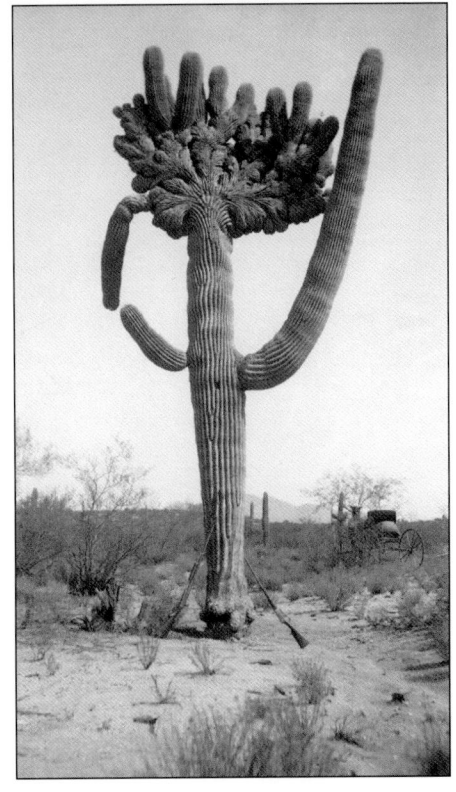

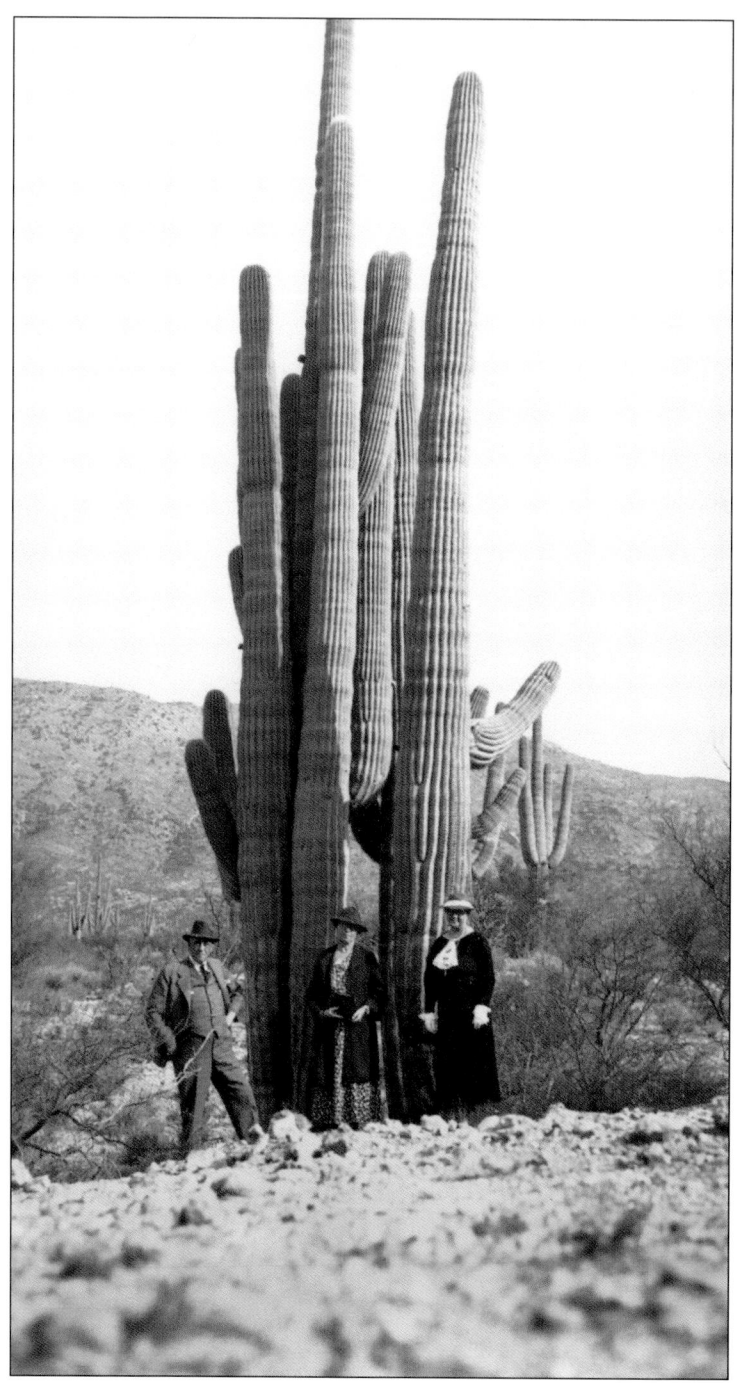

The giant saguaro cactus (*carnegiea gigantea*) stands as one of the best-known symbols of the Sonoran Desert, Arizona, and the American Southwest. For decades, tourists and locals have stopped to get a memorable snapshot next to this huge plant. Saguaro cacti may live for up to 200 years and reach a height of 60 feet. In May 1935, from left to right, Henry Sheldon, Edith Reid, and Mrs. L.A. Upham stood for their photograph next to a grouping of four saguaros on Redington Road, east of Tucson. (AHS PC142f.6 93032.)

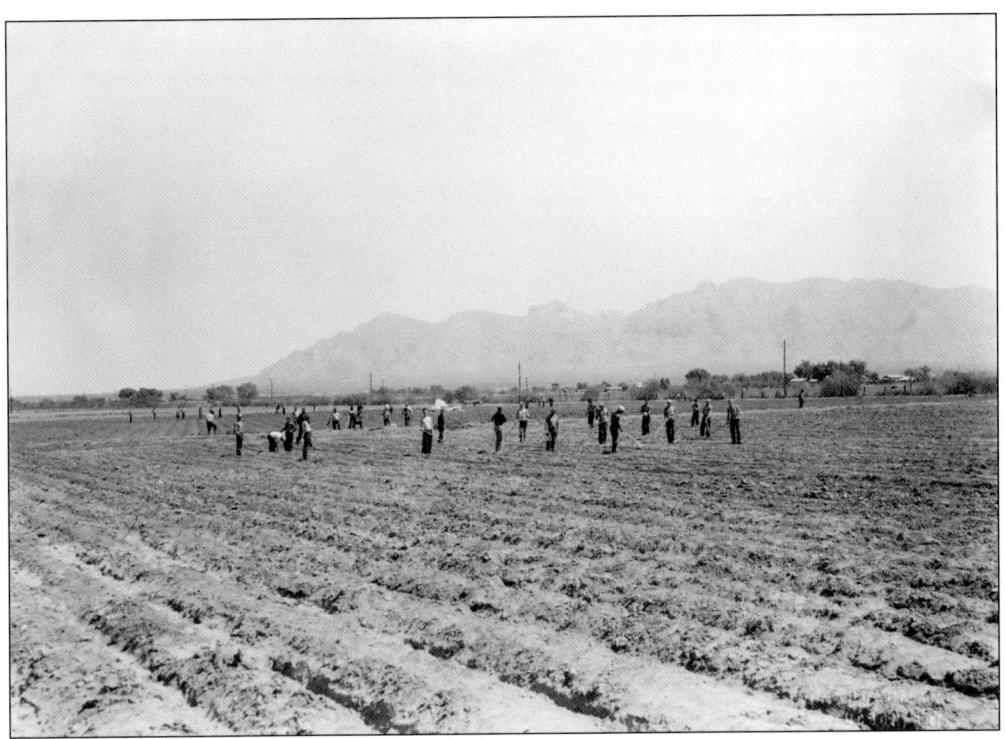

Members of the Civilian Conservation Corps (CCC), founded by Pres. Franklin D. Roosevelt, received $30 per week, plus shelter, meals, and an education. In return, Americans received bridges, parks, buildings, and beautification of the land. In Pima County, the CCC was responsible for, among other things, Sabino Canyon hiking trails, the first building at the Desert Museum, Box Canyon Road, and numerous picnic tables and campgrounds in the Santa Catalina Mountains. Above, men work in a CCC field in an unidentified Tucson camp. Days for CCC workers started at 6:00 a.m. and ended at 4:00 p.m., five days a week. Work meant hard physical labor, building fences, laying pipe, breaking rocks, building roads, and fighting fires. The mess hall, pictured below, gave CCC workers a much-needed respite from their labors. (Above, AHS BN29365; below, AHS 100309.)

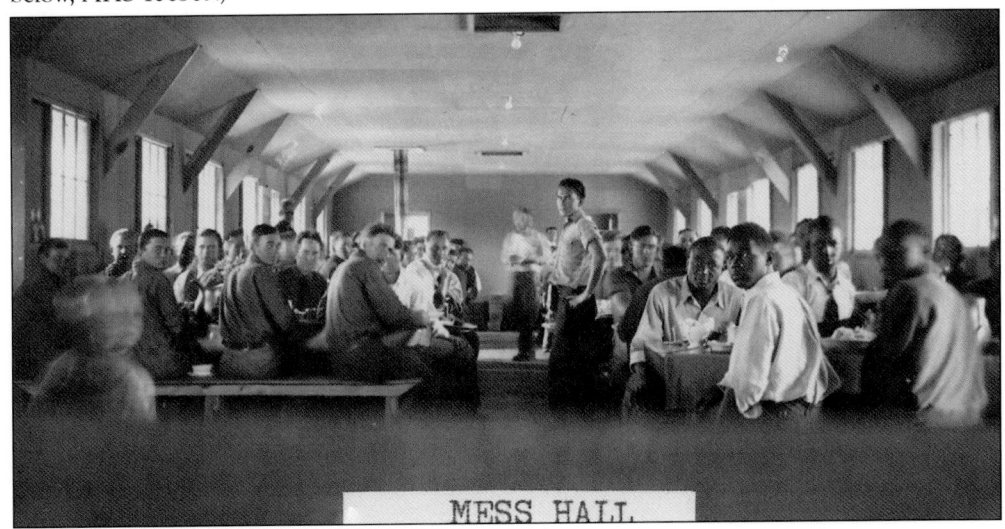

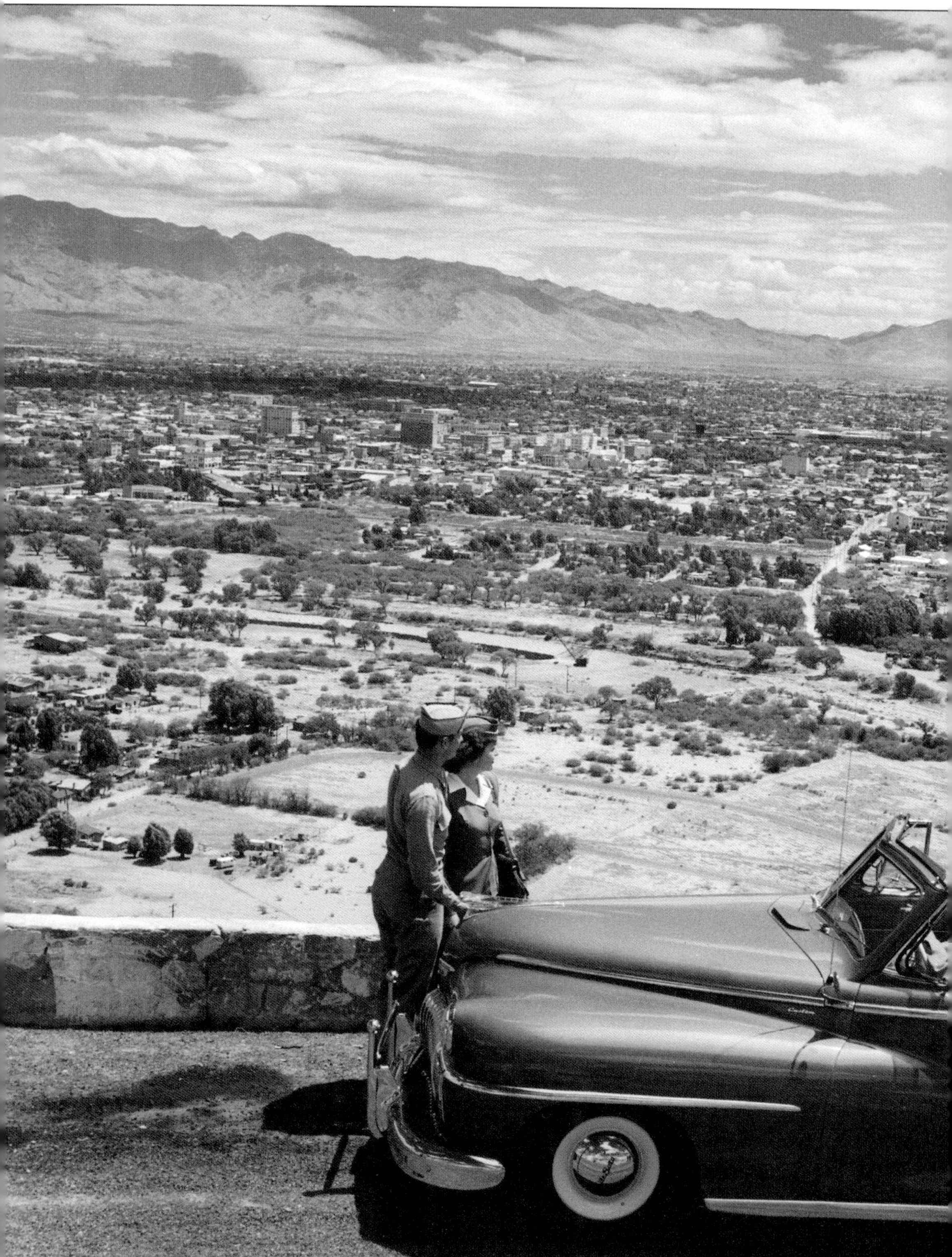

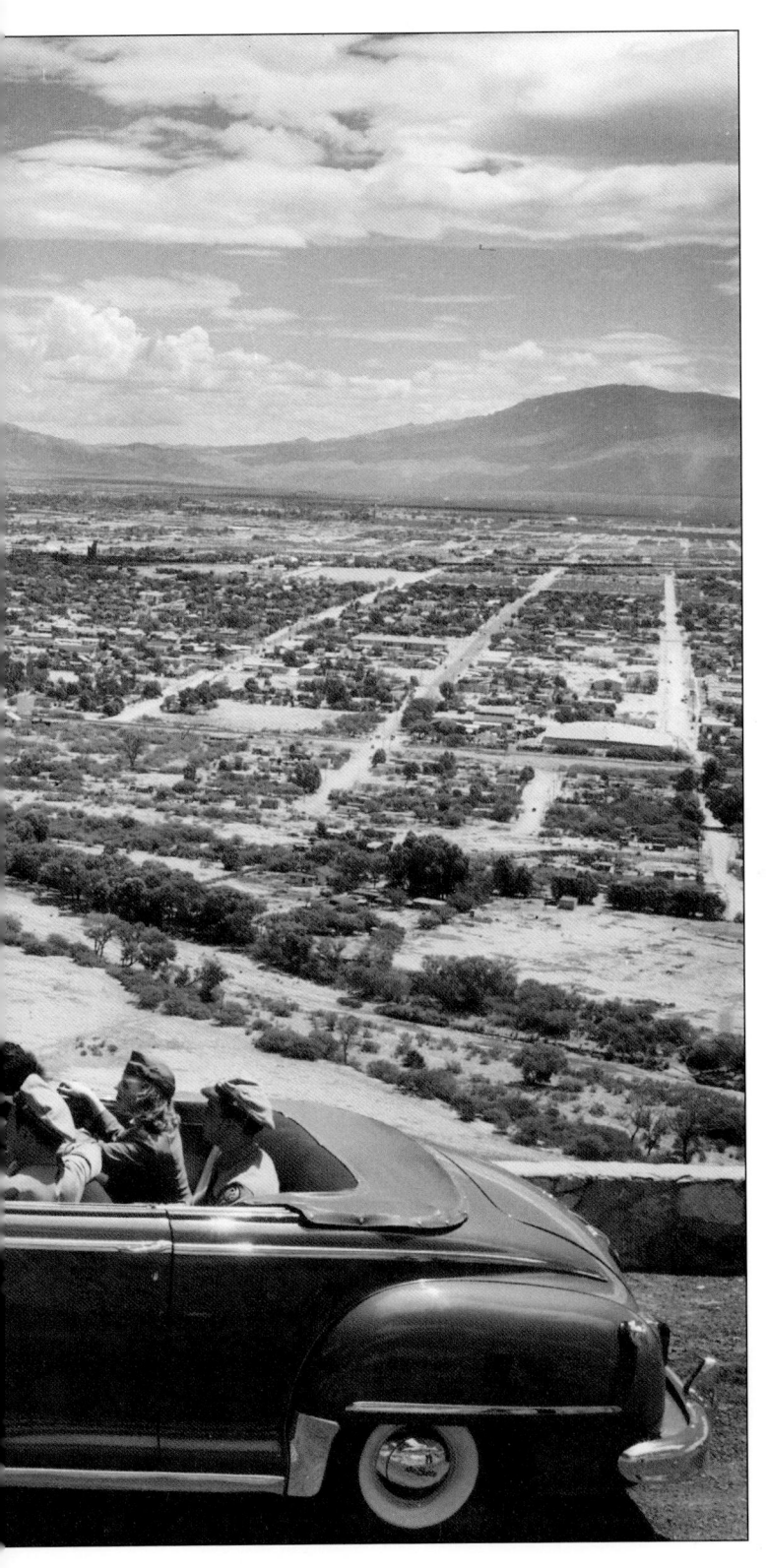

On a day's outing, this group stopped on "A" Mountain, which overlooks Tucson. Also known as Sentinel Peak, it was a place where lookouts once watched for marauding Indian attacks and raised the alarm to those living below. In 1950, around the time this photograph was taken, the population of Tucson was growing rapidly, and urban growth was changing both the nature and size of the city. In postwar boom years, Pima County's population almost doubled every 10 years, and between 1940 and 1970, the population rose from 72,838 to 351,367. In 2012, as the county's population approached 1 million, planning of the county's resources and open spaces became ever more important. (AHS 56423.)

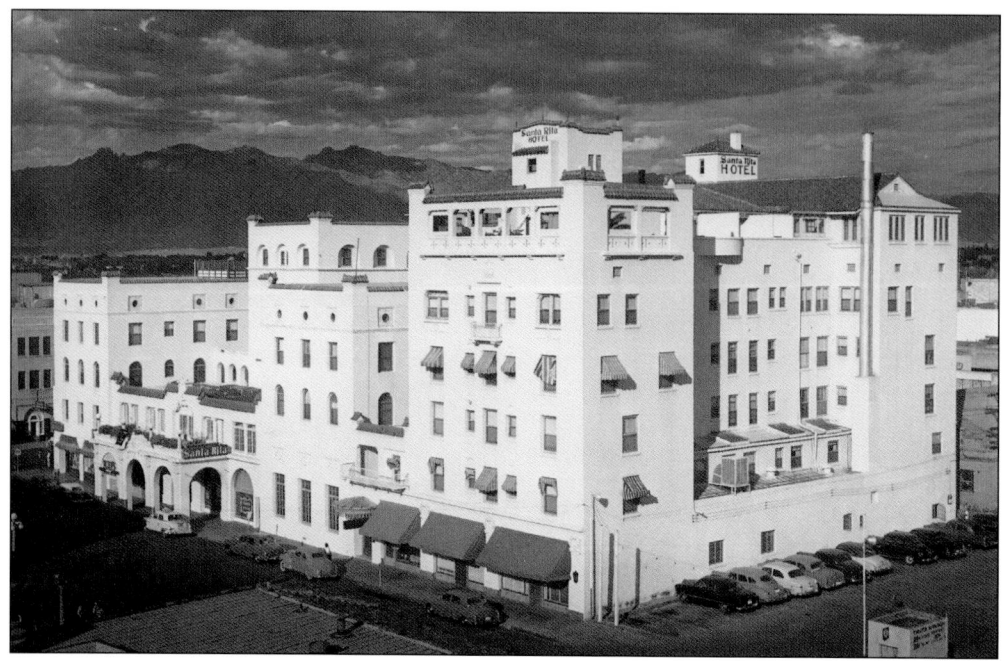

An *Arizona Daily Star* reporter once called the Santa Rita Hotel "the most beautiful hotel in the Arizona Territory." When it opened in 1904, a reported 2,000 Tucsonans came out to celebrate. Over the years, it has hosted a number of celebrities, including actors working at Old Tucson Studios. (AHS MS1255f.139c.)

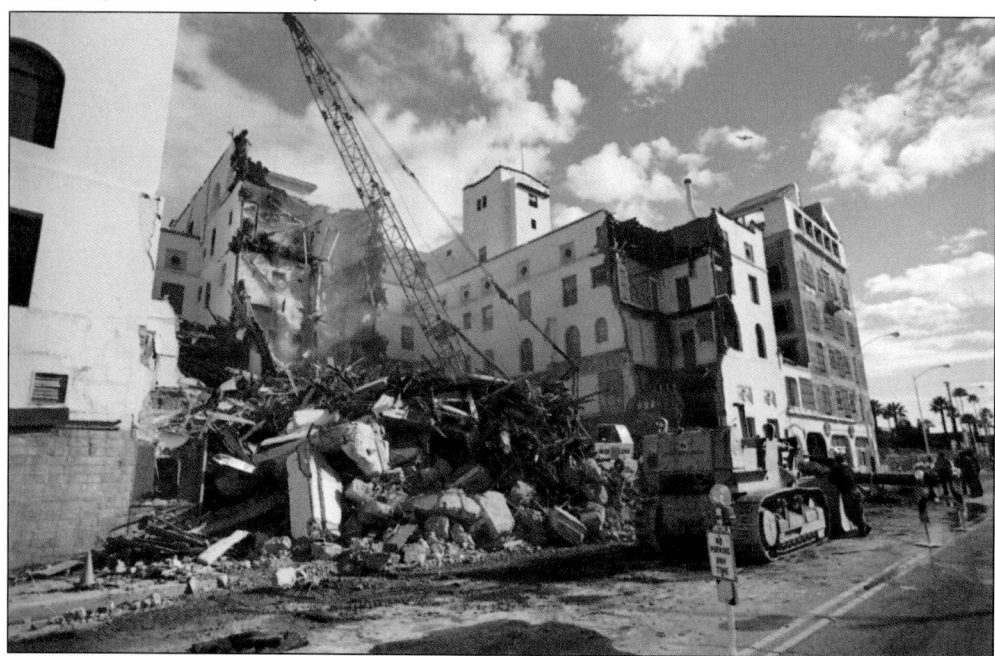

The Santa Rita Hotel underwent a number of changes, including a major reconstruction in 1972. *Arizona Daily Star* photographer Jack Schaeffer was there to document the partial demolition. After being rebuilt, the hotel operated until 2005, when it closed. Its final demolition occurred in 2009 to make way for the new headquarters for Tucson Electric Power. (UA MS435 44997.7.)

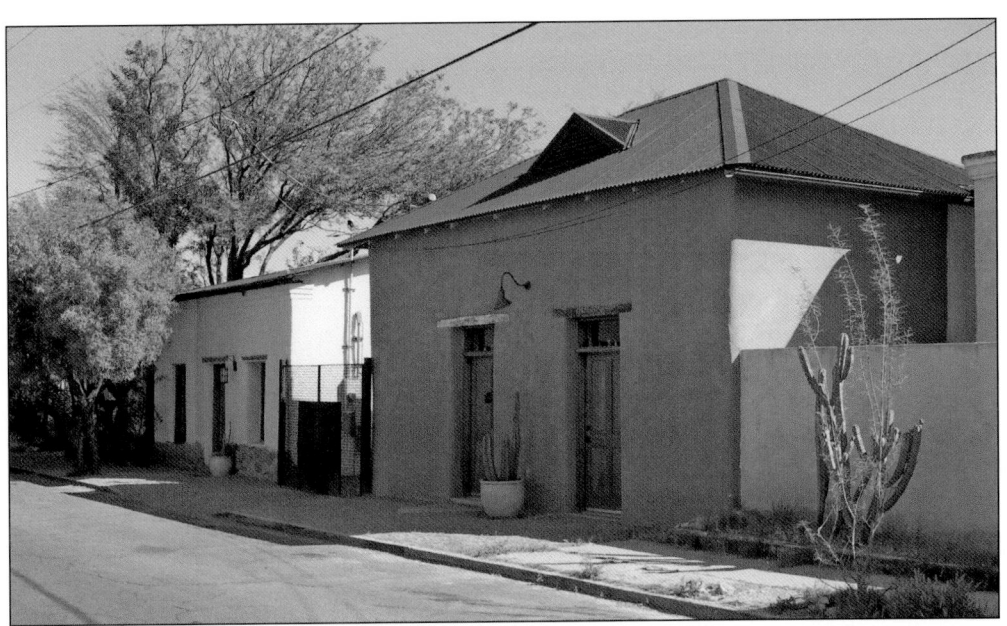

In 1966, Tucson City Council approved a renewal project that led to the demolition of 263 historic buildings. The intent was to improve areas by removing what were viewed as blighted neighborhoods; however, it required the forced removal of some 1,700 citizens, most of whom were poorer Americans of Mexican, African, and Chinese descent. Tucson's period of urban renewal also destroyed long-established social relationships and some of the city's oldest historic barrios, along with irreplaceable buildings. The enormous social upheaval caused by this event proved to be the starting point of Tucson's preservation movement and led to the establishment of protected historic districts, laws, and due process for treatment of historic properties. Some of the old downtown barrios survived, like the ones shown above, and the building shown below was spared to become the Sosa-Carrillo-Frémont House Museum. (Both photographs by Simon Herbert.)

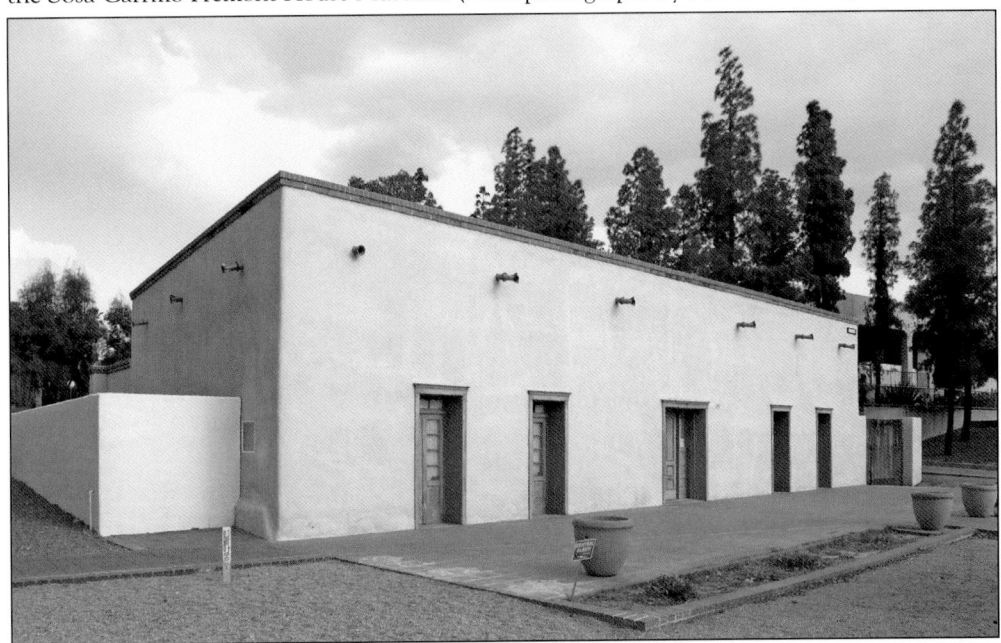

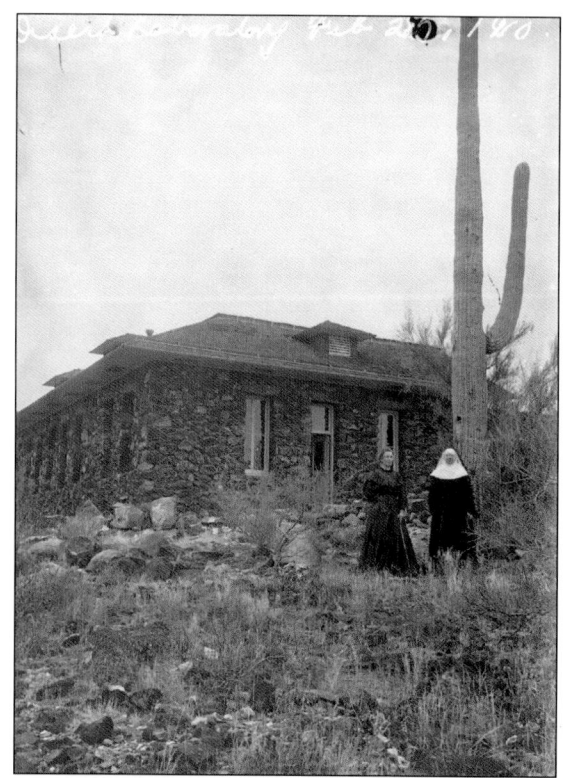

The Desert Laboratory was founded in 1903 by the Carnegie Institute. Sitting atop Tumamoc Hill, an 800-foot-high hill of volcanic rock overlooking Tucson, it is still in operation and remains the premiere center for the long-term study of desert ecology. In 2009, Pima County acquired 320 acres of land on Tumamoc Hill, thus helping preserve the 870-acre site in perpetuity. The photograph shows two unidentified women in front of a Desert Laboratory building in 1910. (AHS MS452F453_B4-92.)

El Tiradito (meaning "outcast") is located in Tucson's Barrio Historico and may be the only shrine in the United States dedicated to a sinner. Legend recalls a love triangle that ended with a man dying at the spot of the shrine. Often called the "Wishing Shrine," local lore states that if a person lights a candle at the site and it remains lit throughout the night, his or her wish will come true. (AHS MS1255f142k.)

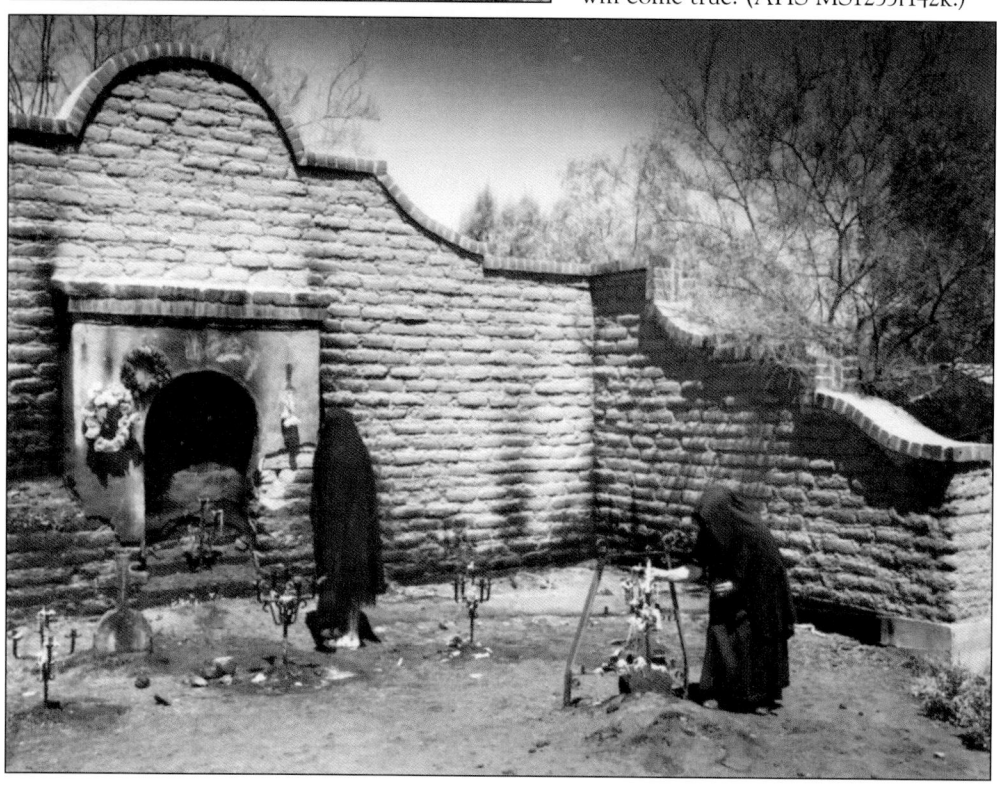

San Xavier Mission was founded in 1692, with construction of the current building taking place between 1783 and 1797. Designated a National Historic Landmark, it remains an active Catholic parish church for the Tohono O'odham. Keeping a special building in good repair is no easy task, and in 1978, the Patronato San Xavier was established to promote conservation of the mission, employing teams of highly skilled local and international conservators. (Photograph by Jill McCleary.)

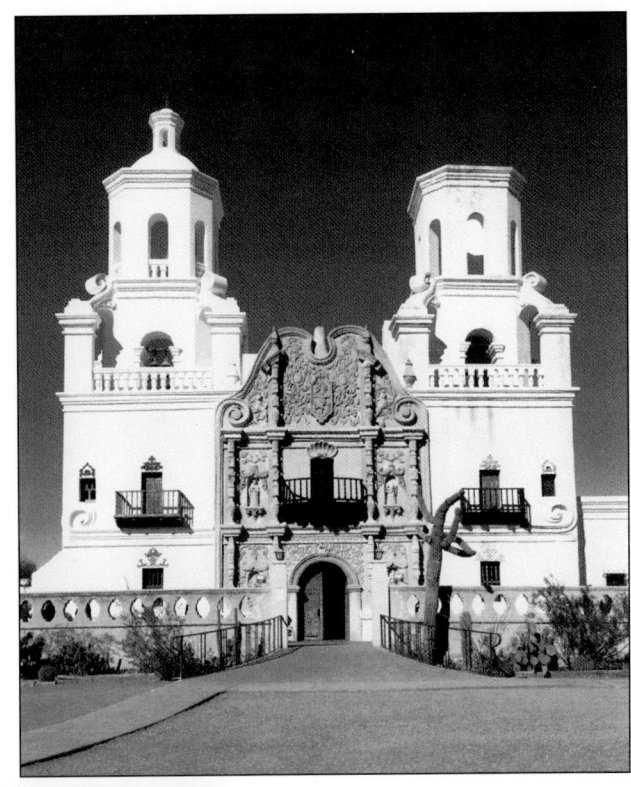

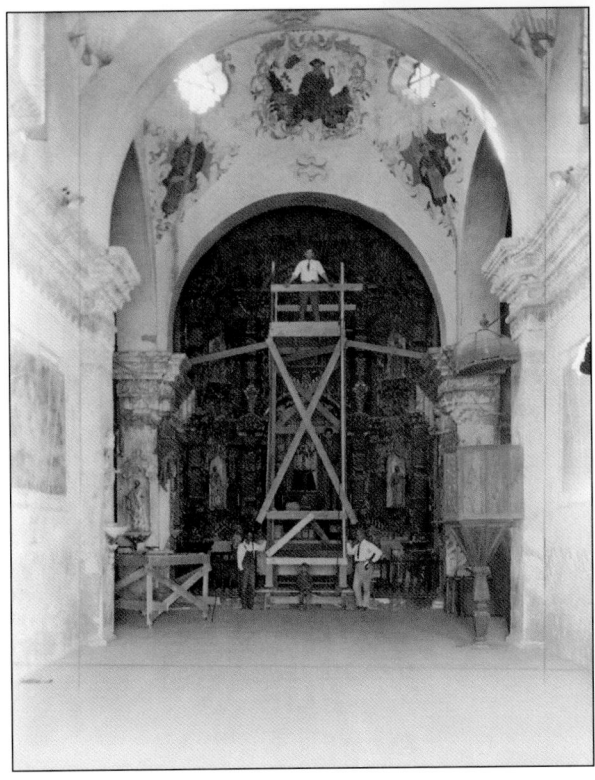

Classical scholar Prentice Duell is shown atop rolling scaffolding inside San Xavier Mission in 1928, as he was overseeing the first photographic documentation of the statuary. More recent conservation efforts have brought the extraordinarily rich Spanish Colonial interior back to life. San Xavier is considered to be the premier example of Spanish Colonial architecture in the United States. (AHS 10410.)

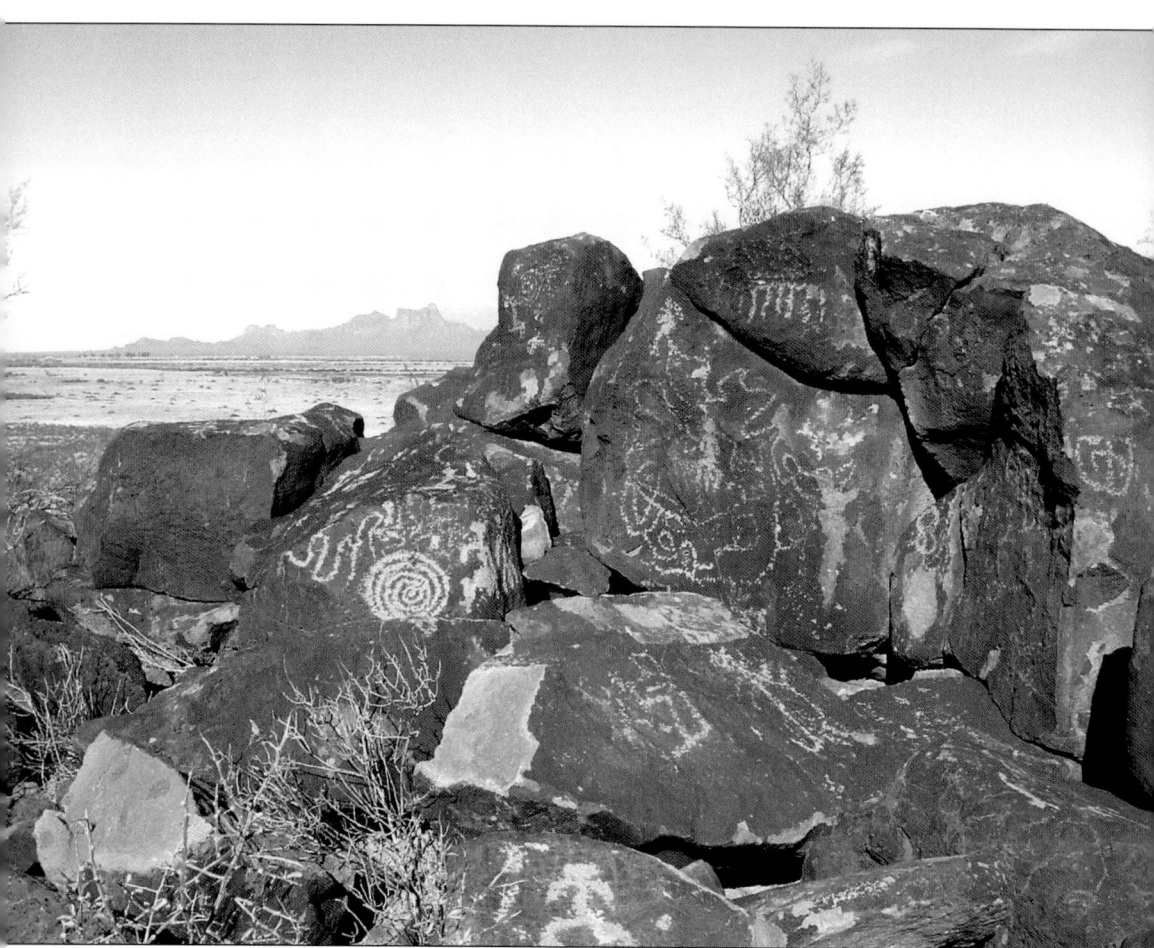

Within the Ironwood Forest National Monument in northern Pima County lie high numbers of preserved petroglyph sites. Sometimes called "rock art," they were made by prehistoric Archaic and Hohokam peoples who resided here or used the area for periodic hunting and gathering between 1000 BCE and 1450 CE. These petroglyphs were made by pecking or lightly striking designs into the black volcanic rock surface using stone tools and include representations of bighorn sheep, snakes, lizards, deer, coyotes, insects, birds, and sometimes people. Also visible are spirals, circles, and other rectilinear or curved designs. While their precise use and meaning are unknown, these sites are important traditional cultural places to the Tohono O'odham, who consider the Hohokam and earlier peoples to be their ancestors. (Courtesy of the Pima County Government.)

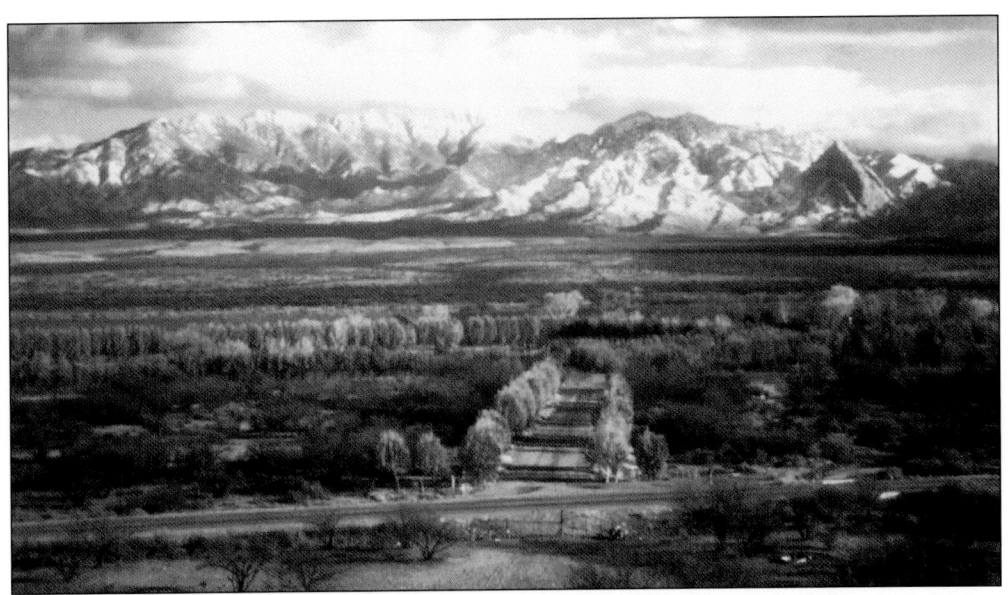

Responding to the loss of critical habitat for endangered species from expansive urbanization and growth in the 1990s, the Pima County Board of Supervisors initiated development of the science-based Sonoran Desert Conservation Plan to balance growth and conservation. Adopted in 1999, the Sonoran Desert Conservation Plan is a blueprint for the conservation of Pima County's natural and cultural heritage and has been recognized as one of the nation's most comprehensive and ambitious conservation and land use planning efforts. It is also the basis for voter-approved bond programs for the acquisition of conservation lands like Canoa Ranch (above), allowing Pima County to retain much of its natural landscape and the unspoiled beauty of the Sonoran Desert. The view below shows Rancho Seco in the Cerro Colorado Mountains in southern Pima County. (Above, courtesy of Deezie Manning-Catron; below, courtesy of Brian Forbes Powell.)

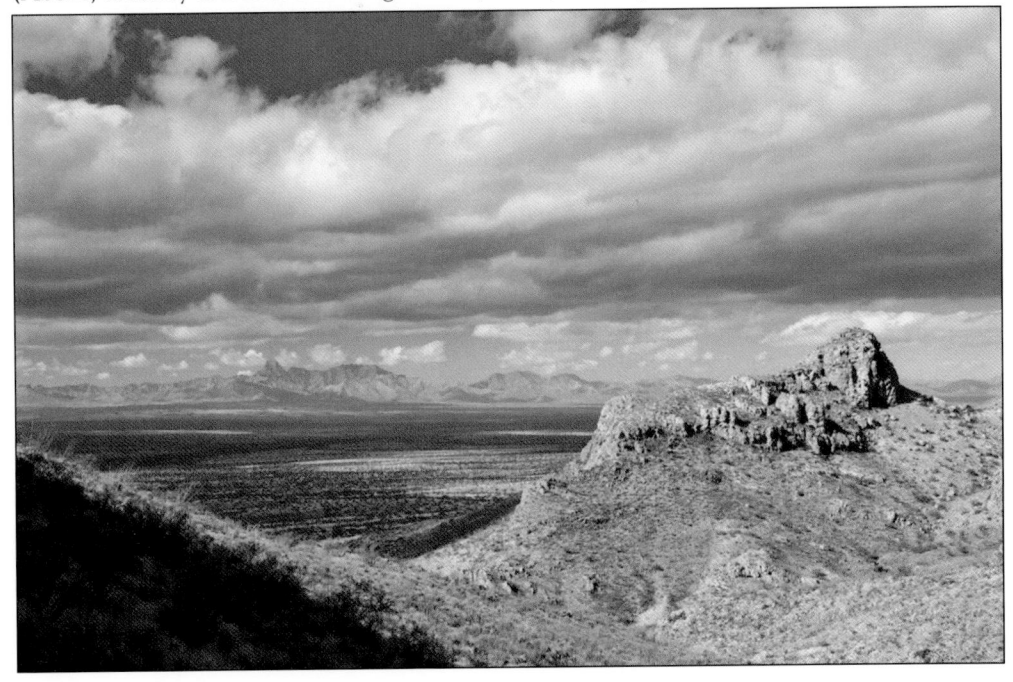

BIBLIOGRAPHY

Canty, Michael J. and Michael N. Greeley, eds. *History of Mining in Arizona*. Tucson: Mining Club of the Southwest Foundation, 1987.

Cosulich, Bernice. *Tucson*. Tucson: Treasure Chest Publications, Inc., 1953.

Lawson, Harry H. *The History of African Americans in Tucson: An Afrocentric Perspective*. Tucson: Lawson's Psychological Services, 1996.

Lazaroff, David. *Sabino Canyon: The Life of a Southwestern Oasis*. Tucson: University of Arizona Press, 1993.

Nequette, Anne M. and R. Brooks Jeffery. *A Guide to Tucson Architecture*. Tucson: University of Arizona Press, 2002.

Officer, James E. *Hispanic Arizona, 1536–1856*. Tucson: University of Arizona Press, 1987.

Santa Cruz Valley Natural Heritage Area Feasibility Study. Tucson: Center for Desert Archaeology, 2005.

Sheridan, Thomas E. *Tucsonenses: The Mexican Community in Tucson, 1854–1941*. Tucson: University of Arizona Press, 1986.

Sonnichesen, C.L. *Pioneer Heritage: The First Century of the Arizona Historical Society*. Tucson: Arizona Historical Society, 1984.

———. *Tucson: The Life and Times of an American City*. Norman: University of Oklahoma Press, 1982.

Tucson: A Short History. Tucson: Southwestern Mission Research Center, 1986.

Udall, Stewart L. *To the Inland Empire: Coronado and Our Spanish Legacy*. Garden City, NY: Doubleday & Company, Inc., 1987.

Wagoner, Jay J. *Early Arizona, Pre-History to Civil War*. Tucson: University of Arizona Press, 1975.

Walker, Henry P. and Don Bufkin. *Historical Atlas of Arizona*. Norman: University of Oklahoma Press, 1979.

Yancy, James Walter. *The Negro of Tucson, Past and Present*. (thesis) Tucson: University of Arizona, 1933.

INDEX

African Americans, 37–39
Ajo, 66, 67
Arizona-Sonora Desert Museum, 108, 109
Baboquivari Peak, 12
Canoa Ranch, 50, 125
Catalina Mountains *see* Santa Catalina Mountains
Chinese, 40, 41
Civilian Conservation Corps, 113
Colossal Cave, 107
county courthouses, 17, 18
Davis-Monthan Air Force Base, 85
DeGrazia, Ettore "Ted," 112
Fort Lowell, 98
Fox Theater, 105
Greaterville, 48, 49
Green Valley, 86
Guerrero, Lalo, 35
Gunsight Mine, 60
Helvetia, 44–46
Hirabayashi, Gordon, 42
Kitt Peak, 108
Marana, 72
Old Tucson, 104
Oro Valley, 97
Pascua Yaqui, 30, 31
Pima County Fair, 110
Prince Chapel African Methodist Episcopal Church, 39
Quijotoa, 54–57, 63
Rialto Theatre, 105
Rillito Racetrack, 106
Rillito River, 74
Sabino Canyon, 88, 89
Saguaro National Park, 112
Sahuarita, 68
St. Augustine Cathedral, 32, 114
San Xavier, 11, 29, 30, 99, 115, 123
Santa Catalina Mountains, 53, 90–94
Santa Cruz River, 76
Santa Rita Hotel, 120
Sasabe, 62
Silverbell, 58, 59
Southern Arizona School for Boys, 83
Steam Pump Ranch, 53
Stone Avenue, 75
Temple of Music and Art, 111
Tohono O'odham, 11, 20–29
Total Wreck Mine, 62
Tucson Mountain Park, 114
Tucson Citizen, 84
Tucson presidio, 14
Tucson Rodeo, 110
University of Arizona, 80–81

DISCOVER THOUSANDS OF LOCAL HISTORY BOOKS FEATURING MILLIONS OF VINTAGE IMAGES

Arcadia Publishing, the leading local history publisher in the United States, is committed to making history accessible and meaningful through publishing books that celebrate and preserve the heritage of America's people and places.

Find more books like this at
www.arcadiapublishing.com

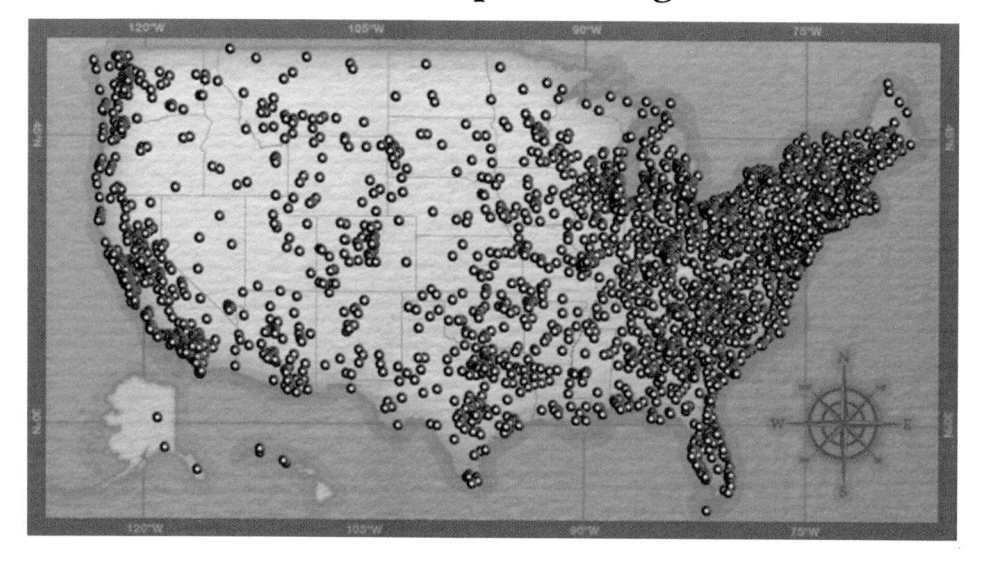

Search for your hometown history, your old stomping grounds, and even your favorite sports team.

Consistent with our mission to preserve history on a local level, this book was printed in South Carolina on American-made paper and manufactured entirely in the United States. Products carrying the accredited Forest Stewardship Council (FSC) label are printed on 100 percent FSC-certified paper.

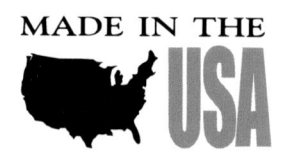

MADE IN THE USA